GALAPAGOS OF THE ANTARCTIC

WILD ISLANDS SOUTH OF NEW ZEALAND

Heritage Expeditions

First published in August, 2009

Copyright © Rodney Russ in text and photographs 2009
Copyright © Aleks Terauds in text and photographs 2009
Copyright © photographs as credited 2009
Copyright © Fiona Stewart in illustration and design 2009

All rights reserved. No part of this book may be reproduced or transmitted in any form or by any means, electronic or mechanical, including photocopying, recording or by any information storage and retrieval system, without prior permission in writing from the publisher.

Heritage Expeditions
53B Montreal Street
Christchurch
New Zealand

Email: info@heritage-expeditions.com
Web: www.heritage-expeditions.com

National Library of New Zealand Cataloguing-in-Publication Data:

Russ, Rodney, 1953-
Galapagos of Antarctica : wild islands south of New Zealand /
Rodney Russ and Aleks Terauds ; photography by Nathan
Russ, Aaron Russ and Aleks Terauds ; illustration and design
by Fiona Stewart.
Includes bibliographical references and index.
ISBN 978-0-473-14635-1(hbk.)

1. Natural history—New Zealand—Subantarctic Islands.
2. Subantarctic Islands (N.Z.)—Description and travel.
3. Subantarctic Islands (N.Z.)—History. I. Terauds, Aleks, 1971-
II. Title.
508.9399—dc 22

Edited by Stephanie Goodwin
Reproduction by Fiona Stewart & Aleks Terauds
Index by Aleks Terauds

Printed in China through Colorcraft Ltd, Hong Kong

GALAPAGOS OF THE ANTARCTIC
WILD ISLANDS SOUTH OF NEW ZEALAND

*To Anne
With Best Wishes
South & Antarctica Voyage.
January 2010
Rodney Russ*

RODNEY RUSS & ALEKS TERAUDS

PHOTOGRAPHY BY: NATHAN RUSS · AARON RUSS · ALEKS TERAUDS

ILLUSTRATION & DESIGN BY FIONA STEWART

TABLE OF CONTENTS

ACKNOWLEDGEMENTS	8
INTRODUCTION	11
The Islands	12
Climate	21
The Southern Ocean	23
CHATHAM ISLANDS	27
Geography and Geology	31
Flora	35
Fauna	41
History	49
BOUNTY ISLANDS	55
Geography and Geology	58
Flora	61
Fauna	63
History	67
ANTIPODES ISLANDS	71
Geography and Geology	74
Flora	77
Fauna	81
History	86
CAMPBELL ISLAND	91
Geography and Geology	94
Flora	96
Fauna	102
History	110

AUCKLAND ISLANDS — 117
Geography and Geology — 121
Flora — 125
Fauna — 133
History — 140

THE SNARES — 149
Geography and Geology — 152
Flora — 155
Fauna — 159
History — 166

MACQUARIE ISLAND — 171
Geography and Geology — 174
Flora — 176
Fauna — 183
History — 190

THE FUTURE — 195
Tourism — 196
A Final Word — 202

BIBLIOGRAPHY — 205
INDEX — 214

MEGAHERBS ON CAMPBELL ISLAND The bright purple flowers of the megaherb *Anisotome latifolia* and the yellow flowers of another megaherb, *Bulbinella rossii* are becoming more common on Campbell Island as they recover from many years of grazing by sheep. *NATHAN RUSS.*

Acknowledgements

It is difficult to know where to begin in acknowledging the contributions that have gone towards making this book a reality. It was over a year in the actual making and it could not have been possible without the advice and generosity of many people.

Many sources were consulted to thoroughly research the text. Several of these are acknowledged in the text and a full list can be found in the Bibliography. However, some need a special mention, particularly those that provided historical information. The two-volumes of Sir James Clark Ross' diary were extremely useful in providing an insight into the islands in the early days of exploration. The comprehensively researched *Murihiki and the Southern Islands* by Robert McNab, *Macquarie Island* by John Cumpston and *Straight Through to London* by Rowley Taylor were consulted extensively and the detail provided in the historical sections would not have been possible without them.

The two volume work – *Subantarctic Islands of New Zealand*, edited by Prof. Charles Chilton was extremely useful in establishing baseline knowledge of the islands in the early days of research. There were also several publications that were published and/or compiled by the New Zealand Department of Conservation including *Chatham Islands Heritage and Conservation* (with a range of contributors) and *Subantarctic New Zealand* by Neville Peat. Other books that were consulted extensively included *Beyond the Roaring Forties* by Conan Fraser and *Whaling and Sealing at the Chatham Islands* by Rhys Richards. The late David Given's unpublished descriptions of the flora were also particularly helpful in compiling the botanical sections.

A number of people generously provided their time, knowledge and advice. Ian (Mo) Turnbull read the early and later stages of the geography and geology sections and contributed significantly to their content. Justine Shaw read the botany sections and also gave us some useful feedback on the Macquarie Island section. Norm Judd, Paul Sagar, Rowley Taylor and Rhys Richards read through later drafts of the island sections and also provided valuable advice. Stephanie Goodwin provided editorial feedback on the entire text and her input on both the structure and content was significant.

The three principal photographers, Nathan Russ, Aaron Russ and Aleks Terauds put together a fantastic working library of images, the best of which make up most of the images used in this book. Kath Walker and Graeme Elliott generously provided a number of images from their time on Adams, Antipodes and Disappointment Islands and without their contribution in this respect it would have been very difficult to illustrate these sections with the appropriate images. Thanks also to Don Merton, Jacinda Amey, Pete Tyree, Jeffrey Stilwell and Russell Thomas for providing important images. Historical images were obtained from a variety of sources and we would like to thank, amongst others, the Alexander Turnbull Library and the National Library of Australia.

"...the most extraordinary is the Pleurophyllum meadow, a community dominated by the large-leafed herbaceous composite, producing a floral display second to none outside the tropics."

Joseph Hooker, 1840

The book design, layout and illustrations were done by Fiona Stewart. Her patience and dedication allowed our ideas and desires to become a reality and her illustrations capture a dimension of these islands that photographs cannot. Aleks Terauds helped to research and write the text and co-ordinated many aspects of the whole project and I thank him for his time and effort.

I would like to thank my 'subantarctic mentors', who have encouraged my enthusiasm for these islands. Three deserve a special mention. Brian Bell, Rowley Taylor and the late Dr. David Given. Without you the 'affair' might have died.

I would also like to thank my parents who taught me the value of wild places, my wife Shirley who supported and encouraged my love of these islands and helped me to achieve my dreams and my two sons, Aaron and Nathan, both of whom have grown to share my passion. Thank you for your support.

Finally to the crew of my vessels, the passengers and the staff of Heritage Expeditions, with whom I have been privileged to work and travel, thank you for sharing the journey.

Rodney B. Russ

RODNEY RUSS
Managing Director
Heritage Expeditions
Christchurch, New Zealand

Bulbinella rossii

GALAPAGOS of the ANTARCTIC

NEW ZEALAND

North Cape
Bay of Plenty
East Cape
Tasman Sea
Cape Egmont
North Island
Cape Farewell
Cook Strait
Hawke Bay
40°S
Cape Palliser
Christchurch
Banks Peninsula
West Cape
Dunedin
South Island
Chatham Islands
Stewart Island
The Snares
Bounty Islands
Antipodes Islands
50°S
Auckland Islands
Campbell Island
Southern Ocean

Macquarie Island

170°E   180°E

0km — 300km

INTRODUCTION

When asked about natural wonderlands of the world, Southern Ocean islands do not immediately spring to the forefront of most people's minds. To try and convey the astounding natural biodiversity of these remote and wild places and to give a sense of how important they are as wildlife refuges, we have termed the seven island groups in this book the 'Galapagos of the Antarctic'. The Galapagos of the Antarctic lie to the south and east of New Zealand, in the great Southern Ocean that encircles Antarctica. They are all in the cool temperate or subantarctic zone and are home to some of the most abundant and diverse wildlife seen on the planet. These islands not only play an important role in the Southern Ocean ecosystem, they also have a rich human history—from their discovery around 200 years ago, through an era of exploitation, until finally today, when they are treasured for their intrinsic value as wild and beautiful places.

Yellow-eyed Penguin

WILD ISLAND SOUTH OF NEW ZEALAND The oceanic islands to the south and east of New Zealand are some of the most remote and biologically diverse islands in the world. Even though the climate is often harsh, they are home to an incredible range of unique plants and animals.

THE ISLANDS

THE GALAPAGOS OF the Antarctic is made up of the Chatham Islands, Bounty Islands, Antipodes Islands, The Snares, Auckland Islands, Campbell Island and Macquarie Island. Macquarie Island—the most southerly of the island groups—is an Australian sovereign territory administered by the state of Tasmania; the other island groups all come under New Zealand jurisdiction.

With the exception of the Chatham Islands, the Galapagos of the Antarctic are often described or referred to as subantarctic islands. Definitions of what makes an island 'subantarctic' vary and are often contentious, but one widely accepted working definition describes subantarctic islands as those that lie within the southern half of the South Temperate Zone, roughly between the latitudes of 47°S and 55°S. The Chatham Islands are clearly not subantarctic and at latitude 44°S, they are considered cool temperate. However, there are strong links between the flora and fauna of the Chatham Islands and the subantarctic islands further to the south, and like the other islands, they are strongly influenced by the surrounding ocean.

BIOGEOGRAPHY

The island groups in the Southern Ocean (excluding those within the Antarctic Sector) can be divided into three distinct geographical regions: the south Pacific Ocean islands (which make up the Galapagos of the Antarctic), the south Indian Ocean islands (Prince Edward Islands, Crozet/Possession Islands, Kerguelen Islands and Heard/McDonald Islands) and the south Atlantic Ocean islands (South Georgia and the Falkland Islands). The total land area of the islands in the south Pacific sector is 186 000 hectares; the southern Indian Ocean group covers a total land area of 805 000 hectares; and then there is the south Atlantic group, which spans over one million hectares.

When you compare the total number of indigenous plant species on the islands in the three geographic regions, the south Pacific group has significantly more, especially when land area is taken into consideration. A similar picture emerges when you compare the number of seabird species of the three regions. Simply put, the islands of the south Pacific are tiny oceanic havens for an abundance of wildlife, the like of which is seen in very few other places around the world.

BIODIVERSITY

The particularly high biodiversity and abundance of wildlife in the south Pacific island groups can be attributed to several factors. Their proximity to New Zealand has undoubtedly facilitated their colonisation by terrestrial species and there are many species that live on these islands and nowhere else. This high number of endemic or unique species is strongly influenced by the geological history and physical isolation of the islands. The Gondwanic origins of the New Zealand islands are also likely to be an important driving force behind high biodiversity, as are the highly productive surrounding waters, heavily influenced by the current systems related to the Antarctic Convergence, where colder waters from Antarctica meet warmer waters from more northerly latitudes.

ROYAL PENGUINS COURTING These two Royal Penguins are courting on the rocky shores of Macquarie Island. This sort of behaviour reinforces the pair-bond which is an important aspect of any successful breeding attempt. *NATHAN RUSS.*

SEA OF YELLOW The bright yellow flowers of the megaherb *Bulbinella rossii* form a sea of yellow on the west coast of Enderby Island. These are the first megaherbs to flower and are at their peak in November and December. *ALEKS TERAUDS.*

Geology

Geologically speaking, there are differences between the islands. The Bounty Islands and The Snares are composed of continental granite, remnants of what was originally part of Gondwana, the ancient supercontinent which eventually split to become the modern continents of the Southern Hemisphere. As such, they are composed entirely of some of the oldest rocks in the subantarctic islands of the region, dating between 100–200 million years old.

The Auckland, Campbell and Antipodes Islands are all of volcanic origin, built on the Campbell Plateau. It has been suggested that they were formed over weak points in the Earth's crust as tectonic plates moved from east to west over underlying hot spots. Geological dating supports this theory, with the Auckland Islands being the oldest of the three at 16–24 million years, then Campbell Island at 6–11 million years and finally the Antipodes at 0.5–1.5 million years. The theory doesn't enjoy universal acceptance, but few alternative theories have been offered. The larger, older islands (Auckland Island and, to a lesser extent, Campbell Island) were glaciated over the last two million years, strongly influencing the shape of their landscape. Today, the Campbell Plateau is the subject of intense scrutiny from the oil industry as global oil reserves diminish and new sources become highly desirable. There is a huge area of potentially oil-bearing sedimentary rocks in this region, and if oil is found then the implications for the surrounding subantarctic islands are likely to be significant.

The Chatham Islands are the exposed part of the Chatham Rise, an elongated submarine platform which split off from Gondwana, together with the Campbell Plateau and New Zealand. The islands that form the group today are the result of 100 million years of volcanic activity, faulting and sedimentation. Although faulting also played a part in the formation of Macquarie Island, it was the movement of the Indian-Australian and Pacific tectonic plates that eventually caused the island to rise above the surface of the ocean. A unique, uplifted piece of largely intact ocean seafloor at the junction of these plates, Macquarie Island is thought to have emerged from the sea around 0.6–0.7 million years ago.

Flora and fauna

Several of the islands in the Campbell Plateau region support a well-developed shrub and/or low tree vegetation and are considered by some botanists to be in the cool temperate zone rather than the subantarctic. Herbaceous plants are a large component of the vegetation on all the islands, with large tussock grasses and robust herbs being particularly conspicuous. Some of these herbs are luxuriant in their growth, with larger leaves, flower heads and often more colourful flowers than their mainland relatives. Sir Joseph Hooker, renowned botanist on the Sir James Clark Ross Expedition and later curator of the Royal Botanical Gardens at Kew, coined the phrase 'megaherbs' when he visited the Auckland and Campbell Islands in the 1840s. The flora of all the islands in the Galapagos of the Antarctic group is quite closely related to the flora of New Zealand.

Seabirds and seals dominate the fauna of the islands, highlighting the strong connections that exist between the marine and terrestrial ecosystems.

NEW ZEALAND (HOOKER'S) SEA LION PUPS Sea lions and fur seals were killed in vast numbers for their skins in the early 1800s on all of the wild islands south of New Zealand. The killing was indiscriminate and in many cases entire populations were wiped out. *AARON RUSS.*

Of the hundreds of bird species recorded breeding on these islands, over 50 are true pelagic species which only come ashore to breed or moult. Included in this number are nine species of penguin, or over half the world's penguin species, four of which are endemic to the region. Of the 13 species of albatross that breed on these islands, only four breed elsewhere. There are at least 25 species of other petrels known to breed on these islands, among them some of the rarest in the world.

The presence of a significant number of endemic species suggests that the island groups have been isolated from each other for long periods of time. Nowhere is this better illustrated than with the cormorants or shags. Each of the islands, with the exception of The Snares and the Antipodes, has their own endemic shag. Other species, like the parakeets for example, also show a high degree of speciation.

Human history

Recent archeological work on Enderby Island in the Auckland Islands suggests that these islands had been at least visited, if not occupied, by early Polynesian seafarers. There is strong oral tradition that early Polynesians also regularly visited the The Snares for the purpose of gathering food. However, it was two British government sponsored expeditions that put the first three island groups of the Galapagos of the Antarctic on the map. Lieutenant Bligh, en route to Tahiti in 1788, sighted a group of rocks, which he named the Bounty Islands after his ship, the *Bounty*. Captain George Vancouver and his second-in-command, Lieutenant William Broughton, discovered The Snares and the Chatham Islands within days of each other in January

GRAVEYARD This graveyard is all that remains of the settlement at Hardwicke in Port Ross, Auckland Island. *RUSS COLLECTION.*

1791. The Antipodes were discovered in 1800, while the increasing demand for new fur sealing grounds led to the discovery of the Auckland, Campbell and Macquarie Islands in the early 1800s.

Common to these island groups—indeed, to all island groups in the subantarctic Southern Ocean—is the impact that sealers had on native animals, birds and plants. Whether intentionally or accidentally, a variety of non-native animals were introduced to all of these islands by the sealers, with the exception of the Bounty Islands and The Snares. The inhospitable nature of the Bounty Islands makes it easy to understand why no introduced animals could establish there, but how or why The Snares escaped these introductions in the long-term remains a mystery and indeed, something of a miracle. Fortunately, smaller islands or islets within most of the island groups were spared the devastating impact of these deliberate or accidental introductions and consequently, a number of indigenous species survived which would have otherwise been lost.

After the sealing era, in which countless thousands of seals were killed, many of the island groups were colonised by entrepreneurs or adventurers looking for other ways to exploit the rich natural resources—from penguin oiling on Macquarie Island, to farming and whaling on and around the Auckland, Campbell and Chatham Islands. Fortunately, the harsh nature of the islands made it difficult for many of these ventures to succeed. With the exception of the Chatham Islands, all the islands were eventually declared Nature Reserves and more recently World Heritage Areas. Several major islands within the Chatham archipelago have now also been declared Nature Reserves and a number of significant Reserves have been established on the main island.

Science and research

Just as dreamers and entrepreneurs were attracted to these islands in the hope that they would prove to be their El Dorado, scientists and naturalists from a multitude of countries have been attracted to their diverse and unique natural histories. The Australian government has maintained a scientific base and metrological station on Macquarie Island since 1948. New Zealand maintained a manned weather station on Campbell Island from the end of the Second World War until 1995, when it was decided that an automated station would be cheaper to run and maintain. Unfortunately, the automated station isn't able to carry out the scientific observations that the station staff did. Chatham Island is the only one of these islands with a permanent human population and scheduled air and shipping services. It no longer has a manned weather station, but because it is relatively easy to get to, there are regular visits by researchers from many disciplines.

Because of their isolation, research on the other New Zealand islands has often been driven by individuals with a passion for their work. Up until the last decade of the twentieth century, the science programs on the New Zealand islands were vetted by the Outlying Islands Committee, a group of people selected for their specialist knowledge of the islands and their expertise in island management. With the formation of the Department of Conservation in 1987, the Outlying Islands Committee was disbanded and the responsibility for science and management passed to the Southland Conservancy. A collective Conservation Management Strategy (CMS) replaced the individual island management plans and a Science Strategy was developed to determine the type and nature of the science that was deemed appropriate.

The Science Strategy spelt the end of the large, multi-disciplinary expeditions to the New Zealand islands and saw the emergence of the 'project based' model of research and management. Sadly, though, this model has limited the opportunities for post-graduates and emerging young scientists to undertake research projects in this unique environment. Consequently, it seems scientists with this kind of training and background will become scarce at a time when these islands and the surrounding Southern Ocean are increasingly being recognised as barometers of the health of the planet.

PARAKEET RESEARCHER Graeme Elliott, of the New Zealand Department of Conservation, attempts to catch Antipodes Island Parakeets as part of a research project on Antipodes Island. *KATH WALKER.*

Macquarie Island research has been managed historically by the Tasmanian Parks and Wildlife Service permit system and logistically through the Australian Antarctic Division. Several generations of scientists from a variety of institutions have lived and worked on Macquarie Island for many years, with a number of long-term monitoring programs still running today.

Many of the recent management projects on these islands have focused on the removal of introduced animals with excellent results. Sheep, cattle, cats and rats have been removed from Campbell Island while cattle, rabbits, mice and goats have also been removed from the Auckland Island group. These eradications have allowed the reintroduction of species like the Campbell Island Teal (*Anas aucklandica nesiotis*) to Campbell Island, which has ensured their long-term survival. Cats and wekas have also been removed from Macquarie Island, with immediate benefits to the seabird populations breeding there.

Tourism

Just as scientists and researchers are recognising the importance of these islands, so are tourists looking for a genuine wilderness and wildlife experience. Tourism to the islands is not new. Some of the earliest tourists traveled on the government inspection ships in the 1890s, but it wasn't until the emergence of expedition cruising, or ecotourism, in the 1980s that demand really increased. The respective governments have responded with rules, regulations and guidelines. Operators are effectively licensed and are allocated quota. Quota currently meets demand but as other operators become interested, this may not be the case in the future. Some groups advocate shutting the islands away due to concerns over the possible impacts of these visitors. However, while tourism is well-managed and continues to create awareness (and also government revenue) it is unlikely to be stopped, unless of course it can be demonstrated that it is having a detrimental impact on the islands.

A WINTERS DAY The plateau of Macquarie Island bears the brunt of the Furious Fifties that bring cold air masses from the south and west. While the plateau region is often blanketed in snow, it rarely settles for long periods due to the wind and rain. *ALEKS TERAUDS*.

CLIMATE

ONE ASPECT THAT the islands south of New Zealand share in common with other Southern Ocean islands is a climate dominated by prevailing westerly winds which circle the globe incessantly at these latitudes. All the island groups described here lie in the Roaring Forties and the Furious Fifties and there is a very good reason that such names have been coined for these regions. Strong to gale force winds, cool temperatures and low sunshine hours are typical features of all these islands.

A HARSH ENVIRONMENT

The wind blows nearly all the time; it shapes the vegetation, it influences where the animals live and it is responsible for the pounding seas that have left their indelible mark on the coastlines. The weather systems that pass through the region generally don't last long but they are frequent and often severe. Campbell and Macquarie Islands, the southernmost of the island groups, are probably hardest hit by the prevailing westerlies. Nothing stands between them and the weather systems that are created deep in southerly latitudes, and those systems often hit these islands with incredible force. Gusts of over 50 knots occur on at least 100 days of the year at these locations and will occasionally reach 80 knots or more. Winds are generally strongest in the winter and spring months and lighter in the summer months. Campbell Island has around 25 days of sunshine a year and Macquarie Island just a few more, at 35 days. On average, that means only two to three hours of sunshine each day.

The average annual temperature on Macquarie Island is just 4°C, while at Campbell Island it is a little higher, at 6°C. Moving further north, the island climates change.

On the Auckland and Antipodes Islands, mean annual temperature is slightly warmer at 8°C, but westerly winds are still common, and overcast and cloudy days predominate. Due to a lack of measurements, the mean annual temperature of the Bounty Islands is not known, but it is estimated to be around 10°C. Sitting closer to the Subtropical Convergence, The Snares are slightly warmer again and the more northerly lying Chatham Islands are the warmest of all the groups, with temperatures frequently rising into the mid-twenties in the summer months. All of the island groups receive around 1000–2000 millimetres of rainfall each year, usually falling as persistent drizzle on the more southerly island groups.

CLIMATE CHANGE

Oceanic islands like these provide ideal environments to investigate climate change. Due to their locations and relatively stable climates, change can often be detected more easily. Combine this with the fact that Macquarie and Campbell Islands have a long history of meteorological observations and they become near perfect climate change study sites. There is little doubt that the climate on the islands is changing, with studies estimating temperature rises of 0.5–3°C over the last 60 years throughout the subantarctic. Not only has the air temperature been found to increase over this time period, but some islands have become drier and recent evidence suggests the surrounding oceans are also getting warmer.

CAMPBELL ALBATROSS Shown here hovering in flight, this species largely feeds on squid that are abundant in the Southern Ocean. *AARON RUSS.*

THE SOUTHERN OCEAN

The Southern Ocean is a vast body of water that encircles the globe. At its centre is the Antarctic ice cap—thousands of cubic kilometres of ice which cools the waters and sets the currents and frontal systems of the Southern Ocean in motion. The Southern Ocean extends up into the South Temperate Zone and is usually considered to reach the southernmost shores of New Zealand and Australia. Throughout most of its range, the ocean is deep and featureless. However, there are ridges and seamounts, undersea trenches and vast abyssal plains. Many of the larger undersea features can be located by the presence of islands like the Auckland, Campbell and Antipodes Islands, which are the exposed, eroded remnants of volcanoes. Macquarie Island is the exposed part of a vast ridgeline that stretches from New Zealand well into the Southern Ocean, rising thousands of metres from the sea floor.

The currents

In the Southern Hemisphere there is a large ocean current system encircling Antarctica known as the Antarctic Circumpolar Current. At the northern border of this current, known as the Antarctic Convergence or Polar Front, warmer waters from northern regions meet colder waters from Antarctica. This current system and subsequent mixing of water masses not only influences the global climate, it also concentrates food in areas known as 'fronts', creating reliable food sources for many animals.

Seabirds and seals also feed in waters over shelf areas, where deeper and shallower waters mix, creating upwellings that are again high in nutrients and food. All the islands considered here, with the exception of Macquarie Island, are located on either the Campbell Plateau or Chatham Rise, with an average ocean depth of between 400-1000 metres. They are sometimes referred to as the New Zealand continental shelf islands. The currents that circumnavigate the globe at these latitudes must all rise to pass over these shelf areas, creating further mixing of deeper and shallower waters and again, increasing productivity in the area.

Together with the Campbell Plateau and Chatham Rise, the South Island of New Zealand also has a major influence on the surrounding ocean and this in turn influences the waters surrounding the nearby islands to the south. Warmer waters from the East Australian Current flowing through the Tasman Sea are blocked by the South Island, effectively allowing the cooler, less salty waters from the subantarctic to move into the region south-east of the mainland.

FULMAR PRION This small prion is hunting for small fish or crustaceans on the surface of the ocean. *ALEKS TERAUDS.*

FLYING BENEATH WAVES Penguins evolved from a common ancestor with petrels, and what were once wings have become high powered flippers that propel them through the water at great speeds with amazing manoeuvrability. *AARON RUSS.*

The Subtropical Convergence marks another boundary between these warmer and colder waters and curves around the South Island of New Zealand, up the east coast, then east again at the Chatham Rise. The Chatham Rise also has a blocking effect on warmer waters from northerly latitudes heading south. With the combination of the warmer and colder waters mixing and the upwelling effect of the Chatham Rise itself, it is little wonder that the waters in this region are renowned as some of the most productive in the world. Seabirds and other marine organisms travel to this area in their thousands to take advantage of the bountiful supply of food.

Marine life

The waters of the Southern Ocean are rich in marine life. At the base of this ecosystem is phytoplankton—tiny plant-like organisms that form the building blocks of all oceanic food chains. Zooplankton feed off phytoplankton, making them the second link in the marine food chain. Zooplankton include small, shrimp-like creatures called krill which provide food for a multitude of animals, including whales, albatrosses, seals and penguins.

Squid is another fundamental part of the Southern Ocean food chain and is one of the main food sources for a whole variety of animals, particularly the albatrosses and seals who range vast distances over the ocean in search of this prey. The distribution of plankton, krill and squid, and therefore the animals that eat them, is strongly associated with the currents and frontal system of the Southern Ocean. The congregations are patchily distributed and this is why many of the animals that inhabit the Southern Ocean have developed the ability to travel long distances.

CHATHAM ISLANDS

REKOHU, WHAREKAURI • 43°–45°S • 176°35'E • 96 700 ha • 210 m a.s.l

Lying around 900 kilometres east of Christchurch, New Zealand, the Chatham Islands are extremely isolated from all other land masses. The first people probably arrived on the Chathams sometime in the fourteenth century. These Polynesians, who were to become known as the Moriori, developed a peaceful and sustainable way of life which would change very quickly with the arrival of Europeans, who plundered the marine life. The terrestrial biome also suffered considerably in the first 150 years of European and Maori occupation and as a consequence the islands are a shadow of their former selves. However, even as a shadow they retain natural values that are outstanding amongst islands of the world. The Chatham Islands occupy an interesting position, where two of the world's great oceans meet, creating a unique ecosystem not seen anywhere else in the world.

Magenta Petrel

THE CHATHAM ISLANDS Covering almost 100 000 hectares, this island group is the largest of the wild islands to the south and east of New Zealand. It is also the most northerly, with a temperate climate, and the only one to have permanent, non-transitory human settlement.

CHATHAM ISLAND The landscapes of the Chatham Island are diverse, and many of them have been changed irrevocably by the presence of humans. Long sandy beaches are common, as is farmland, shown here to be reverting to a more natural state. *RUSS COLLECTION.*

RANGATIRA CAVES Cavernous weathering in soft volcanic breccia and ash laid down during volcanic eruptions ca. 3-5 million years ago has formed these large caves on the coast of Rangatira in the Chatham Islands. *ALEKS TERAUDS*.

GEOGRAPHY AND GEOLOGY

The Chatham Islands as they stand today are the only parts of the Chatham Rise that are above water. As such, they provide a unique window into this underwater feature. The islands are geologically diverse, shaped predominantly by volcanic activity, uplift, erosion and sedimentary deposition over millions of years. The fossil record is rich, particularly from between 30–90 million years ago.

Geography

The Chatham Islands consist of four main islands and seven smaller islets. Chatham Island (Rekohu) is by far the biggest at approximately 90 000 hectares. The next biggest, with an area of 6300 hectares, is Pitt Island (Rangiauria), which sits around 20 kilometres south-east of the main island. South-east Island (Rangatira) lies just off the south-east coast of Pitt Island and has an area of 218 hectares. Mangere Island is the next biggest at 113 hectares and it lies off the west coast of Pitt Island. Smaller islets that make up the Chatham Islands include Little Mangere (Tapuaenuku), Castle Rock and Sail Rock, which are all clustered around Mangere Island. Outlying islets include The Sisters, The Pyramid, The Forty Fours and Star Keys.

Chatham Island has no large mountains, reaching a maximum elevation of just over 200 metres in the south. The southern hills are the eroded remains of a large volcano and are partly mantled by peat. This peat layer developed during and since the last glaciation, which ended about 14 000–16 000 years ago, and it extends over much of the northern part of the island, studded with isolated volcanic hills.

Over 20 per cent of Chatham Island is covered by water, with lagoons and lakes common features. The largest is Te Whanga Lagoon, which has periodically been open to the sea and which dominates the eastern side of the island. Small lakes are also common on the periphery of the wetlands. The coastline is a mixture of sweeping white, sandy beaches interspersed with cliffs or rock shorelines in the north, while spectacular cliffs are common in the south.

Pitt Island is higher, drier and more rugged than the main island, mainly covered with low-lying bush and undoubtedly still recovering from the damage that humans caused by clearing much of the native forest. High, steep cliffs are prominent along the southern coastline of the island.

DINOSAUR BONES The sedimentary rocks of the Chatham Islands are rich in fossils. These fossils were recently unearthed along a remote stretch of beach on the Chatham Islands. *JEFFERY D. STILWELL.*

Origins

Around 100 million years ago the New Zealand continental land mass, which include the Chatham Rise, lay on the margin of the supercontinent Gondwana. The Chatham Rise (and the Chatham Islands) were formed during the fragmentation of the edges of the supercontinent between 65–100 million years ago. Over long periods of time, varying sea levels and volcanic activity significantly changed the shape of the land masses that now form the Chatham Islands; by around 65 million years ago the land bridge that connected the Chatham Islands to mainland New Zealand had been completely severed.

The islands that we now know as the Chathams are the result of repeated episodes of volcanic eruption over the last 80 million years, together with uplift along several major faults that are thought to have begun to move around 100 million years ago.

The southern region of Chatham Island and much of Pitt Island are the eroded remnants of a large, broad volcano that probably peaked in activity some 70–80 million years ago. Several cliffed islands west of Pitt Island—Mangere, Little Mangere, Castle and Sail Rocks—are the wave-eroded remnants of another large, but more recent Pliocene volcano. Volcanic rocks from this time period also form Rangatira, The Pyramid and Star Keys.

Geology

Dating from its long association with the New Zealand land mass (and accordingly, Gondwana), very old continental rocks are exposed in places on the Chatham Islands. Produced deep beneath the earth under huge pressure and extremely high temperatures, these metamorphic rocks are known as Chatham Schist (and greywacke) and form the bulk of the spectacular northern coastline and the outlying Western Reef. The Forty Fours—New Zealand's easternmost emergent land mass—are also wave-eroded remnants of greywacke.

Basalt lava flows associated with Chatham Island's southern volcano are known as the Southern Volcanics and they form the bulk of the southern half of the main island. This southern tableland is built from layer upon layer of basalt lava flows and these are spectacularly exposed on the south coast, north of Pitt Strait.

Between the northern schists and southern uplands, the majority of the central section of Chatham Island is made up of sedimentary rocks now covered in peats. These were deposited in shallow water during volcanic activity around 60–70 million years ago, and comprise a mixture of volcanic ash, breccia and limestone deposits typical of open ocean conditions. Younger volcanoes continued to form in northern Chatham Island up until a few million years ago, forming the characteristic cone-shaped hills in the north of the island.

The Fossil Record

Due to the extended periods of time when much of the island group was under water, the sedimentary rocks on the Chatham Islands are rich in fossil material. There are fossils here that are not found anywhere else in the world, including mainland New Zealand. However, the oldest fossil-bearing rocks on the island are not marine, but date from over 100 million years ago when the Chatham Islands were still part of Gondwana. Found on northern

THE PYRAMID One of several small islands off Pitt Island that are the remnants of a larger volcano, The Pyramid is a plug of volcanic rock known as phonolite. *NATHAN RUSS.*

Pitt Island, these rocks—known as the Tupuangi Formation—were largely deposited in rivers and estuaries, and contain fossil spores and pollen of mosses, conifers and early flowering plants similar to beeches. The oldest marine fossils known from the Chathams are also found on Pitt Island and were formed during eruptions which deposited volcanic sand into a shallow sea. They contain tiny, ancient, many-limbed organisms reminiscent of squid.

The Te Whenga Limestone so prevalent throughout central Chatham Island is also rich in fossils; in fact most are formed by the aggregation of the shell-like hard parts of marine invertebrate organisms. Other fossils in the limestone include fragments of sea urchins and sharks' teeth. Fossilised bones of marine vertebrates, including reptiles, birds and dinosaurs, have also been found in another formation—the Takatika Grit—on the northern coast. Associated with the Te Whanga Limestone is another sedimentary layer, formed of volcanic ash during another episode of volcanic activity and known as Red Bluff Tuff. This distinctive red-brown rock contains fossil marine organisms not found anywhere else in the southern hemisphere.

CHATHAM ISLANDS

FORGET-ME-NOTS The Chatham Island forget-me-not (*Myosotidium hortensia*) is an iconic species of the island group and is not found anywhere else in the world.
AARON RUSS.

FLORA

Before the arrival of Europeans, the Chatham Islands had a unique and highly distinctive native plant community. Around 325 species of flowering plant are indigenous to the Chatham Islands, with a further 215 known as 'naturalised exotics' that grow wild. Several plant species are yet to be named and the mosses, lichens and fungi are poorly known. David Given and Ian Atkinson described the vegetation and major habitat types on the Chatham Islands in the Department of Conservation publication *Chatham Islands: Heritage and Conservation* and this should be consulted for a more detailed description of the flora and plant communities. Although the changes wrought by European colonisation make it difficult to accurately picture the original vegetation, enough survives today to provide clues about the nature of the pristine vegetation. Changes associated with human occupation of the islands— including fire, introduced animals and plants and the wholesale clearing of native vegetation—have made many of the plants, and sometimes whole communities, threatened and in danger of extinction on the islands today.

Before settlement

The pristine vegetation of Chatham Island, Pitt Island and Rangatira was dominated by broadleaf forests along most coasts and peat forming forests inland. On the main island, extensive low-lying or gently sloping land surfaces provided ideal conditions for peat formation and were interspersed with rushes and moorlands. There were also numerous tarns and lagoons—some brackish—leading to well-developed wetland vegetation types. In addition, due to its location and climate, at some sites on Chatham Island peat has been forming more or less continuously for perhaps tens of thousands of years. Some peat columns on the main island provide a virtually continuous pollen record of changing vegetation and climate over a time span that is hard to match elsewhere in the New Zealand region. Many of the threatened plant communities on the Chatham Islands are unique, and once gone will be impossible to replace.

The coast and outlying islets

Most of the smaller islets around the Chathams (like The Sisters, The Forty Fours, Star Keys and The Pyramid) are extremely exposed to wind and associated spray, with very little soil and consequently very few plants. The exceptions are a large groundsel (*Senecio radiolatus radiolatus*), which grows in loose soil, and the Chatham Island button-daisy (*Leptinella feathersonii*), which is rare but distinctive in rock crevices.

Throughout the Chathams, but particularly to the south of the larger islands and on the smaller islands, there are areas of native cliff plants characterised by the small endemic shrubs Dieffenbach's koromiko (*Hebe dieffenbachia*) and Chatham Island koromiko (*H. chathamica*), often with the endemic grasses *Poa chathamica* and *Festuca coxii*. Conspicuous endemic herb species such as the Chatham Island forget-me-not (*Myosotidium hortensia*) and soft speargrass (*Aciphylla dieffenbachia*) are also found in inaccessible places where there is no grazing. Other plants that grow on the coastal cliffs and rocky shorelines include the endemic ice plant (*Disphyma papillatum*) and the Chatham Islands geranium (*Geranium traversii*). Many other species also occur around the coastal region, including the Chatham Island korokio (*Corokia macrocarpa*), Chatham Islands mingimingi (*Cyathodes robusta*) and kawakawa (*Macropiper excelsum*). Further away from the splash zone, other species start to appear like the soft speargrass and leatherwood scrub or keketerehe (*Olearia chathamica*).

The dune community

On Chatham Island impressive sand dunes dominate much of the coastal landscape and although they used to be largely held together by the native pingao (*Desmoschoenus spiralis*) and endemic herbs such as Chatham Island forget-me-nots, sowthistle (*Embergeria grandiflora*) and the southern nettle (*Urtica australis*), grazing by stock has largely eliminated these species. Most of the dunes that were once covered with this vegetation are now dominated by the introduced marram grass (*Ammophila arenaria*). Inland from the grass zone, other small shrubs, including sand daphne or toroheke (*Pimelia arenaria*), begin to dominate.

On consolidated sands further inland, Chatham Islands mingimingi often predominates. A little further inland, the first trees to become established are the Chatham Islands akeake (*Dodonaea viscosa*) and mahoe (*Melicytus chathamica*), then karamu (*Coprosma chathamica*), matipo (*Myrsine chathamica*) and kopi (*Corynocarpus laevigatus*). These trees form a tight and dense canopy typical of dune forests that are buffeted by strong winds with a heavy salt load. Lush herbaceous vegetation made up of the Chatham Island button daisy and *Carex trifida*, often with the groundsel, is found on highly fertile soils associated with nesting or burrowing oceanic sea birds. This vegetation was formerly widespread on many coastal sites.

Wetlands

Wetlands are a common feature on Chatham Island as water draining from inland areas towards the ocean is often trapped behind dunes to form lakes or wetter areas. In these areas the rushes *Leptocarpus* spp. and *Sporadanthus* spp. prevail. *Leptocarpus* rushlands usually include patches of herbaceous turf where several grass species are present. These herbaceous turf areas also dominate large areas of the lagoon shore and seasonally wet hollows. Where there is little water movement, mossfields of *Sphagnum* and scattered inaka (*Dracophyllum paludosum*) develop. In wetter areas, the sedge *Eleocharis acuta* is more common. In areas of high water flow and good nutrient input, several species of flax and *Blechnum* ferns predominate. Estuarine rushlands composed of *Eleocharis acuta*, *Baumea rubiginosa* and *Leptocarpus* spp. form in the lower reaches of some streams and small lagoons.

Peat areas

Further inland on Chatham Island, peat is present beneath both tarahinau (*Dracophyllum arboreum*) forest and stands of the bamboo rush *Sporadanthus traversii*. The latter has extremely well-developed root systems which may extend up to a metre below the surface. The accumulations of peat are very prone to fire and can burn underground for several years. Following the arrival of the Moriori, these peat fires became a familiar part of the landscape and increased even further following the arrival of Europeans. It is likely that the increase of fire eliminated much of the tarahinau forest in the low-lying peat areas.

The mostly inaccessible upland peat areas, which form a large part of the southern main island, are hilly and covered by tarahinau forest up to 15 metres high. Sheep, cattle and pigs wander through this forest, ensuring that any new seedlings have little chance of surviving into trees. Consequently, recruitment into the forest is largely dependent on seedlings that have established as epiphytes on tree fern trunks. The tree ferns wheki-ponga (*Dicksonia fibrosa*) and wheki (*D. squarrosa*) are found throughout the wetter forested areas. The gully tree fern (*Cyathea cunninghamii*) grows up to 12 metres in height on a long slender trunk, with soft curved fronds up to 3 metres long. The tree ferns themselves are not palatable to grazing stock and as such they dominate areas of the forest in some of the valleys where grazing occurs.

Volcanic hills and lowlands

In the northern part of Chatham Island, the once tarahinau-forested volcanic hills and lowlands are now a mixture of bracken fernland, gorse scrub and some coarse pasture. Like the wetlands, nutrient availability largely determines the plant assemblages and in areas of low nutrients, bracken forms a patchwork mosaic with tangled ferns and *Baumea* rushes. Despite wholesale clearing and grazing, odd forest remnants remain scattered throughout the Chatham Island group. On the better drained soils, especially where peats mix with coastal sand, tall broadleaf remnants are characterised by kopi, matipo, karamu and akeake. Chatham Islands lacewood (*Pseudopanax chathamicus*), also known as hoho, is widely distributed, while the nikau palm (*Rhopalostylis* sp.), ribbonwood (*Plagianthus regius* var. *chathamicus*), akeake and kowhai (*Sophora microphylla*) are more localised in their distribution. Several species still depend on the fertile soils that are only found where there are high densities of burrowing petrels.

On southern Pitt Island, tarahinau is the dominant forest tree on the more peaty soils. *Dracophyllum* forests like these have low biological diversity due to deep acidic beds of litter and thick peat. Increasing diversity really only comes from the narrow ribbons of mixed broadleaf forest in the gullies winding through the uplands.

Marine plants

There are over 140 species of marine plant around the shores of the Chatham Islands. There are two species of bull kelp—the Antarctic bull kelp (*Durvillaea antarctica*) and a second endemic species, *Durvillaea chathamensis*. The Antarctic bull kelp dominates the lower intertidal platforms around the rocky coastline, while the endemic species occurs in deeper, more subtidal waters. Other species of large kelp include *Lessonia tholiformis* and *Macrocystis pyrifera*. The former tends to grow in deeper water of up to 15 metres, while the latter usually forms thick underwater forests in more sheltered locations. There are numerous species of algae that utilise the shelter of the larger kelps. These 'understorey' species include several smaller brown, red and green algae. Coralline red algae are the most common understorey algae and are found throughout the coastal water column.

RARE REMNANTS Dense forests such as these once dominated the landscape of the Chatham Islands. Since the arrival of humans the extent of these areas has been severely reduced, but they still survive in small patches. *ALEKS TERAUDS*.

THE PAREA Native to the Chatham Islands, this pigeon survives in very small numbers, with only a few hundred birds comprising the entire population. In recent years, predator control and stock exclusion fencing in the Tuku Valley have resulted in improved breeding success and an increase in numbers. *NATHAN RUSS.*

FAUNA

Due to the repeated submerging and emerging of the islands that make up the Chatham Island group, many of the animals evolved without competitors over a relatively short evolutionary time period. Considering the lack of predators and the almost unparalleled productivity in the surrounding waters, it is little wonder that fossil bones in the older dunes suggest the Chatham Islands were once the most important breeding site for petrels anywhere in the world. Unfortunately, human colonisation has taken its toll and over 20 bird species are thought to have become extinct since the arrival of humans. Today, there are 52 native bird species, 18 of which are endemic. There are no native mammals or reptiles on the Chatham Islands (except for a skink on The Pyramid), but there are a myriad of introduced animals, both feral and domesticated.

Albatrosses

The Chatham Albatross (*Thalassarche eremita*) breeds annually on The Pyramid, at the southern end of the Chatham Island group. In 2004, the population was estimated to be at around 4500 breeding pairs. A distinctive looking albatross with a dark grey head and bright orange/yellow bill, it is listed as 'critically endangered' by the International Union for Conservation of Nature (IUCN) as it only breeds in this one location and is known to be caught and killed on longline fishing vessels.

Apart from a small number of breeding pairs in southern New Zealand, the entire world population of the Northern Royal Albatross (*Diomedea sanfordi*) also breeds in the Chatham Island group. A population of around 6500 pairs breeds mainly on The Forty Fours, Big Sister Island and Little Sister Island. The northern race of the Buller's Albatross (*Thalassarche bulleri*) also breeds on the plateau basins of The Forty Fours, and the cliffs of Big Sister and Little Sister Islands, with a total population thought to number around 1500–2000 breeding pairs. Several other species of albatross have been observed breeding in the Chatham group, but only in very small numbers.

The Chatham Island Taiko

The Chatham Island Taiko or Magenta Petrel (*Pterodroma magentae*) was thought to be extinct for over a century until David Crockett and his team rediscovered it in the Tuku Valley on the main Chatham Island in 1978. Since then it has been the subject of intensive management involving local people, scientists and hundreds of fieldworkers. In 2004 there were estimated to be 10–15 pairs, in known burrows, that attempt to breed each year and the total population is thought to be in the vicinity of 100–150 birds, making it one of the rarest petrels in the world. Due to the generosity of the Tuanui family, who donated the land for the 1239 hectare Tuku Nature Reserve, the main breeding site of this species is now a protected area, with fences and predator control measures being undertaken.

The Chatham Petrel

The Chatham Petrel (*Pterodroma axillaris*) is a medium-sized petrel that was once widespread over the Chatham Island group. While it is impossible to estimate their pre-human population size, it is likely to have been much larger than the 1000 breeding pairs that survive today in the forests of Rangatira. In the same forests there are hundreds of thousands of nesting Broad-billed Prions (*Pachyptila vittata*) and they tend to out-compete the Chatham Petrel for burrows, putting further pressure on this small and vulnerable population.

OTHER PETRELS

The large, albatross-sized Northern Giant Petrel (*Macronectes halli*) breeds on The Sisters and The Forty Fours, with an estimated population size of around 2000 breeding pairs. Many of the smaller petrels are no longer present on Chatham Island or Pitt Island due to predation by feral animals such as pigs, cats and rats. The absence of introduced predators on many of the smaller outlying islands has allowed the formation of large colonies of Sooty Shearwaters (*Puffinus griseus*), with their main breeding population on Little Mangere. Subantarctic Little Shearwaters (*Puffinus assimilis elegans*) are also present, but in much lower numbers, and are largely restricted to Star Keys.

Other petrels that breed on the Chatham Islands include tens of thousands of the southern subspecies of the Common Diving Petrel (*Pelecanoides urinatrix chathamensis*), Grey-backed Storm Petrels (*Garrodia nereis*) and White-faced Storm Petrels (*Pelagodroma marina maoriana*). White-faced Storm Petrels are estimated to breed in numbers approaching one million pairs, with over 80 per cent of the population in the forested areas of Rangatira. Other medium-sized petrels include small numbers of Black-winged Petrel (*Pterodroma nigripennis*), Broad-billed Prions, Fairy Prions (*Pachyptila turtur*) and the endemic subspecies of the Fulmar Prion (*Pachyptila crassirostris pyramidalis*).

OTHER SEABIRDS

Two endemic cormorants (also known as shags) breed on the Chatham Islands. Chatham Island Shags (*Phalacrocorax onslowi*) breed in colonies on coastal stacks of the main island and around many of the smaller outlying islands. Census estimates vary, with a total breeding population of between 200–800 pairs. The Pitt Island Shag (*Phalacrocorax feathersoni*) also breeds in small colonies on most of the islands of the Chatham group, with a total population of approximately 500–700 pairs.

Around 200 pairs of Subantarctic (Brown) Skua (*Catharacta lonnbergi*) breed on Rangatira and Mangere Island. Gulls present in the Chatham group include Southern Black-backed Gulls (*Larus dominicanus*) and Red-billed Gulls (*Larus scopulinus*), while several hundred pairs of the White-fronted Tern (*Sterna striata*) breed on the steep cliffs and rock islets. A subspecies of the Little Blue Penguin (*Eudyptula minor chathamensis*) breeds around the coastal areas of most islands in the group.

SHOREBIRDS AND WADERS

The Chatham Island Oystercatcher (*Haematopus chathamensis*) is another species that only breeds on the Chatham Islands. While being one of the rarest oystercatcher in the world, this species is found right around the northern and southern coasts of the main island and many of the smaller islands. In response to proactive management, numbers of this species have increased since 1987 and today there is thought to be at least 250 birds in the population. The New Zealand Shore Plover (*Thinornis novaeseelandiae*) breeds in low numbers around the coast of Rangatira and is listed as

CHATHAM ISLAND BIRDS (clockwise from top left) Chatham Albatross, New Zealand Shore Plover, White-fronted Tern, Chatham Island Oystercatcher.

MORE CHATHAM ISLAND BIRDS (clockwise from top left) 'Old Blue' the matriach of most Black Robins alive today, Chatham Island Tui, Chatham Island Red-crowned Parakeet, Chatham Island Tomtit.

'endangered' by the IUCN. This species has also benefited from proactive management and reintroductions have seen its range expand to Mangere and other islands around New Zealand.

White-faced Herons (*Ardea novaehollandiae*) also breed on the Chatham Islands and have most likely benefited from the clearing of forest into pasture. Several species of migrant wader also spend time on the Chatham Islands. Freshwater birds include the Black Shag (*Phalacrocorax carbo*), Black Swan (*Cygnus atratus*), Feral Goose (*Anser anser*), Grey Duck (*Anas superciliosa*), Mallard (*Anas platyrhynchos*), Pukeko (*Porphyrio melanotus*), Spotless Crake (*Porzana tabuensis*), Marsh Crake (*Porzana pusilla*) and the Pied Stilt (*Himantopus himantopus*).

Forest birds

The forest birds of the islands have suffered greatly from habitat clearance and the introduction of feral animals. Many are endemic and large numbers of those remaining exist only in very small populations on outlying islands. Proactive management strategies have allowed many of these populations to be pulled back from the brink of extinction. One such species, the Chatham Island Snipe (*Coenocorypha pusilla*), became extinct on Mangere Island in the 1880s but was reintroduced there in 1970. More recently, 20 birds were introduced to the Ellen Elizabeth Preece Conservation Covenant on Pitt Island. There is now an estimated breeding population of around 1000 breeding pairs throughout the Chatham Islands. The Parea (*Hemiphaga chathamensis*), one of the worlds largest and heaviest pigeons, has also suffered near-extinction. Today, they are largely confined to the southern forests of the main island. A census in 1995 estimated there were 150 birds and it is thought that numbers have increased since this time.

ALBATROSS RESEARCH CAMP This camp on Little Sister Island was used as a base by Wildlife Service staff to study the breeding biology of the Northern Royal Albatross. *RUSS COLLECTION.*

Parakeets and Warblers

There are two endemic parakeets on the Chatham Islands: Forbes Parakeet (*Cyanoramphus forbesi*) and Chatham Island Red-crowned Parakeet (*Cyanoramphus novaezelandiae chathamensis*). The Forbes Parakeet has a yellow crown and narrow red frontal band above the bill and is one of New Zealand's rarest parakeets. Besides the risk from habitat clearance and feral animals, it is also at risk of losing its identity through hybridisation with the more common Chatham Island Red-crowned Parakeet. The Chatham Island Warbler (*Gerygone albofrontata*) is another endemic species that breeds on most of the islands of the group, inhabiting the entire range of native forests.

SAVING THE BLACK ROBIN Don Merton (shown above) was a key member of the team that worked to save the Black Robin on the Chatham Islands. DON MERTON.

CHATHAM ISLAND SNIPE Were re-introduced to Mangere Island from Rangatira in 1970. This chick was evidence of their success on Mangere Island. DON MERTON.

THE BLACK ROBIN

The Black Robin (*Petroica traversi*) is probably one of the best known of the Chatham Island endemics. For many years it was restricted to a tiny population on Little Mangere Island, protected by high cliffs and inaccessible breeding locations. The entire population of just seven birds was removed from this island in 1976 and taken to Mangere Island, where chicks were fostered out to other species so that productivity could be increased. This was very successful and today there are small but viable populations on Mangere Island and Rangatira, with current estimates of over 200 birds in the population. Recent attempts have been made to establish a third population on Pitt Island.

OTHER LAND BIRDS

The Chatham Island Fantail (*Rhipidura fuliginosa penita*) and the Chatham Island Tomtit (*Petroica macrocephala chathamensis*) are considered endemic subspecies, with the former breeding on Chatham and Pitt Islands while the latter is largely restricted to Pitt Island, Rangatira and Mangere Island. The Chatham Island Tui (*Prosthemadera novaeseelandiae chathamensis*) is another endemic subspecies that once bred on most of the islands but is today restricted to a small population on Rangatira.

The Chatham Island Pipit (*Anthus novaeseelandiae chathamensis*) is the only endemic open country species in the Chatham Island group. Other open country species that are native to New Zealand include the Australasian Harrier (*Circus approximans*), the Buff Weka (*Gallirallus australis hectori*), the Banded Dotterel (*Charadrius bicinctus*), Spur-winged Plover (*Vanellus miles novaehollandiae*) and the Welcome Swallow (*Hirundo tahitica neoxena*). Of these species, the Buff Weka is of particular note as it has been wiped out from its former range on mainland New Zealand and now only survives in good numbers on the Chatham Islands. At least a dozen other open country species that are non-native to New Zealand have made their way to the Chatham Islands and established breeding populations.

Marine mammals

The New Zealand Fur Seal (*Arctocephalus forsteri*) was once numerous throughout the Chatham Island group, but by about 1810 foreign sealers had killed most of them for their skins. Today, several thousand fur seals are estimated to live on the island group, with most breeding on the smaller outlying islands. However, numbers prior to the arrival of Europeans are thought to have been far higher. The New Zealand (Hooker's) Sea Lion (*Phocarctos hookeri*) was also much more common before the arrival of Europeans and today they are seen only occasionally. Leopard Seals (*Hydrurga leptonyx*) and Southern Elephant Seals (*Mirounga leonina*) are also seen as occasional visitors.

The three most common species of whale seen around the Chatham Islands are Sperm Whales (*Physeter macrocephalus*), Southern Right Whales (*Eubalaena australis*) and Long-finned Pilot Whales (*Globicephala melas*). All were targeted by early foreign whalers and thousands of Sperm Whales and Southern Right Whales were killed. Today, the legacy of this indiscriminate slaughter remains, with only a few individuals of each species sighted each year. Pilot whales are more commonly observed, often in schools of hundreds.

Introduced mammals

Although Polynesian Rats (*Rattus exulans*) reached the Chatham group in the canoes of the Polynesian settlers, today they are restricted to the most inaccessible parts of the southern tablelands on Chatham Island. Sheep, cattle, pigs and goats occur in both domestic and feral states on the main island and on Pitt Island, and Australian Brush-tail Possums (*Trichosurus vulpecula*) are also prolific and destructive on the main island. European rabbits (*Oryctolagus cuniculus*) and Stoats (*Mustela erminea*) have not been introduced, but two species of rats (*Rattus norvegicus* and *Rattus rattus*), European Hedgehogs (*Erinaceus europaeus*), Feral Cats (*Felis cattus*) and House Mice (*Mus musculus*) have become well-established on the main island. Cats and mice are also present on Pitt Island but no rats.

Terrestrial invertebrates

Over 700 species of insect have been recorded on the Chatham Islands. Like the birds and plants, endemism is high and around 20 per cent are considered endemic, with many groups that are abundant on the New Zealand mainland completely absent. The forested areas of Rangatira probably host the largest biodiversity of insects, particularly large, ground-dwelling forms like wetas, cockroaches, many species of beetle and a giant spider, found nowhere else.

Among this group of Moriori, photographed in 1877, were survivors of the Maori invasion of 1835. Other members of the group include descendents of survivors. Alfred Martin album, Canterbury Museum. 19XX.2.481

The Pitt Island farm of Frederick Hunt, was one of the first established in the Chatham Islands. Alexander Turnbull Library, Wellington, New Zealand. PA1-q-041-29

Lt. William Broughton was the first European to discover the Chatham Islands. He landed in 1791 and named the island group after his ship. Columbia River Maritime Museum, Astoria. 1977.98

Once Europeans arrived on the Chatham Islands the Moriori came into contact with people from other countries and cultures for the first time. This photograph illustrates the mixed communities that developed in the 19th century. Alfred Charles Barker collection, Canterbury Museum. 1957.13.20

One of the most famous early sheep farmers, Thomas Ritchie, first arrived on the Chatham Islands in the 1840s. Alexander Turnbull Library, Wellington, New Zealand. F- 0021-120mm -9-1

HISTORY

OF ALL THE island groups covered here, the Chatham Islands are unique as the only group to have permanent, non-transitory human settlement. It seems likely that the more equitable climate associated with its relatively northerly latitude is largely responsible for this and the associated rich human history.

Early settlers

It appears that the Chatham Islands were first settled by Polynesians sometime in the fourteenth century. These early Polynesian settlers evolved quite differently from their relatives who settled on mainland New Zealand. On the Chathams Islands they abandoned horticulture, developed their own dialect, ceased to have chiefs and later outlawed warfare and killing. These people eventually became known as the Moriori and they developed a distinct way of life well suited to making good use of available food sources. Like the first European visitors, they also exploited the seals that were living on the islands, but did so with a much better understanding of how such practices could be sustained in the long term.

Europeans arrive

Europeans first visited the Chatham Islands in 1791. Lieutenant Broughton was second-in-command on a voyage from New Zealand to Tahiti and on discovering the Chatham Islands he named them after his ship. He only made one landing, at Kaingaroa in the north, where he and his crew were greeted by around 200 unarmed natives. Although it seems that the meeting was initially good-natured, relations later deteriorated and one of the Moriori was killed. Broughton departed the same day.

Despite this negative beginning, a Moriori council decided, in typical fashion, that if foreigners returned they would be met with an emblem of peace. Accordingly, sealers who visited the coast of the Chatham Islands in ensuing years found the Moriori hospitable and willing to assist them in their ventures.

The sealing industry

The first definitive record of foreign sealing on the Chatham Islands was when Captain Folger in the *Topaz*—an American ship looking for new sealing grounds—landed there in November of 1807 and took around 600 seal skins. It seems likely that sealing continued sporadically over the next few years, but records are hard to come by. Most of the sealing on the Chatham Islands occurred between 1810 and 1835. Not only was sealing carried out, but trading between Europeans and Moriori, who had collected skins, was also a lucrative business. However, before long the foreigners impact disrupted Moriori social, religious and economic life. In particular the Europeans brought with them diseases like measles and influenza, and the Moriori, having no natural immunity, suffered greatly from these introductions.

The Maori invasion

The Maori invasion in 1835 was one of the most significant events in the history of the Chatham Islands. In New Zealand, the Europeans desire for land and the introduction of firearms from 1820 onwards widened the traditional Maori tribal wars and eventually engulfed the Chatham Islands. In 1835, a Sydney brig, the *Lord Rodney* was seized by around 400 Maoris from two mainland tribes—Ngâti Mutunga and Ngâti Tama—in Port Nicholson, Wellington. After initially declining to help them escape local wars by migrating elsewhere, Captain Harwood eventually made two trips to the Chatham Islands, where he deposited 7 canoes, 70 tons of seed potatoes, 20 pigs and around 900 Maoris. The Maoris settled in quickly and began to spread through the island, encroaching on the Moriori food resources.

Even though the Moriori outnumbered the invaders by almost two to one, a Moriori council decided not to kill anybody and offer no physical resistance as killing was against their religion. The Maori began to 'walk the land', killing and eating many Moriori, enslaving them and taking title to their land. Dispirited by the suffering already brought upon them by the European diseases, many of the Moriori lost hope, feeling that the future of their race was threatened. Although the Maori conquered the Moriori they did not stay satisfied within the narrow confines of the Chatham Islands and within five years the Maori tribes fell to fighting amongst themselves.

The first whalers

After sealing became less profitable due to low seal numbers in the early 1830s, whaling became the dominant industry, beginning in the Chatham Islands in the late 1830s. One of the first successful whaling trips in the area was led by an American, Captain George Littlewood, who stopped at the Chatham Islands in 1839 and took six Southern Right Whales, one Sperm Whale and six Long-finned Pilot Whales in a month. A year earlier, the French whaler *Jean Bart* had a bloody interaction with the Maori people on the island, resulting in the death of all 40 crew.

The publicity surrounding this apparent massacre probably helped to draw attention to the Chatham Islands as a rich whaling ground and in 1839 and 1840, dozens of whaling vessels visited their productive waters.

The mildness of the winter season and the abundance of provisions made the Chatham Island grounds particularly appealing to whalers. It seems that initially Southern Right Whales were the principal targets, and later Sperm Whales. Both shore whaling and bay whaling was carried out and killing was indiscriminate, including females and calves. By 1839 whalers had depleted most of the Southern Right Whale stocks visiting the island.

Traders and farmers

In 1840 the New Zealand Company, a commercial venture set up to foster immigration to the New Zealand colonies, sent representatives to purchase Chatham Island land from the Maori conquerors in order to settle large numbers of Europeans there. Dr. Ernst Dieffenbach, the German naturalist accompanying this expedition, was the first scientist to visit the island and describe the flora and fauna. He was also one of the first to bring the plight of the Moriori to a much wider audience.

The British government overruled the New Zealand Company purchase in 1842 and the Chatham Islands were officially gazetted as part of New Zealand. Missionaries began to settle permanently in 1842 and over the next 50 years had considerable success in converting much of the population to some form of Christianity.

In the early 1840s, several trading stations were set up on the Chatham Islands to service the whaling industry, forming the base for many of the whaling activities between 1840 and 1844. Several farming ventures were also established around this time, not only on the main island but also on Pitt Island and Rangatira. In 1842, an Englishman named Frederick Hunt set up what proved to be one of the longer-term ventures on Pitt Island and his descendents still farm the island today. Two of the islands' most famous sheep farmers, Thomas Ritchie and Edward Chudleigh, also arrived on the Chatham Islands in the 1840s and established stations.

Associated with the increase in industry and associated farming practices was wholesale clearing of much of the forested areas on Chatham Island, Pitt Island, Mangere Island and Rangatira—not only for timber and firewood, but also to make way for more grazing ground. This indiscriminate clearing had a dramatic effect on the indigenous wildlife, irretrievably altering whole ecosystems by causing localised extinctions and removing significant breeding habitat and food for a variety of birds and animals. Foreign settlers also introduced pigs, cats, rodents and Australian Brush-tailed Possums, which contributed to the extinction of the native wildlife. Farmers imported livestock and used blackberry, gorse and boxthorn for shelter belts and these noxious weeds also seeded and spread rapidly.

The ocean whalers

With the depletion of the Southern Right Whale stocks, the whaling industry shifted to focus on Sperm Whales in the productive waters around the islands. American ships dominated this seasonal industry and in the latter half of the 1840s it became less common for these ships to actually stop at the Chatham Islands—they tended to

An unknown photrapher captured this scene at Torotore in the Chatham Islands in 1910. Alexander Turnbull Library, Wellington, New Zealand. C- 24355-1/2

Waitangi, on the main Chatham Island is the biggest settlement in the island group today. Here, around 1916, it was little more than a collection of farmsteads. Alexander Turnbull Library, Wellington, New Zealand. PAColl-1619-03

Sheep farming was one of the main land based industries on the Chatham Islands in 1919 when this photograph was taken. Alexander Turnbull Library, Wellington, New Zealand. G- 3244-1/1

cruise slowly through the area, taking what they could en route to the North Pacific whaling grounds. Some whaling ships did stop, however, and one longer lasting legacy of the whaling industry was that the Chatham Islands developed a thriving agricultural trade in pork and potatoes—a trade that expanded in the 1850s and 1860s to include the developing New Zealand colonies like Wellington, and even Sydney and the Australian goldfields.

After a lull through the 1850s, the 1860s saw a revival in Sperm whaling, with reliable grounds discovered south of Pitt Island. It was not unusual to see over 20 ships on the grounds in high season and trading on the Chatham Islands also peaked during this period, with ships traveling through the area as much for the good supplies as for the whaling. Whaling declined in the latter part of the 1860s and early 1870s although a few American ships continued to visit the Pitt Island whaling grounds until 1886. Hundreds, if not thousands of Sperm Whales were killed over this time period and the effect on the population of this extremely long-living creature was dramatic.

Early government

Lawlessness prevailed around the whaling stations, where the living was harsh and crude, and the islands became well-known for the brutal behaviour of the European settlers and the fighting between the Maori tribes. An attempt to bring law and order to the islands, and to curb liquor smuggling into New Zealand via the Chatham Islands, was made by appointing the first Resident Magistrate, Archibald Shand, in 1855. In 1863, Captain William Thomas was appointed to this position and from all accounts was much more effective than his predecessor. The most notable amongst his many achievements was convincing the Maoris to accept New Zealand rule and to release their Moriori slaves. The Native Land Courts sat at Waitangi for the first time in 1868 and 1870 and confirmed the Maori tribes right of ownership on the grounds of conquest. By now the totally demoralised Moriori population was much reduced, and they were awarded only half a dozen tiny reserves on which to subsist.

The fishing industry

The next resources to be exploited around the Chatham Islands were fish and shellfish, particularly Blue Cod (*Parapercis colias*). Intensively fished from 1910 to the 1950s, few regulations were in place to ensure that catches were sustainable, with considerable overfishing and resource depletion resulting. In the 1960s the focus shifted to crayfishing and within the first five years this resource was also seriously depleted by unsustainable catches. More recently, fisheries like scallops and paua have contributed significantly to the Chatham Island economy. Regulations are now in place to ensure that fishing stocks are better protected, although many local fishermen still resent the large quotas held by non-Chatham Islanders which channel few resources back into the local economy.

Indigenous culture today

The last of the full-blooded Moriori died in 1933. Many of the descendents continue to identify as Moriori and since the late 1860s Moriori, Maori and Pakeha have lived peacefully alongside each other on the Chatham Islands. However, since the 1980s a cultural revival of sorts has taken place, with Moriori and Maori tikanga, values and language being retrieved from the past and taught to members of the younger generation. In particular the opening of the spectacular Moriori Kopinga Marae in 2005 has served as a rallying point for descendents of Moriori on the island and those living in New Zealand and beyond.

Through the latter half of the twentieth century, the inhabitants of the island slowly came to terms with the fact that the wanton destruction of plant and animal life, both on land and in the sea, could not continue indefinitely. Even though the Chatham Island economy is largely supported by farming and fishing, more and more people are realising that these exploitative lifestyles are not incompatible with conserving the island's outstanding natural values for subsequent generations. Many landowners are fencing off remaining stands of bush on their land and in some cases forest regeneration is relatively rapid.

Recent research and management

The presence (and value) of predator-free offshore islands was recognised in the early 1950s. The late Sir Charles Fleming was a major advocate of these islands as refuges. He played an important role in convincing the New Zealand Wildlife Service, which had recently received new statutory powers under the Wildlife Act of 1953, to purchase and reserve Rangatira and Mangere Island. Contributions of funds from the New Zealand Forest and Bird Society helped to sway the last government doubters, who were unsure of the value of the purchases. Later, both of these island reserves were to play a major role in the

DAVID CROCKETT On New Year's Day 1978, with the first two Chatham Island taiko to be captured. *RUSSELL THOMAS.*

protection of several of the world's rarest birds and these success stories have encouraged other initiatives, with further reserves being gazetted.

Today, the Department of Conservation maintains a field station on the Chatham Islands, which employs a number of local people. The island group has its own Conservation Management Strategy and Conservation Board to advise the government on conservation issues. Tourism is becoming more important and has the support of many local people. Most amenities that are found on mainland New Zealand can now be obtained on the islands, although many of the things that mainlanders take for granted only arrived in the last two to three decades. Nevertheless, urban and industrial developments remain relatively low-key and in terms of its natural values, Chatham Island remains the northern jewel in the crown of the islands south of New Zealand.

BOUNTY ISLANDS

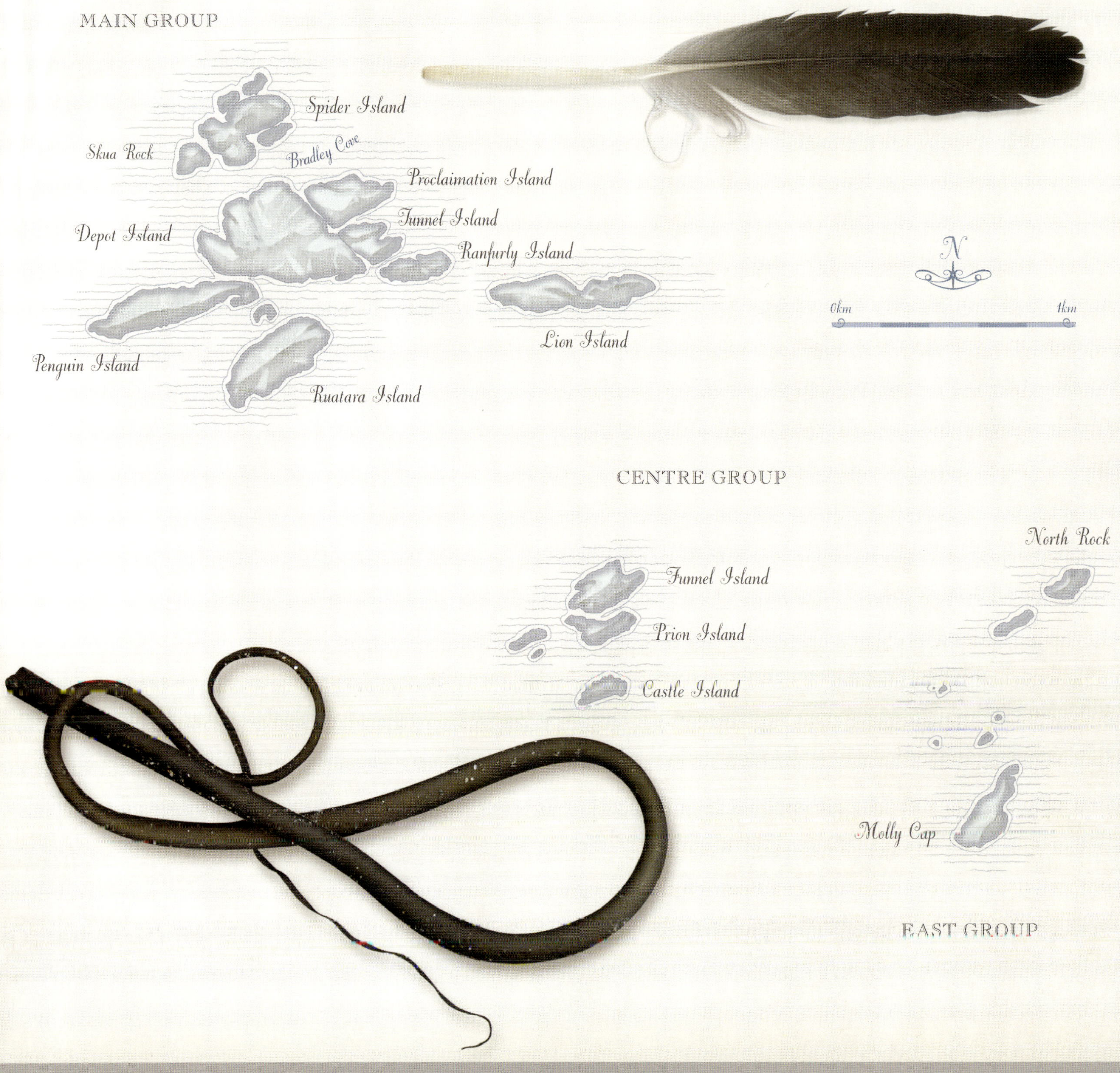

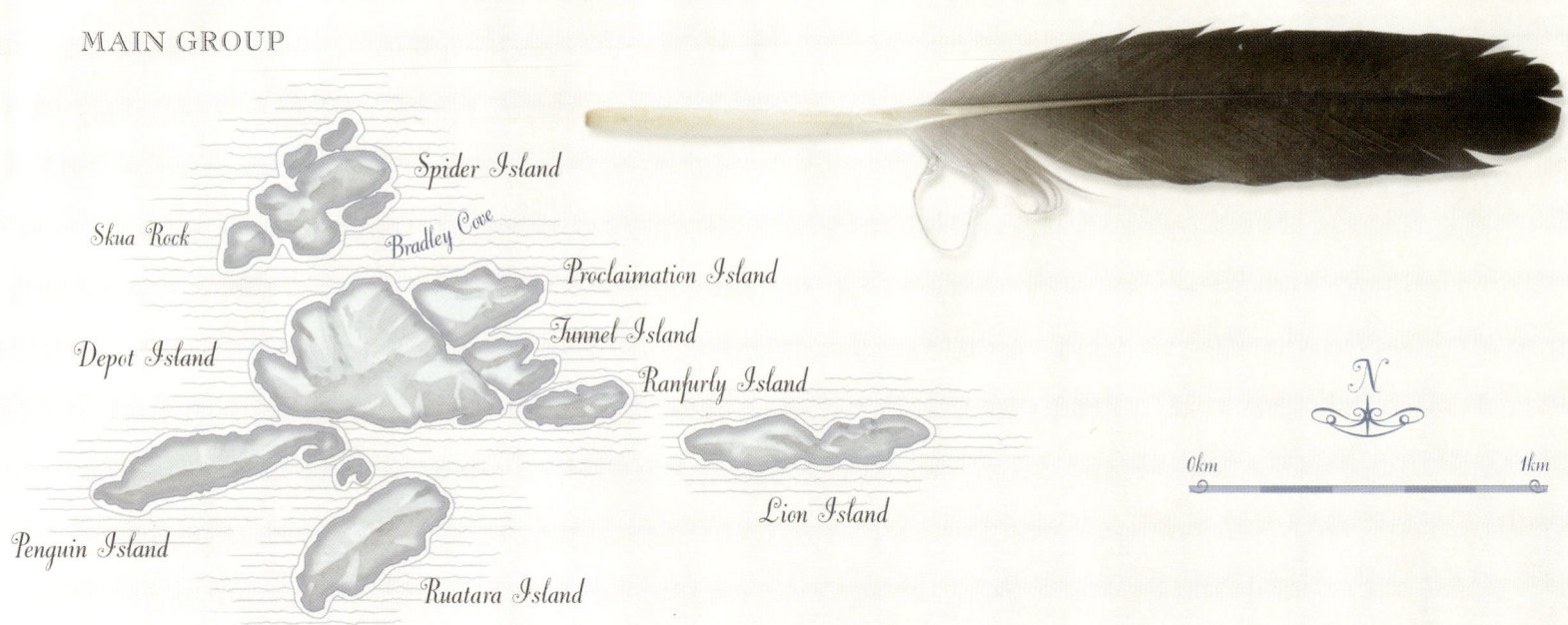

BOUNTY ISLANDS

47°45'S • 179°02'E • 135ha • 88m a.s.l

The Bounty Islands are situated approximately 650 kilometres south-east of the southern end of New Zealand. They are an ancient oceanic remnant of Gondwana and the small, wave-battered rocks, islets and small islands that remain above the surface of the ocean look and feel like they are from another time. The Bounty Islands are the smallest island group of all New Zealand's subantarctic islands, covering only 135 hectares in area. Despite the inhospitable environment, they are an important breeding site for thousands of seabirds and seals. The seals are recovering from almost wholesale extermination carried out by sealers in the early 1800s, but numbers are still well below pre-exploitation levels. Today, the islands are rarely visited, except from a distance, as the small islands offer little in the way of shelter for safe anchorages, and the steep-sided, smooth rocks make landing difficult. In the harshest weather, there are very few places on the islands that are beyond the reach of the waves and the flying spray, and as such there is very little vegetation.

Bounty Island Shag

THE BOUNTY ISLANDS The smallest of the wild islands south of New Zealand, the Bounties, as they are often known only cover 135 hectares. Due to the inhospitable environment very few plants grow there.

NO ROOM TO MOVE With animal life filling almost every available space on the exposed parts of the Bounty Islands, albatrosses and penguins have learnt to live side by side. *ALEKS TERAUDS.*

GEOGRAPHY AND GEOLOGY

THE BOUNTY ISLANDS are remote—the closest landmasses are the South Island of New Zealand 650 kilometres to the north-west, the Chatham Islands 450 kilometres to the north, and the Antipodes Islands 165 kilometres to the south. Unlike most other oceanic islands south of New Zealand, the Bounty Islands were not formed by volcanic action; they are made of basement granite and contain some of the oldest known exposed rocks in the subantarctic region. The main islets can be divided into three groups, or clusters, and are low-lying, reaching a high point of only 88 metres above sea level.

GEOGRAPHY

Depending on the definition of when a rock becomes an island, the three groups that comprise the Bounty Islands are made up of 15–22 distinct islands or islets. The northernmost group is known as Main Group, where eight islands lie tightly clustered together. The largest of these is Depot Island, which was the site of the castaway depot that was first established in 1886. At 800 metres long, this island dominates the group. Other islands in the Main Group include Ruatara and Penguin Islands to the south-west of Depot Island, Lion and Ranfurly Islands to the south-east, Proclamation Island lying just off the north-east coast and Spider Island and Skua Rock to the north.

The Centre Group, about a kilometre to the south-east of the Main Group, is made up of three main islets. Funnel Island is the largest, followed by Prion Island and Castle Island, but all are relatively small, covering just a few hectares in area. The East Group is made up of Molly Cap and North Rock, two widely spaced islets to the east of the Centre Group.

ORIGINS

The Bounty Islands are the only exposed portion of the Bounty Platform on the eastern edge of the vast, submerged Campbell Plateau. The Campbell Plateau was originally adjacent to Marie Byrd Land in Antarctica as part of the Gondwana supercontinent, but it started to move away around 80 million years ago. The rocks of the Bounties are thus more like those of west Antarctica than most of New Zealand. As the eastern edge of the Campbell Plateau was gradually submerged, the granites were eroded away to the small remnants which make up the Bounty Island group we see today. As the Bounties are an exposed portion of an underwater platform, the waters immediately surrounding the island groups are just a few hundred metres deep. The mixing that results from the influx of deeper waters into these shallower regions causes higher marine productivity, which is ideal for sustaining the thousands of birds and seals that live and breed on the island group.

GEOLOGY

The Bounty Islands are made of pale grey, coarse-grained granite, formed during the Jurassic period, around 180 million years ago. This granite, into which some slightly younger, fine-grained granite and basalt dykes have intruded, provides a rare exposed example of the basement lying beneath the sedimentary rocks that form much of the Campbell Plateau. The granite originally formed under enormous pressure deep in the Earth's crust. During uplift, this pressure was released and the granite fractured along cracks or 'joints' to form the angular blocks that are characteristic of the island group. Over time, the granite has been worn into a polished, slippery surface, not

THE BOUNTY ISLANDS The coarse granite that forms these cliffs cooled and crystallised deep in the Earth's crust some 180 million years ago. As it cooled and shrank, it fractured along planes or "joints", which now control the shapes, slopes and angles of these spectacular cliffs. *AARON RUSS.*

just by the constant pounding of waves, but also by the movement of countless numbers of seals and birds over thousands of years.

Due to their small size and wave-washed nature, there is very little soil development on the islands. A film of hard, polished guano, also known as phosphatic mudstone, covers the rocks on the larger islands, making them extremely slippery. The winter rains tend to wash away most of the guano, which is deposited by the high concentrations of birds and seals in the summer months. These rains fill hollows with water, which soon turns into an organic mud formed by a combination of decaying carcasses, moulted penguin feathers, excreta, food scraps, guano and seaweed.

FOREST OF KELP The long and tangled fronds of the Antarctic bull kelp ring the edges of the Bounty Islands. These fronds can grow up to 20 metres in length and can withstand the relentless pounding of the surf and spray. *ALEKS TERAUDS.*

FLORA

Few plants can survive in the inclement terrestrial environment of the Bounty Islands and for many years it was thought that algae and crustose lichens represented the only plant life. Green algae generally forms in the small freshwater rock pools and two genera have been identified—*Prasiola* and *Chlamydomonas*. The crustose lichens are common on many of the more sheltered rocky surfaces and species tentatively identified to date by botanist Colin Meurk include *Verrucaria maura*, *Pertusaria* sp. and *Candelaria* sp.

A recent discovery

In November 2004, Jacinda Amey and co-workers discovered 13 large, bushy plants of Cook's scurvy grass (*Lepidium oleraceum*) in rock crevices of Funnel Island (Centre Group), with another single plant sighted on top of Molly Cap (East Group). Historically speaking, these islands are rarely visited and it is difficult to ascertain when these plants first became established. However, the plant observed on the top of Molly Cap was clearly visible and it is likely that this, at least, was a relatively recent introduction. Possible vectors for this plant include wind and/or European Starlings (*Sturnus vulgaris*), which have recently established breeding populations on the island group.

Marine plants

Algae and lichens abound around the intertidal and near-shore environments of the Bounty Islands. Antarctic bull kelp (*Durvillaea antarctica*) ring the bases of almost every island, and its long, thong-like tendrils often reach 20 metres or more out to sea. These kelp forests are held onto the rock face by holdfasts, which can reach huge proportions and are the kelp equivalent of roots, enabling these plants to withstand the pounding of the waves. Below this kelp zone the diversity increases, with a range of red and brown algal species, including *Marginariella parsonii*, a brown algae with strap-like fronds, found only around the coast of the Antipodes and Bounty Islands.

COOK'S SCURVY GRASS This is the only vascular plant that has been found on the Bounty Islands and only occurs on two islands of the group. *AARON RUSS.*

SALVIN'S ALBATROSS The Bounty Islands are the main breeding ground for this species, and it nests in large colonies across the island group. There is some evidence that the population has declined over the last 30 years. *NATHAN RUSS.*

FAUNA

At first sight, the sheer density of life on the Bounty Islands, particularly during the summer months, threatens to overwhelm the senses. The sight, noise and smell of this huge concentration of biomass all congregated on a few small granite rocks in the middle of the ocean almost defies belief. On approaching the Bounties, the first thing that a visitor sees are the thousands of albatrosses circling and calling. On closer approach, even more albatrosses can be made out nesting on the ground, and amongst these the penguins, shags, gulls and prions who also call this group of rocks home; it's a wonder there's any room for the fur seals. In fact, it is one of the largest breeding colonies of New Zealand Fur Seals (*Arctocephalus forsteri*) in New Zealand waters. A fortunate by-product of the inhospitable nature of the Bounty Islands is that there are few introduced animals, with the self-introduced European Starling being the only representative.

Penguins

The Bounty Islands and the Antipodes Islands are the only two places in the world where Erect Crested Penguins (*Eudyptes sclateri*) breed. In the seabird survey of 1978, it was estimated that there were over 115 000 pairs of this species breeding throughout the Bounty Island group. In a more recent census, researchers estimated that there were around 28 000 pairs breeding there. Again, different census methodologies make it difficult to draw too many conclusions from the differences. Nevertheless, due to its restricted breeding range and likely decline, the species is listed as 'endangered' by the IUCN. There are no records of other penguins breeding on these islands.

TERRITORIAL DISPUTE A Salvin's Albatross and Erect Crested Penguin square up to each other in a territorial dispute. *ALEKS TERAUDS.*

Albatrosses

The Bounty Islands are the world's main breeding ground of the Salvin's Albatross (*Thalassarche salvini*), which breeds in large colonies across the island group. They tend to concentrate above the areas that are wave-washed, utilising the broader slopes and ledges. The Salvin's Albatross is one of the 'Shy complex' of albatross species, along with the Chatham Albatross (*Thalassarche eremita*), White-capped Albatross (*Thalassarche steadii*) and Shy Albatross (*Thalassarche cauta*). Salvin's Albatross forage widely over the Southern Ocean, especially in the non-breeding season when they are thought to disperse eastwards to the eastern Pacific Ocean and the coast of South America.

In a census carried out in 1978 by the first group to land and spend time on the Bounty Islands in over 95 years, Chris Robertson estimated that there were approximately 76 000 pairs of this species across the island group. In 1997, Department of Conservation field workers Andrea Booth and Jacinda Amey estimated that there were around 31 000 pairs. Unfortunately, as is often the case with censuses that are separated by long time periods, different methodologies and base maps confound direct comparisons. It does seem likely that there has been some decline over this time period, however, which is why the IUCN has listed this species as 'vulnerable'.

OTHER PETRELS

Due to the difficulties in conducting comprehensive censuses, it is often hard to know exactly which species are actually breeding on the island group, and even more difficult to ascertain population numbers. So, while Snares Cape Petrels (*Daption capense australe*) and Fulmar Prions (*Pachyptila crassirostris*) are known to occur there, it is very difficult to estimate actual numbers. The 1978 census estimated there were over 7000 breeding pairs of the latter species.

The sea to the north of the Bounty Islands is often full of petrels taking advantage of the nutrient-rich and productive waters. Commonly observed species include the White-chinned Petrels (*Procellaria aequinoctialis*), Soft-plumage Petrels (*Pterodroma mollis*), White-headed Petrels (*Pterodroma lessoni*), Grey-backed Storm Petrels (*Garrodia nereis*), Black-bellied Storm Petrels (*Fregetta tropica*), southern Common Diving Petrels (*Pelecanoides urinatrix chathamensis*) and both forms of the Little Shearwater (*Puffinus assimilis* [*elegans*]). Due to a lack of breeding habitat, none of the above species are thought to breed on the Bounty Islands. The Northern Giant Petrel (*Macronectes halli*) is also observed frequently in nearby waters, or preying on the penguin colonies. Like many of the other petrels, it is not known to breed here and most individuals are probably from the nearby breeding grounds on the Antipodes Islands.

Of special note is the Chatham Petrel (*Pterodroma axillaris*), which is thought to use these waters as an important feeding ground and is regularly observed in mixed flocks with species such as Cook's Petrel (*Pterodroma cookii*), Black-winged Petrels (*Pterodroma nigripennis*) and Great-winged Petrels (*Pterodroma macroptera*). In addition, large numbers of the White-faced Storm Petrel (*Pelagodroma marina maoriana*) have been observed, often with mixed flocks of Broad-billed Prions (*Pachyptila vittata*) and Fulmar Prions. Less commonly observed petrels recorded in the area include the Kerguelen Petrel (*Lugensa brevirostris*) and Juan Fernandez Petrel (*Pterodroma externa*).

OTHER SEABIRDS

The Bounty Island Shag (*Phalacrocorax ranfurlyi*), which breeds on many islets of the group, is one of the rarest cormorants in the world. A census conducted in 1978 estimated there were between 500 and 600 pairs and the species is wholly restricted to this island group. More recent attempts to count the number of nests—made of seaweed and marine debris and found on some of the steeper cliff areas throughout the island group—have resulted in much lower estimates and the current population status is largely unknown. Several other breeding sea birds that can be found in small and scattered number are the Subantarctic (Brown) Skua (*Catharacta lonnbergi*), Southern Black-backed Gulls (*Larus dominicanus*), Red-billed Gulls (*Larus scopulinus*) and Antarctic Terns (*Sterna vittata bethunei*).

NEW ZEALAND FUR SEAL BULLS These adult males tend to congregate at the edges of the islands where there are fewer birds. Nevertheless, space is still relatively scarce and confrontations often occur between rival bulls. *ALEKS TERAUDS.*

Seals

New Zealand Fur Seals are the only mammal breeding on the Bounty Islands. They were hunted almost to extinction in the early decades of the 1800s. The population recovered slowly following this early exploitation, but another period of sealing in the 1880s again removed all the seals that were present. Since that time the population has recovered, although it is unlikely that numbers have reached pre-exploitation levels. Following a 1994 aerial census, Rowley Taylor estimated that there were over 4000 pups born annually on the islands, with a total population of somewhere between 19 500 and 27 500 seals. This is by far the biggest breeding colony in New Zealand waters and represents a very important site for this species.

Terrestrial invertebrates

Considering the nature of the environment, the terrestrial invertebrates of the Bounty Islands are diverse, with at least 18 different species of insect from 16 different families. Many of these are flightless and most depend on decomposing organic matter, excreta, or parasitic relationships to survive. Notable members of this group include an endemic flightless beetle (*Bountya insularis*) and an endemic flightless weta (*Ischyroplectron isolatum*). Two species of moth and two species of spider have been discovered to date. Only a few collections of the insect fauna from the Bounty Islands have been made and it is likely that future visits will add more species to the current list.

Captain Hooper and a group of boys surrounded by penguins on the Bounty Islands, circa 1910. Alexander Turnbull Library, Wellington, New Zealand. F- 56479-1/2

HISTORY

When the residents of the West Indies applied to the King of England to have the bread-fruit tree (*Artocarpus altilis*) introduced amongst them, he duly sent Lieutenant Bligh, Captain of the *Bounty*, to obtain plants from the Society Islands and return with them to Jamaica. Due to bad weather, Bligh avoided the usual route around Cape Horn and took the Cape of Good Hope route, reaching Tasmania on 20th August 1788. A month later, he passed the southern part of New Zealand and 'discovered a cluster of small rocky islands' which he promptly named the Bounty Islands. Captain Bligh described the islands as 'bare and desolate, with the inability to afford any vegetable production'.

The sealing era

Being as bare and desolate as they were, the Bounties were not immediately deemed suitable for human habitation, even though the number of seals there were undoubtedly tempting for the seal hunters that abounded in the late eighteenth and early nineteenth centuries. The American sealing vessels the *Perseverance* and the *Pilgrim*, under the command of Captain Delano, visited the islands on 7th November 1804. On arrival, the strong westerly gale that had accompanied them all the way from The Snares continued unabated. They observed numerous shoals and a number of areas with broken water and became quickly convinced 'that it was a very dangerous place for a ship to come near to'. Captain Delano noted the presence of shags and gulls and a few seals. At this stage of the sealing era, the abundance of seals on the larger islands did not make it appealing to land gangs on the smaller, more inhospitable islands like the Bounties.

The first sealing gang landed on the Bounty Islands in 1807. They were from the schooner *Brothers* and spent a few months living ashore before eventually returning to Sydney with a bountiful harvest of 38 000 skins. The *Santa Anna*, skippered by Captain William Moody, was next to visit and after leaving Sydney in the latter half of 1807 she stopped at the Bay of Islands to take on the Maori chief Ruatara. The *Santa Anna* then sailed for the Bounty Islands, where Ruatara and 13 others were landed, most probably in February 1808.

In May 1808, nearly four months after landing the men, the owners of the *Santa Anna* were contacted by Captain Moody, calling their attention to the fact that the men would undoubtedly be in need of relief. It was reported in the press (*Sydney Gazette*, 15th May 1808) that the *Commerce* had sailed from Sydney on 6th February 1808 to relieve the gang, but this was likely to be a company response to allay public concerns about the group and the supposed relief voyage never reached them. It was not until about September 1808 that the whaler *King George* under the command of Captain Chace, reached the Bounty Islands and afforded some relief to the stranded men. The *Santa Anna* returned to the island in November 1808 to find that the men had undergone extreme suffering from thirst and hunger and three had died. Remarkably, they had managed to obtain 8000 skins during their 9 months ashore and after loading their catch aboard, they set sail for London.

While sealing on the Bounty Islands peaked in 1807 and 1808, when over 40 000 skins were taken, it continued sporadically until the 1820s. Over this time period at least 50 000 skins were taken from these islands, and given the difficulties in obtaining accurate records from this era it is likely that the number is greater than that. On an exploratory sealing and whaling voyage in 1831, Captain J. Biscoe in the *Tula* landed on the Bounty Islands and found few seals. However, he did find remnants of recent European occupation, including a hut made out of the wings and skins of birds, suggesting that sealers had inhabited the islands relatively recently. They only saw five seals during this visit, indicative of the thorough extermination of fur seals on these small and inhospitable islands.

Castaway depots and scientists

The absence of seals, together with the remote and barren nature of the islands, meant that there was little incentive for humans to visit through much of the 1800s. Although the New Zealand government nearly made the embarrassing and ill-informed mistake of offering it up as a farming lease in the late 1800s, it was quickly withdrawn when those doing the offering realised that it was completely devoid of vegetation.

The first visit to the Bounty Islands after the sealing era appears to be in 1865 by the *Victoria*, searching for castaways and only one sailor was briefly landed. On the second voyage of this nature, in 1868, the steamer *Amherst* tried but was unable to land on the islands due to extremely strong winds. The first castaway depot was built on Depot Island in 1886 by the New Zealand government, and thereafter regular checks to the islands were made up until 1927. Several scientists took advantage of this regular shipping and Thomas Kirk and Frederick Chapman were some of the first to visit the Bounty Islands for this

The S.S *Hinemoa* was one of the few ships to visit the Bounty Islands in the early 1900s. Here it was photographed by Henry Wright in New Zealand. Alexander Turnbull Library, Wellington, New Zealand. G-20530-1/1

Walter Armiger Bowering, more commonly known as the Earl of Ranfurly, made several important discoveries on the New Zealand subantarctic islands, including the Bounty Islands Shag. Alexander Turnbull Library, Wellington, New Zealand. B-055-003

purpose in 1890. A notable visit was also made in 1900 by the Earl of Ranfurly, who was the Governor of New Zealand at the time. He obtained a berth on the government resupply steamer the *Hinemoa* and, accompanied by the naturalist Professor Frederick Hutton, he set out with the aim of collecting specimens of New Zealand birds for the British Museum. On this voyage, he discovered the Bounty Island Shag, which was subsequently named after him (*Phalacrocorax ranfurlyi*).

Another notable visit facilitated by the government steamers was made by the botanist Leonard Cockayne in 1903. In a remarkable winter voyage, Dr. Cockayne visited all of the southern New Zealand islands with the exception of The Snares, and collected extremely valuable botanical and zoological specimens from the Bounty Islands. While the landmark scientific expedition organised by the Philosophical Institute of Canterbury did not land on the rocky shores of the Bounty Islands, the geology and some of the molluscs that were dredged up from the near-shore environment were described in the comprehensive publication that followed.

Recent science and management

In 1961 the Bounty Islands were given reserve status by the New Zealand government on the basis of their remarkable natural values. The first post-war visit to the Bounty Islands was organised by Alex Black in his launch *Alert* in 1950. In 1962 the renowned naturalist Sir Robert Falla led a New Zealand Oceanographic Institute expedition to the island group and in 1978, the first major scientific visit was made as part of the BAAS (Bounty, Antipodes, Auckland and Snares) Expedition. Three scientists camped on Proclamation Island and studied the ecology of the birds breeding there. Underwater collections and aerial photographic surveys were also made during this landmark expedition, which was supported by the HMNZS *Waikato*. The navy ship HMNZS *Monowai* also provided logistic support for an expedition in 1985, when accurate, land-based surveying and aerial photography allowed detailed topographic maps of the island to be prepared for the first time. Lichens and algae were also collected from the Bounty Islands on this voyage.

In more recent times there have been two scientific expeditions where members stayed ashore, but in both cases their support vessel stayed in the vicinity. Gerry Clark on board the *Totorore* provided transport and support for an expedition that attempted to census the albatross, penguins, shags and prions over the summer of 1997–98. In 2004, well-known wildlife photographer Tui de Roy and Mark Jones funded an expedition in their own yacht, under permit from the Department of Conservation, to take photographs for a book on albatrosses. This expedition also carried field workers who undertook a limited amount of scientific research.

Because these islands are visited so infrequently, annual tourist visits by Heritage Expeditions have provided one of the few opportunities to collect information. In 2006, kelp samples were collected for University of Otago researchers to assist with the investigation of an undescribed species of bull kelp which grows in the surrounding waters. Visits to the Bounty Islands are strictly controlled by guidelines laid down in the Conservation Management Strategy and landings are only allowed under permit from the New Zealand Department of Conservation.

ANTIPODES ISLANDS

Antipodes Islands

49°41'S • 178°45'E • 2100ha • 366m a.s.l

The Antipodes Islands are situated approximately 870 kilometres south-east of New Zealand. Originally named the Penantipodes by early explorers, this island group is almost directly opposite London, on the other side of the globe. Even though it was a major hunting ground for fur seals in the early 1800s, it remains one of the most pristine of all the island groups, with very few introduced animals or plants present today. It is the youngest of all the volcanic islands, and yet despite its relatively small size and young geological age, the Antipodes hold a diverse range of flora and fauna. The main island is a major breeding ground for the New Zealand endemic Antipodean Albatross (*Diomedea antipodensis*) and is also home to one of the rarest parakeets in the world. Due to its relatively pristine nature, the island group has been designated a Special Nature Reserve and the New Zealand government only allows landing under special permit.

Antipodes Island Parakeet

ANTIPODES ISLANDS This relatively small island group was formed by volcanic eruptions in the last 1.5 million years. The main island dominates the group, although there are several smaller islands scattered around the coast.

COURTSHIPS DISPLAY These Antipodean Albatrosses usually mate for life. The formation of a strong pair bond through courtship displays such as these is an integral part of the breeding process. *KATH WALKER.*

GEOGRAPHY AND GEOLOGY

Geologically speaking, the Antipodes are young. Thought to have emerged from the ocean as a result of volcanic activity around 1–2 million years ago, they are entirely volcanic in origin and largely formed of ash and lava deposits. Erosive forces have shaped the islands since their formation and today the group is composed of a main island and several smaller surrounding islands.

Geography

The Antipodes Islands rise up from the edge of an underwater feature known as the Bounty Platform—a submerged peninsula of a massive underwater region called the Campbell Plateau. To the east and south of the island the ocean becomes deep very quickly. The main island, Antipodes, measures around 7 kilometres by 5 kilometres, covers an area of just over 2000 hectares and comprises over 95 per cent of the land area of the island group. To the north-east lies Bollons Island, which at around 50 hectares is the largest of the small islands. Adjacent to Bollons Island is Archway Island; the shapes of these two islands dramatically illustrate their volcanic origins, with the old crater rim clearly visible above the surface of the waves. There are four smaller islands within 2 kilometres of the main island. Leeward Island lies close to the east coast, while Orde Lees Islet and the two islands that comprise the Windward Islands lie off the west coast.

Steep cliffs, hundreds of metres high, encircle the main island, which rises to its highest point at Mount Galloway, 366 metres above sea level. The centre of the island is an undulating plateau mantled by peat, alternating between hilly terrain and deep gullies. Remnants of volcanic cones and craters are present throughout the landscape, the most striking being a large, steep-sided crater around 150 metres in diameter above the aptly named Crater Bay on the north-east coast. To the north of Crater Bay is Stella Bay and then Anchorage Bay, the latter being one of the few spots where visiting ships can find some shelter and people can get ashore, protected from the westerly and southerly winds which predominate in this part of the world.

The erosive force of the ocean has left its mark right around the coastline, which is peppered with sea caves and rock stacks. Some of the caves in the sea cliffs are exceptionally large, and the biggest—named Remarkable Cave by Captain Fairchild in 1886—arches to 90 metres above sea level. Wave-cut platforms are also observed at the lower margins of some cliffs. In the few places where the cliffs do not meet the water, basalt boulders form beaches which slope steeply down to the sea. The harsh, black volcanic cliffs are in sharp contrast with the undulating green hills of the interior and on first approach these cliffs give the island a dramatic and somewhat ominous appearance.

Origins

The main island was formed during two volcanic periods, dating from 0.5–1.3 and 0.16–0.4 million years ago. The older eruptive period is thought to have been more of a fire fountain than a succession of lava flows. Huge amounts of ash deposited from these older eruptions form the bulk of the underlying rock on the main island. Over thousands of years these ash deposits have been eroded and then overlain by lava from younger volcanoes, the remnants of which can be clearly seen around the main and surrounding islands. Many of the high cliffs that

BASALT CLIFFS Harder bands in the coastal cliffs of the Antipodes are composed of dark grey to black basalt, which erupted from numerous volcanic vents to form tabular lava flows. The vertical cracks are joints formed as the larva cools. *ALEKS TERAUDS.*

surround the island include columnar jointed basalt lava flows, the result of thick, syrupy lava cooling. There is no sign of the Antipodes being affected by glaciation, although the numerous deep gullies are clear evidence of erosion caused by the flow of fresh water.

Geology

Due to the nature of the islands' formation, all of the rock on the Antipodes is of volcanic origin, composed almost entirely of lavas and pyroclastic rocks. Pyroclastic comes from the Greek meaning 'fire' and 'broken' and these types of rocks were brought up from deep within the Earth's crust during volcanic eruptions. Rare fragments of the underlying basement granite have also been found in the accumulations of volcanic rubble, torn from the crust beneath and brought up to the surface during violent eruptions. These fragments show the basement rock that the Antipodes Islands are built on to be similar to the Bounty Islands, but slightly younger (~130 million years). Well-exposed examples of the columnar jointed lava flows are apparent in the cliffs of Anchorage Bay and the long tongue of lava that makes it way to sea level at South Bay. Like most of the other larger islands, a layer of peat, up to 5 metres thick, blankets the undulating interior plateau.

TUSSOCKS AND FERNS While Antipodes Island is dominated by tussock and ferns, sedges in wet seepages and low shrubs in sheltered sites help create a colourful patchwork of vegetation. *KATH WALKER.*

FLORA

There are over 150 species of plant on the Antipodes Islands, of which only three, possibly four, are endemic. Nearly half of these are vascular plants, with mosses, liverworts and lichens comprising the bulk of the remaining species. All the plants that grow on the Antipodes had to make their way across the oceanic barrier that has separated the island from other landmasses since its formation, and wind and birds are the most likely methods of transport. Unlike many of the other islands, the flora of the Antipodes has not been affected by long-term grazing and is thought to be relatively intact. The main vegetation communities can be categorised as tussock grassland, scrubland, swamps and bogs. Megaherbs are common in the wetter areas, but there are no trees and only a couple of shrub-like species. A complete list of the current flora known from the Antipodes Islands and a detailed summary of the historical botanical research is provided by Eric Godley in his seminal manuscript *The flora of the Antipodes Islands*, published in the *New Zealand Journal of Botany* in 1989.

Species Composition

The terrestrial plant species on the Antipodes are dominated by flowering plants, of which there are thought to be over 50 species. Four of these are considered to be introduced; the annual meadow grass (*Poa annua*), the chickweed *Stellaria media*, the weedy daisy *Sonchus asper* and the wild turnip (*Brassica rapa*). Grasses, sedges and rushes make up 16 species and in terms of abundance these dominate the landscape. Four orchids have been identified to date. Of the other flowering plants, 25 have been identified as herbaceous, two as semi-woody species and only two as shrub species. Both of the latter species are *Coprosmas*, with *C. rugosa* forming scattered areas of stunted shrubland in sheltered gullies or protected by the tall tussock grass. Some researchers consider this species on the Antipodes to be an endemic form of the mainland species and as such it is sometimes referred to as *C. rugosa* var. *antipoda*, or even *C. antipoda*. The other endemic species—the gentian *Gentiana antipoda*, the groundsel *Senecio radiolatus antipodus* and the chickweed *Stellaria decipiens* var. *angustata*—are also flowering plants.

Ferns are common components of the flora of the islands, with 17 species present. There are three species of the small primitive plants known as lycopods, closely related to the ferns. Relatively few species of fungi have been identified, with only two species recorded to date. Terrestrial algae are also rare, with only three species found. Bryophytes are common and diverse, with 37 liverwort species and 21 species of moss identified. Lichens are also relatively abundant, with 17 species found.

Coastal rocks and cliffs

The steep cliffs that ring much of the island are largely bare of vegetation, with the exception of crustose lichens, easily identifiable by their white colour, stark against the dark basalt cliffs. Plant life also colonises the rock cracks and crevices and includes the cushion plant *Colobanthus muscoides*, the succulent *Crassula moschata*, the rush *Isolepis aucklandica*, New Zealand wild celery (*Apium prostratum*) and the small coastal daisy *Leptinella plumosa*. Some of the wetter areas of the coast cliffs and rocky shores are covered in mats of glistening wet moss. Where there is more soil, particularly towards the tops of the cliffs, larger plants such as the tussock grasses *Poa foliosa* and *Poa litorosa* and the sedge *Carex trifida* start to become more common. As the cliffs and rocks merge into the plateau region, in many places the vegetation turns into an almost homogenous tussock meadow.

Grasslands

Tussock grasslands composed largely of *Poa litorosa* dominate the undulating plateau region of the main island. Underneath these grasslands the soil is almost entirely composed of a thick peat layer. The large tussock grass grows over head height in many places, particularly closer to the coast, and they grow so closely together in the wet peaty soil that early visitors to the island soon found it was easier to walk on the tops of the pedestals than try and make their way between them. Tussock grass also dominates on some of the steeper coastal slopes, and in wetter areas the dominance is shared by another tussock, *Poa foliosa*. Several other species live in amongst these grassland ecosystems. The large fern *Polystichum vestitum* grows in a semi-tree fern form and is one of the more common plants seen amongst the *Poa* fields, co-dominating in many areas. The tender green fern *Histiopteris incisa* is also common in some areas, while the smaller ferns *Asplenium obtusatum* and *Blechnum durum* form luxuriant mats between tussock pedestals. The distinctive bluey-green bidi-bidi *Acaena antarctica* is another species that coexists with the tussock grass, and it tends to grow over the tussock pedestals.

The tussock grass and the ferns provide a sheltered, damp environment perfect for low-growing plants like the smaller ferns mentioned above, small herbaceous plants like *Epilobium* spp., the filmy fern (*Hymenophyllum multifidum*), lycopods, liverworts and a variety of mosses. Lichens are also a common feature of the thriving ecosystem beneath the larger vegetation and several species are abundant. The tussock fields are not an unbroken formation and throughout these areas small bogs are common where a variety of plant species, particularly the megaherbs, also thrive. Examples of plants that live in these areas include *Anisotome antipoda*, the megaherb daisy *Pleurophyllum criniferum* and the sedge *Carex ternaria*. The white and purple flowers of the megaherb

GRASSLANDS Tussock grass meadows, interspersed with ferns, dominate the landscape of Antipodes Island. *KATH WALKER.*

A. antipoda, which is related to the carrot, are distinctive against the uniform green and browns of the tussock fields. Also in many of these boggy areas is the megaherb *Stilbocarpa polaris*, also known as the Macquarie Island cabbage. It forms dense stands, with thick juicy green stems and bright green leaves providing further relief from the relative drabness of the seemingly endless tussock. Also scattered throughout the tussock grasslands and bogs is the endemic gentian *Gentiana antipoda*.

Other vegetation communities

Three main types of swamp are common on the Antipodes Islands. The first is a coastal swamp, dominated by the sedge *Carex appressa*. The closely related *C. sectiodes* also forms another type of swamp, while the third type of swamp, which occurs in more inland areas, is composed of the small *Blechnum* fern and a third species of *Carex*, *C. ternaria*. *Coprosma rugosa*, the only erect woody plant on the island, forms scrub patches in gullies and is often associated with large patches of *Polystichum* ferns. The nutrient input from burrowing petrels and nesting albatrosses also influences the vegetation. Abandoned albatross nests form fertile habitats for early colonisers such as the liverwort *Marchantia* sp., the herbaceous species *Epilobium* sp. and *Acaena minor,* and the chickweed *Stellaria decipiens* var *angustata*. Groups of giant petrels also provide nutrient-rich grounds and in these areas the daisy *Senecio radiolatus antipodus* is abundant.

Due to the relatively low-lying nature of the island, exposed areas above 300 metres are generally still covered with peat, and bare areas of gravel known as fell field or feldmark are uncommon. In these areas, tussock grasslands give way to the herbfield, where the megaherbs *Pleurophyllum* and *Stilbocarpa* become common, albeit in a more stunted form than the luxuriant stands that grow in the lower-lying areas. There are also thick patches of the semi-woody plant *Coprosma perpusilla*, with several species of the smaller inland sedges like *Luzula crinita* and *Uncinia hookeri* also present. Although few observations have been published on the freshwater plants, a collection from a deep green pool at the base of Reef Point contained considerable amounts of the green algae *Chlorella*, a small amount of the unicellular flagellate *Chlamydomonas* and what may have been yellow-green algae belonging to *Tetrakentron* or *Goniochloris*.

Marine plants

One hundred and sixteen species of marine algae have been recorded from the Antipodes Islands. Antarctic bull kelp (*Durvillaea antarctica*) is one of the most common species and it can be found in the intertidal zone at the base of the basalt cliffs. A second species of bull kelp, yet to be formally described but similar to *Durvillaea antarctica*, grows deeper, tending to inhabit more sub-tidal regions. The taxonomy of the bull kelps is currently under review by researchers at the University of Otago and the unknown species in the Antipodes is in the process of being described. Another kelp species only found in the Antipodes and Bounty Islands is *Marginariella parsonii*. It has brown, strap-like fronds and is found on submerged rocks in shallow waters (3–5 metres deep) around the coastline.

ERECT CRESTED PENGUINS When arriving or just after leaving land, Erect Crested Penguins often come together in large associations called 'rafts'. This may be a way of ensuring 'safety in numbers' and help protect them against predators. *AARON RUSS*.

FAUNA

The Antipodes group are free of all introduced mammals except for the House Mouse (*Mus musculus*). Consequently, the islands are home to a large number of breeding birds, particularly burrowing petrels, with the peaty soils that blanket the island providing an ideal nesting habitat. The Antipodes are one of only two breeding grounds for the Erect Crested Penguin (*Eudyptes sclateri*) and they are also home to the Antipodean Albatross (*Diomedea antipodensis*). The lack of introduced predatory mammals means that several populations of land birds have thrived and there are two species of parakeet and several other endemic subspecies. The island was a site of extensive sealing in the early 1900s and the small population of fur seals present today is a testament to the wholesale extermination that occurred.

Penguins

The endemic Erect Crested Penguin (*Eudyptes sclateri*) breeds around the coastlines of the island group, sharing the entire world population with the Bounty Islands. In 1978, the population was estimated at over 200 000 pairs on the two larger islands, but a more recent census of the two populations in the 1990s suggested that breeding numbers have declined significantly to approximately 80 000 pairs. While differences in census methods confound direct comparisons, there is little doubt that a decline has occurred and for this reason the species is listed as 'endangered' by the IUCN. While reasons for the decline are unclear, it is thought to be related to a decreased survival rate due to changes in the marine environment.

The Rockhopper Penguin (*Eudyptes chrysocome*) also breeds on the main, Bollons and Archway islands. Like populations on other New Zealand islands, this population has undergone a significant decline, from around 50 000 pairs in 1978 to less than 5000 pairs in 1995. Satellite tracking by researchers from the New Zealand National Institute of Water and Atmospheric Research showed that females generally foraged within 60 kilometres from their nests and chicks were fed on average once per day.

Albatrosses

The islands that form the Antipodes are the world's main breeding ground for the endemic New Zealand species, the Antipodean Albatross. In a 2002 Department of Conservation report, Kath Walker and Graeme Elliott estimated that there were approximately 9000 breeding pairs of this species, based on counts conducted throughout the early to mid 1990s. These birds nest all over the plateau of the main island, only avoiding areas of tall vegetation and bare, exposed tops of hills and ridges. The *antipodensis* split from the Wandering Albatross complex is relatively recent. Considered to be the most unique species of the group, it shows obvious differences between the sexes and the adults retain juvenile-like plumage (especially the females). Like most other albatross species, the Antipodean Albatross is thought to be at risk from mortality due to interactions with long-line fisheries and this could be responsible for recent declines in population numbers.

Other albatrosses breeding on the groups include the Black-browed Albatross (*Thalassarche melanophrys*) and White-capped Albatross (*Thalassarche steadii*), each represented by a small colony on nearby Bollons Island (approximately 100 and 20 pairs respectively).

The Light-mantled Sooty Albatross (*Phoebetria palpebrata*) breeds mainly around the coastal cliffs of Antipodes, Bollons and Leeward Islands and although the inaccessible nature of their nests makes population estimates problematic, researchers estimate that there are in the vicinity of 200–300 breeding pairs.

OTHER PETRELS

While the albatrosses are the larger members of the petrel family to breed on the Antipodes, it is the smaller petrels that dominate in terms of abundance and diversity. The Antipodes Islands are home to the biggest breeding colony of Grey Petrels (*Procellaria cinerea*) in New Zealand. This species lays its eggs in winter, with most chicks fledging by October. It breeds throughout the island group in various-sized colonies, with preliminary surveys suggesting a total population of around 50 000 breeding pairs on the main island. Other smaller petrels include the White-chinned Petrel (*Procellaria aequinoctialis*), Soft-plumage Petrel (*Pterodroma mollis*) and White-headed Petrel, (*Pterodroma lessonii*) as well as the Fairy Prion (*Pachyptila turtur*) and Subantarctic Little Shearwater (*Puffinus assimilis elegans*).

If the high numbers that are observed at sea provide any indication of the breeding populations of these species, then they are likely to be present in significant numbers throughout the island group. The Black-bellied Storm Petrel (*Fregetta tropica*), Grey-backed Storm Petrel (*Garrodia nereis*) and the southern subspecies of the Common Diving Petrel (*Pelecanoides urinatrix chathamensis*) are also thought to breed in large numbers, but due to their cryptic burrows it is very difficult to obtain an accurate population estimate. Relatively small breeding populations of the Snares Cape Petrel (*Daption capense australe*) and Sooty Shearwater (*Puffinus griseus*) are found on Bollons Island and the main island respectively. The Northern Giant Petrel (*Macronectes halli*) also breeds on the island, with population estimates between 200 and 300 breeding pairs.

OTHER SEABIRDS

There are several other seabird species that can be found in small and scattered numbers around the Antipodes group. These include the Subantarctic (Brown) Skua (*Catharacta lonnbergi*), Southern Black-backed Gull (*Larus dominicanus*) and Antarctic Tern (*Sterna vittata bethunei*). Population estimates vary, but skua numbers are thought to be in the vicinity of 50–100 pairs on the main island and Bollons Island. The Campbell Island Shag (*Phalacrocorax cambelli*) and Bounty Island Shag (*Phalacrocorax ranfurlyi*) have been observed, but no breeding has been recorded.

LAND BIRDS

The Antipodes Islands are the breeding ground for one of the world's rarest parakeet, the endemic Antipodes Island Parakeet (*Cyanoramphus unicolour*). Also present is an endemic subspecies of the Red-crowned Parakeet, sometimes known as Reischek's Parakeet (*Cyanoramphus novaezelandiae hochstetteri*). The Antipodes Island Parakeet is the largest of the parakeets in the New Zealand region and is almost entirely green, without the red or yellow colour markings that characterise most of the other species. The two endemic parrot species have quite different diets and are not thought to interbreed

ANTIPODES ISLAND BIRDS (clockwise from top left) Antipodean Albatrosses courting, Northern Giant Petrel fledgling, Light-mantled Sooty Albatross chick, Antipodes Island Red-crowned Parakeet

ANTIPODES ISLAND PARAKEET The largest of all the parakeets in the New Zealand region, this endemic species is entirely green, with no head colour typical of most of its close relatives.
KATH WALKER.

Another species endemic to the island is the Antipodes Island Snipe (*Coenocoypha meinertzhagenae*), a relatively small, long-billed bird that lives in amongst the tussock grass. Several thousand pairs are thought to breed on the main and outlying islands of the group. The only other endemic bird species on the island is a subspecies of the New Zealand Pipit (*Anthus novaeseelandiae steindachneri*). Again, there are thought to be several thousand birds in the breeding populations of the larger islands of the group. Other self-introduced land birds that appear to be breeding in small numbers include the Mallard (*Anas platyrhynchos*), Dunnock (*Prunella modularis*), Redpoll (*Carduelis flammea*) and European Starling (*Sturnus vulgaris*).

SEALS

In his numerous visits to the island group, Rowley Taylor has documented the progress of the recolonisation of the New Zealand Fur Seals (*Arctocephalus forsteri*). After being effectively wiped out in the early 1800s, it has taken almost 200 years for the seals to recolonise the islands and numbers are still significantly less than pre-exploitation levels. Today, some 2000 fur seals visit the island group each year, with numbers peaking during March. The majority of these seals are yearlings and juveniles and only a few pups are born each year. The slow rate of increase in seals here has led to speculation that the island group may not have been a significant breeding site prior to exploitation and that it may have been used primarily as a haul-out site for thousands of yearling and juvenile seals. Unfortunately, due to lack of evidence, it is impossible to test this hypothesis. In addition to New Zealand Fur Seals, a few Subantarctic Fur Seals (*Arctocephalus tropicalis*) and Leopard Seals (*Hydrurga leptonyx*) regularly visit. Small numbers of Southern Elephant Seal (*Mirounga leonina*) also breed on the island, with up to 100 pups being born each year.

INTRODUCED ANIMALS

Even though livestock was introduced sporadically in the late 1800s and early 1900s, the only introduced animal to survive on the Antipodes group today is the House Mouse. It is restricted to the main island, with higher numbers in summer attributable to higher food availability and lower survival of the young during the winter months. Although mice are known to be voracious invertebrate predators, their impact on the invertebrate fauna of the Antipodes is difficult to measure. However, the differences in the invertebrate fauna of the main island compared to mouse-free Bollons Island suggests that mice significantly influence the abundance and composition of the invertebrates.

TERRESTRIAL INVERTEBRATES

The terrestrial invertebrate fauna of the Antipodes group is diverse. There are 150 species of insect and 20 arachnids. Around 30 per cent of all the insects are eco-parasites, living mainly on a variety of bird species. Twenty of the insect species are considered endemic; nine of these are beetles, four are moths and one is a weta. The weta was only recently discovered, on Bollons Island in the mid 1990s. A high percentage of the moth species are also found on the south island of New Zealand and for many of these the Antipodes marks the southern extent of their distribution. Other groups of invertebrates represented on the Antipodes include isopods, amphipods and collembola.

HISTORY

On her last voyage home from Port Jackson to England, the HMS *Reliance*, under the command of Captain Waterhouse, came across an island group to the south-east of New Zealand on 26th March 1800. Captain Waterhouse described the main island as a 'desolate, mountainous and barren island, with scarcely any vegetation' and also noted the presence of a small island at the north-eastern end of the larger one. He initially named the island group the Penantipodes due to its proximity to the antipodes of London. Before departing, Captain Waterhouse also noted the presence of numerous seals.

The fur sealers

The seals brought the next visitors to the island. First to arrive were the Americans, looking for fur seal skins to sell to the lucrative Chinese market. In 1805 the schooner *Independence*, under the command of I. Townsend, landed three sealing gangs totaling around 31 men, some of whom stayed on the island for over two years. In subsequent years, the Antipodes—or Penantipodes, as they were often still known—were visited by numerous sealing gangs, who exacted a heavy toll on the seals there. For a time, the islands had a reputation as one of the richest sealing grounds in the world. In fact, over a two year period (1806-1807) nearly 200 000 skins were taken from these islands.

As with all other examples of this industry, the extermination of the seals was efficiently brutal and quick. Within a few years the number of seals had diminished considerably, and new sealing grounds further south took the focus away from the Antipodes. Sporadic visits were made over the next 25 years but catches were never comparable to those obtained in the first few years.

Castaway depots and scientists

The Antipodes experienced something of a human hiatus between 1830 and 1865. Prompted by a spate of shipwrecks on the Auckland Islands, provincial government steamers visited the island in 1865 and 1868, looking for survivors of shipwrecks. During the latter voyage the government representative, Henry Armstrong, set fire to the tussock grass to alert any possible castaways of their presence. A small cache of stores were also left on the island at the conclusion of that visit. In the late 1870s, the building and servicing of the castaway depots was taken over by the New Zealand government and their ships made regular visits to most of the islands, paving the way for better access for scientists. Apart from the government steamers, there were few visitors to the Antipodes until the penguin skin trade of the early 1880s rekindled interest in these islands.

The first botanical collections of the Antipodes were made in 1890 by the botanist Thomas Kirk. In 1895, Sir James Hector and Professor Thomas Jeffrey Parker visited all the subantarctic islands, including the Antipodes, on a government steamer and made collections and notes on the geology. Extensive collections of living plants were also made on this trip, some of which made their way to the Royal Botanical Gardens at Kew. The Earl of Ranfurly, accompanied by Professor Hutton, visited the Antipodes in 1900 and collected birds for the British Museum. Another significant botanical visit was made in 1903 by Leonard Cockayne, who for the first time noted some of the winter aspects of the vegetation. Staff from the American Museum of Natural History visited the island in 1926 during the Whitney South Sea Expedition in the *France*.

The botanist, Thomas Kirk, visited mot of the wild islands south of New Zealand in the late 1800s. Alexander Turnbull Library, Wellington, New Zealand. F-41850-1/2

It was on this voyage that one member of the expedition is reported to have shot 51 birds early one morning, afterwards remarking 'which is the most I have ever shot before breakfast'. An interesting insight into the attitudes of the 'naturalists' of the day.

The Antipodes continued to be visited by government steamers up until 1927. During these visits livestock were often landed in an attempt to provide potential food for shipwrecked sailors. However, livestock were not able to survive here for extended periods as they were on Campbell and Auckland Islands, and so never established viable, long-term populations.

Shipwrecks

The *Spirit of Dawn* was wrecked on the south-west coast of the main Antipodes Island in thick fog in September 1893. The vessel sank before the lifeboats could be lowered and the captain and four of the crew drowned, but the remaining officers and men eventually managed to get into one of the lifeboats and make it to shore. Unfortunately they didn't find the castaway depot at the northern end of the island and after nearly three months of eating raw penguin, penguin eggs and roots of the Macquarie Island cabbage, they were rescued in late 1893 by the government steamer *Hinemoa*. Another wreck occurred in 1908 when the French *President Felix Faure* came to grief on a reef at the north-east of the island. The 22-man crew made it to shore safely in a lifeboat and were sustained by the stores of the castaway depot and the native wildlife, including albatrosses, penguins and shellfish, before being rescued two months later by the HMS *Pegasus*.

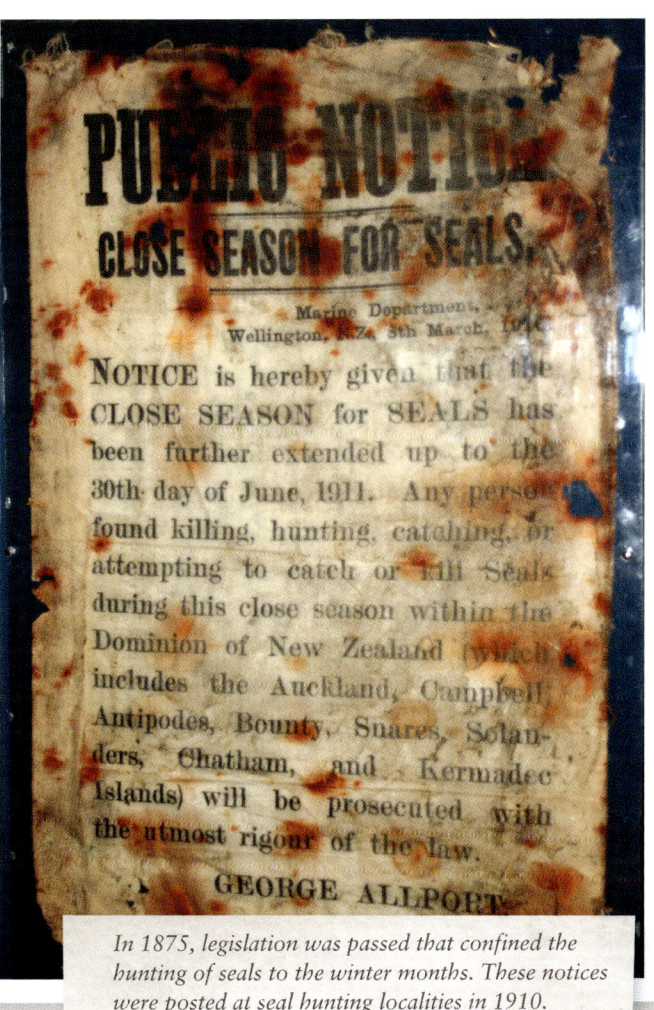

In 1875, legislation was passed that confined the hunting of seals to the winter months. These notices were posted at seal hunting localities in 1910. Southland Museum and Art Gallery. 06225sm

ANTIPODES ISLANDS 87

More recently, shipping tragedy was again associated with the island when the *Totorore* disappeared. In May 1999, Gerry Clark and Roger Sale sailed from Lyttelton for the Antipodes with two albatross researchers aboard. After landing the researchers, Gerry anchored the *Totorore* in Alert Bay for the next seven nights. On the radio schedule on the night of 11th June, Gerry mentioned that he intended to take the *Totorore* to South Bay as soon as conditions permitted. The vessel was not heard from again. Due to his considerable experience in the Southern Ocean, a search was not mounted until 18th June and on 21st June wreckage from the yacht was found in South Bay. To this day the cause of the wreck remains unknown and it will be remembered as one of the most tragic events in the island's history.

The twentieth century and beyond

Like its nearest island neighbour, the Bounty Islands, the Antipodes were little visited after the end of the castaway depot resupply. It wasn't until 1938 that the next visitors called at the Antipodes Islands. The Royal Research Ship *Discovery 11* visited in January of that year during a circumpolar voyage from Cape Town. Nobody landed, but the team carried out oceanographic research. The USCG cutter *Northwind* made an unscheduled visit to the island en route from Antarctica in 1947 and although they only spent a few hours ashore, they managed to collect over 50 live penguins, which they brought back to New Zealand.

The first scientific expedition to land on the Antipodes was in 1950 when a privately-funded group, organised by Alex Black and led by Sir Robert Falla, landed and stayed on the island for six days in November. They searched extensively for fur seals but only found one old male ashore. In those days the main way of obtaining information about birds was to kill and collect specimens and 89 individuals were collected, both on land and at sea. Expeditions were also made by staff from the New Zealand Oceanographic Institute in 1962 and 1965 and the research vessel *Eltanin* called in briefly in January 1967. A number of specimens were collected, including some flowering plants and ferns that are now in the US National Arboretum in Washington.

In 1969 John Warham led a significant expedition to the Antipodes with the aim of learning more about this island group. Up to this point, the island group was the least studied of all the New Zealand subantarctic islands. The findings from this expedition added considerably to the general knowledge of the island, including vegetation, invertebrates, birds, mammals and evidence of past human contact. This expedition also marked the beginning of ecologist Rowley Taylor's long association with the island, an association that culminated with his recent book on the Antipodes and Bounties Islands, *Straight Through to London*, published by Heritage Expeditions.

The New Zealand Wildlife Service BAAS (Bounty, Antipodes, Auckland and Snares) Expedition of 1978, led by Brian Bell, was the next expedition of significance. It was during this visit that the new Lands and Survey hut was built near the site of the old castaway depot. Small boats taken as part of the expedition also allowed the outlying islands to be investigated in more detail than many the earlier visits. It was, however, the last of the multidisciplinary expeditions and the nature of research on this and other island groups changed considerably after this time.

GERRY CLARK AND *TOTORORE* Many recent research trips to the Antipodes Islands would probably not have been possible without the skill and local knowledge of the late Gerry Clark in his yacht the *Totorore*. JACINDA AMEY.

A number of brief visits were made to the Antipodes throughout the 1980s, including Television New Zealand's Natural History Unit, who were producing a two part series entitled *Islands*. In 1985, the National Film Unit visited the Island on the HMNZS *Monowai* during the filming of their production *Beyond the Roaring Forties*. Several scientists accompanied this expedition, which stayed for four days.

In February 1994, a privately-funded expedition sailed to the islands on Gerry Clark's yacht *Totorore*, its main aim being a census of the Antipodean Albatross population and other associated albatross research. The party stayed until March and Gerry returned to the islands later that year with more scientists, searching for the breeding grounds of the Chatham Island Taiko (*Pterodroma magentae*). In February 1995, Gerry and a party returned to the Antipodes to complete the Antipodean Albatross census. A second Taiko searching expedition also visited the island in 1995 and concluded that 'no Taiko were breeding on the Antipodes'. In January 1996, albatross researchers Kath Walker and Graeme Elliott began a long-term study into the effects of commercial long-line fishing in the Southern Ocean on the Antipodean Albatrosses. This project ran until 2005, with annual visits to the island.

The New Zealand Ministry of Fisheries has recently provided funding for two projects on the Antipodes Islands, both of which are being undertaken by National Institute for Water and Atmospheric Research (NIWAR). There are plans to fund research into White-chinned Petrels for five years and Grey Petrel research has received two years funding. There are concerns that the long-line fishing industry is having an impact on both these species.

Campbell Island

MOUTERE IHUPUKU • 52°35'S • 169°10'E • 11400ha • 569m a.s.l

Campbell Island is one of New Zealand's better known oceanic islands, situated 700 kilometres south of New Zealand. Despite its southerly location, it has a rich human history and has been visited almost continuously since its discovery by Europeans in 1810. This prolonged presence of people has had a marked impact on the island, particularly on its flora and fauna. From the sealers and whalers who settled there in the early years, to the farmers who tried to make it a viable agricultural resource, the legacy of humans on Campbell Island is one of environmental change and rarely for the good. In recognition of this fact, in more recent times steps have been taken to try and return the island to a more natural state. The removal of sheep, cattle and more recently, the eradication of rats, has given the island a chance of returning to a more pristine condition. Despite the impact of humans, the island remains a wonderland of diverse animals and plants.

Campbell Island Teal

CAMPBELL ISLAND Formed by volcanic action between six and eleven million years ago, Campbell Island is New Zealand's southernmost subantarctic island and famous for the diversity of megaherbs that occur there.

CAMPBELL ISLAND With the unmistakeable yellow flowers of *Bulbinella rossii* in the foreground, the imposing west coast cliffs of Campbell Island recede to the north, with Mt Azimuth forming the highest point. *ALEKS TERAUDS.*

GEOGRAPHY AND GEOLOGY

The Campbell Island group is the second largest of New Zealand's subantarctic island groups and includes one main island and a number of small islets, covering around 11 400 hectares in total. Like the Antipodes Islands and Auckland Islands, Campbell Island is almost entirely volcanic in origin; it is much older than the Antipodes and somewhat younger than the Auckland Islands.

Geography

Campbell Island is an exposed portion of the southern margin of the Campbell Plateau, a large feature that dominates the underwater landscape south of New Zealand. To the west is an oceanic trench, several kilometres deep, which separates the Campbell Plateau from the Macquarie Ridge. Macquarie Island, 700 kilometres south-west of Campbell Island, is the only exposed portion of this huge submarine ridgeline.

The main island dominates the Campbell group, with a total area of 11 311 hectares. Dent Island, off the west coast, with an area of 23 hectares, and Jaquemart Island, off the south coast, with an area of 19 hectares, are the largest of the small islands. Other smaller islands and islets of the group include Isle de Jeannette Marie, Gomez Island, Wasp Island, Monowai Island, Survey Island, Folly Island and Hook Keys.

The volcanic origins of the main island are not immediately obvious from its appearance. In contrast to the Antipodes, the greater age of the Campbell Island volcano means that many of its original features have been eroded away. However, the western coastline and outwardly radiating ridgelines on the plateau are reminiscent of a volcanic cone, and with a bit of imagination the original shape of the volcano can be traced. The bays and inlets on the eastern side are fiords of glacial origin, with Perseverance Harbour and North-east Harbour being the largest. In fact, Perseverance Harbour nearly cuts right through the island, coming to within a few kilometres of the western coastline. Steep, high cliffs ring the west and south-west coasts, which only really flatten out briefly in North-west Bay. The high cliffs have also been formed by massive erosion, with numerous caves and arches formed by the relentless action of pounding waves.

The higher parts of the island are dominated by long, gently-sloping ridgelines and radial valleys that tend to run from west to east and which define the fiord-like inlets. The high points of these ridgelines are Mount Honey (the highest point of the island at 569 metres) and Mount Dumas in the south, Mount Lyall in the centre and Mount Fizeau in the north. Mount Azimuth, Mount Faye, Menhir and Mount Paris are other notable peaks. Peat, several metres deep in places, blankets the island. Wetter areas are common, with swamps and tarns present in many of the flatter parts of the island.

Origins

Built on the ancient basement rock of the Campbell Plateau, Campbell Island is the eroded remnants of a shield volcano that erupted between 6 and 11 million years ago, during the Miocene epoch. The radiating pattern seen in the volcanic rocks indicates the centre of the volcano was between North-west Bay and Dent Island. Marine erosion has removed most of the western half of the volcano, and today the scarp in that Mount Coast is all that remains of the central caldera.

Beeman Hill, inland from Perseverance Harbour, is a remnant volcanic plug left over from more recent volcanic action.

While the volcanic rocks influence the landscape, Campbell Island has also been shaped by more recent glacial action during the ice ages of the Pleistocene epoch. Although the thick blanket of peat that covers the island masks finer details and makes it difficult to identify some glacial evidence, there is little doubt that the U-shaped valleys, moraines and cirques were formed by the action of ice during the last two million years.

Geology

The basement rock underlying Campbell Island is mica schist, which at 400–600 million years old is the oldest rock known from the Campbell Plateau and New Zealand. Some of this rock, veined by quartz, is exposed at Complex Point in North-west Bay and more is poorly exposed on the eastern shore of Garden Cove. Overlying the schist is a younger sequence of sedimentary rocks deposited between 70 and 25 million years ago. These sedimentary rocks include sandstones, mudstones, conglomerate and limestone. The best outcrops of the limestone are in the white cliffs to the north of North-west Bay. Numerous basaltic dykes from later volcanic action intrude the sedimentary rocks in many places. Another feature of these marine sedimentary rocks is that they hold a significant number of fossils, which are generally uncommon on many of the other subantarctic islands.

The sediments in the south-west portion of the island include two different formations. The first, at Garden Cove in Perseverance Harbour, is 30–100 metres thick and

WEST COAST CLIFFS Little vegetation grows on these high steep cliffs that ring the west coast of the island. *NATHAN RUSS.*

comprised of conglomerate, sandstone and mudstone, initially deposited in a non-marine environment that appears to have become marginally marine between 70 and 55 million years ago. The fossils contained within this deposit are particularly interesting as their ages span the Cretaceous–Tertiary boundary (widely believed to mark the extinction of the youngest dinosaurs and a huge number of other organisms) and include spores, pollen, dinoflagellates, foraminifera and radiolarians. The overlying Tucker Cove Formation is 100–200 metres thick and consists of limestone, sand and chert (flint) nodules. It contains a diverse array of microfossils from 55 to 30 million years ago.

Overlying the limestone and covering around half of the island is the Shoal Point Formation, a partly marine deposit of pyroclastic volcanic sediment, composed mainly of ash and scoria, which also includes fossils. This, in turn, is covered by lava flows on the higher ridges and north-eastern part of the island. Menhir is an intrusion of a coarse, dark rock known as gabbro, which is the solidified remains of the magma chamber beneath the Campbell volcano.

FLORA

The plants of Campbell Island have long been affected by the presence of people. From the burning of the slopes when looking for castaways, to the extended periods of stock grazing, the vegetation has been altered significantly from its original form. Nevertheless, removal of cattle and sheep from the island, and more recently the eradication of the rats in 2001, have had a major positive impact. Today, the island's tussock fields and megaherbs are once more beginning to thrive. Well over 200 species are recognised on the island, with 140 species of vascular plant, 119 species of moss and numerous lichens and liverworts. In addition to the obvious, unnatural impacts of people and associated animals, the pattern of vegetation growth is largely driven by topography, climatic factors and the nutrient content of the soil.

History of botanical study

The earliest botanical collections from Campbell Island were made by Sir Joseph Hooker during the voyage of the *Erebus* and the *Terror*, led by Sir James Clark Ross in 1840. On this voyage, Hooker spent the best part of three days ashore and collected almost 200 species, including 68 flowering plants and 72 mosses and liverworts. These collections, together with those from the Auckland Islands, were published in the first volume of the seminal work *Flora of Antarctica*.

Botanists did not visit the island again until the French Transit of Venus Expedition in the summer of 1874–75. In 1883, John Buchanan visited the island and made a large collection of species and five years later, Andreas Reischek and the photographer William Dougall spent four days there. While no plant specimens were collected on this visit, Dougall's photographs are invaluable today as a pre-pastoral record of the vegetation.

Botanists Thomas Kirk and Frederick Chapman visited the island briefly in 1890, while Leonard Cockayne went there in the winter of 1903 and was one of the first to document the damage from pastoral practices. The next visit was the landmark Philosophical Institute of Canterbury Expedition, which landed a group for just over a week on the island in 1907. The descriptions to come from these two visits were some of the most extensive since Hooker's visit. The Cape Expeditions of the Second World War provided the next real opportunity for botanists to visit the island and Jack Sorenson conducted botanical studies during this time and eventually published an account of the general botany of Campbell Island and a checklist of the vascular flora. In 1961, Eric Godley led a party of botanists and zoologists to the island and he again revisited the island in 1969, after which he published observations on the flora and new records. A visit to the island in the 1970s by another party made collections of the lichen and bryophyte flora and further observations on the vascular plants.

Over the last forty years many botanists—too numerous to list here—have visited the island. Their contributions have been significant, with few areas of the main or outlying islands remaining unsurveyed. David Given and Colin Meurk made a number of visits over this time and have contributed significantly to recent knowledge of the plants and plant communities on the island, while recent studies and publications by M.S. McGlone have clarified broad changes in the vegetation over the last 13 000 years.

MEGAHERB FLOWERS One of the most common megaherbs on Campbell Island is *Pleurophyllum speciosum*, a member of the daisy family, whose bright purple flowers dominate the landscape in many places during summer. *NATHAN RUSS.*

VEGETATION BANDS Altitude and aspect are two important factors that determine where plants grow on Campbell Island. The dark green *Dracophyllum* scrub is dominant in lower altitudes while in higher, more exposed areas, tussock grasses dominate. *ALEKS TERAUDS.*

Coastal plants

Maritime communities occur close to sea level and include salt marsh on the edges of harbours, rock fields encrusted with lichens and mosses, and a combination of turf and cushion plants on rocks near the waterline. The tussock grass *Poa foliosa* and megaherbs *Anisotome latifolia* and *Stilbocarpa polaris*, together with the fern *Blechnum durum*, also grow together close to the coast. Many of the coastal communities are influenced by the animals that inhabit these environments, with bright green *Poa ramosissima* common on the steep banks around bird colonies and the herbs *Callitriche antarctica* and *Montia fontana* thriving in abandoned elephant seal wallows. Some of these boggy coastal areas are also home to rafts of the grasses *Agrostis capillaris* and *Deschampsia chapmanii*, the coastal daisy *Leptinella plumosa* and the liverwort *Marchantia berteroana*.

Sub-alpine plants

Above the coastal zone is a transitional zone that corresponds to the sub-alpine zone in New Zealand. It is very restricted in distribution and is characterised by a dwarf forest of *Dracophyllum scoparium* and *D. longifolium*, with *Coprosma* species and *Myrsine*. In more sheltered places these trees can attain a height of 5 metres and are large enough to form a low canopy of foliage and branches. Tree growth and distribution are limited by the ever-present high winds combined with cool temperatures. *Dracophyllum* forest may dominate up to about 180 metres above sea level in sheltered areas and these forests have greatly increased their range since the 1940s by

STATION IN THE SCRUB The boardwalk down to the abandoned meteorological station provides easy access while protecting the vulnerable vegetation from damage. *ALEKS TERAUDS*

colonising tussock meadows made vulnerable through the burning and grazing of *Chionochloa* tall tussock vegetation. A single introduced spruce tree grows on the island and has the distinction of being the loneliest tree in the world according to the *Guinness Book of Records*.

Low alpine plants

The low alpine areas include patches of *Chionochloa* tall tussock grassland, scattered areas of dwarf *Dracophyllum* scrub and a number of localised vegetation assemblages made up of tall tussock, dwarf scrub and boggy areas of turf and cushion plants. These boggy areas are largely composed of *Isolepis* sp. and *Oreobolus* cushions. Lowland bog composed of tussock and cushion plants are fairly common on broad ridges and saddles at low altitudes and are usually surrounded by dense scrub or separated by deep, entrenched gullies brimming with tall scrub or dwarf forest. These features have often been referred to as 'lanes' and they are also found on the Auckland Islands.

Swampy areas of *Coprosoma-Myrsine* shrubland, often growing with the tall sedge *Carex appressa* and *Blechnum* ferns are also common in the low alpine zone, mainly on peat slips, around tarns and other wetter areas. Another widespread feature of the low alpine zone is the *Bulbinella rossii*–turf meadow. The dark green leaves and yellow flowers of *B. rossii* are a distinctive feature of this environment and the plant forms a dark green swathe on the summer landscape between the bronze upper alpine rush herbfields and the lighter coloured tussock meadow. The distribution of this largely unpalatable plant increased due to the preferential grazing of other species by sheep.

HEBE BENTHAMII Only found on Campbell Island and the Auckland Islands, this plant, with its unique indigo flowers, was first discovered and described by renowned botanist Joseph Hooker. *ALEKS TERAUDS*

HIGH ALPINE PLANTS

About 50 species of plant on Campbell Island are restricted to the upper alpine habitats and the vegetation of this zone forms a mountain summit, tundra-like mosaic. The tall rush-herbfield association is dominated by the rush *Marsippospermum gracile* and *Bulbinella rossii* (seasonally), but a wide range of grasses, forbs, lichens and bryophytes form a dense, turf-like understorey. Before the arrival of grazing animals, the megaherbs *Pleurophyllum speciosum*, *Anisotome antipoda* and dwarfed *Stilbocarpa polaris* were more common components of this association.

Two other species of *Pleurophyllum*—*P. criniferum* and *P. hookeri*—also occur on the island, with the latter more commonly found in the higher, more exposed locations. The distribution of these extremely palatable megaherbs has increased in recent years with the absence of grazing animals and they dominate in some areas. The presence of grazing animals has had a big impact on these higher areas, where trampling of fragile assemblages followed by wind erosion has allowed other, more grazing-tolerant species to colonise the exposed peat. Due to the slow growth rate of many plants in these regions, the recovery will take a long time. In addition, due to the unnatural succession it is likely that some of these areas will never completely return to their pristine state.

INTRODUCED (ALIEN) SPECIES

Introduced plants form a large proportion of the flora on Campbell Island and their status has been regularly assessed. Traditionally, alien plants are divided into four main categories: transient aliens, persistent aliens, restricted naturalised and widespread naturalised.

ALPINE MEGAHERBS The impact of years of trampling and grazing by livestock has had long lasting impacts, especially in the more delicate alpine areas of Campbell Island. Megaherbs like these *Pleurophyllum* spp. are slowly starting to recolonise in places. *ALEKS TERAUDS*

The jointed rush (*Juncus articulatus*) is classified as a persistent alien species, as is the deadnettle (*Lamium purpureum*), the monkey-flower (*Mimulus guttatus*) and the spiny sowthistle (*Sonchus asper*).

There are three restricted naturalised species considered to threaten the native components of natural communities. These are the grass (*Arrhenatherum elatius*), the marsh foxtail (*Alopecurus geniculatus*) and the lotus, *Lotus pedunculatus*. The grass has already established in the tall sedge swamp at the head of Tucker Cover, along with another weedy grass, *Holcus lanatus*. The marsh foxtail has also formed an extensive stand in the salt marsh-wallow area at the head of Tucker Cove and the lotus has gradually been spreading in the vicinity of the old Tucker Camp.

Today, the greatest concentration of alien species occurs in the environs of the upper Perseverance Harbour. There is, however, a hardy widespread naturalised element, which has penetrated and established in the low alpine hinterland, albeit in generally modified vegetation.

Marine plants

A diverse range of kelps and algae grow around the coast of Campbell Island, with over 100 species present. Around 80 per cent of these species are also found around the New Zealand mainland. Like most of the subantarctic island groups, Antarctic bull kelp (*Durvillaea antarctica*) is one of the more common species and while it is present around much of the exposed coast, it also grows in the sheltered regions of the bays and harbours.

FAUNA

Since the 1940s, Campbell Island has been almost permanently occupied, allowing intensive research into the animals living there. It is one of the most important nature reserves for breeding seabirds in the world and in addition to being the main home of the Southern Royal Albatrosses (*Diomedea epomophora*), five other albatross species breed there, including the endemic Campbell Albatross (*Thalassarche impavida*). The island is also home to thousands of penguins, several species of burrowing petrel, a diverse range of land birds, seals and even one species of galaxiid fish. Many of the albatrosses and penguin counts were conducted or coordinated by Peter Moore and much of the following information has been obtained from his Department of Conservation reports.

Penguins

A significant conservation issue facing the island is the disastrous population crash of the Rockhopper Penguin (*Eudyptes chrysocome*). In the early 1940s the population was estimated to be between one and two million breeding pairs. The most recent census, in 1985, found the number of breeding birds had declined by 94 per cent, to around 100 000 pairs. The decline is attributed to changing oceanic temperatures and subsequent changes in food resources, possibly related to the southwards shift of the nutrient-rich Antarctic Convergence. The island is also an important nature reserve for one of the world's rarest penguins, the Yellow-eyed Penguin (*Megadyptes antipodes*). The most recent survey of breeding birds, conducted in 1988, estimated that there were around 490–600 breeding pairs, or around one-quarter of the world population. However, in a 1998 study of penguins coming ashore, Peter Moore and co-workers estimated that there had been a decline of 41 per cent in the number of individuals in the population.

Albatross

Almost the entire world population of the Southern Royal Albatross, estimated at around 8000–9000 pairs, breeds on Campbell Island. The island is also the only breeding ground for the endemic Campbell (Black-browed) Albatross, which nests in mixed colonies with Grey-headed Albatrosses (*Thalassarche chrysostoma*), mainly around the north coast, from North-east Harbour to Courrejolles Point. Photographs of colonies and ground counts have been used to census these species since the 1940s. Estimates from the mid to late 1990s suggest there are around 24 600 pairs of the Campbell Albatross, with a total population of over 70 000 individuals. There are around 12 000 breeding pairs of the biennially breeding Grey-headed Albatross in total, with 6000–9000 pairs nesting each year.

Low numbers of the Black-browed Albatross (*Thalassarche melanophrys*) also breed on Campbell Island, with occasional interbreeding occurring with the Campbell Albatross. A small breeding population (<20 pairs) of the Antipodean Albatross (*Diomedea antipodensis*) are also scattered around the island. The sixth albatross species breeding on the island is the Light-mantled Sooty Albatross (*Phoebetria palpebrata*), with an estimated population of at least 1600 pairs breeding each year on coastal cliff and offshore islets.

CAMPBELL ALBATROSS This species only breeds on Campbell Island in large colonies, mainly in the northern part of the island where over 20 000 pairs are estimated to breed. *AARON RUSS.*

SOUTHERN ROYAL ALBATROSSES Like most of the larger albatrosses, courtship displays are an important part of finding a mate. During summer, particularly late in the day, it is not unusual to see several young males vying for the attentions of one or two females. *ALEKS TERAUDS.*

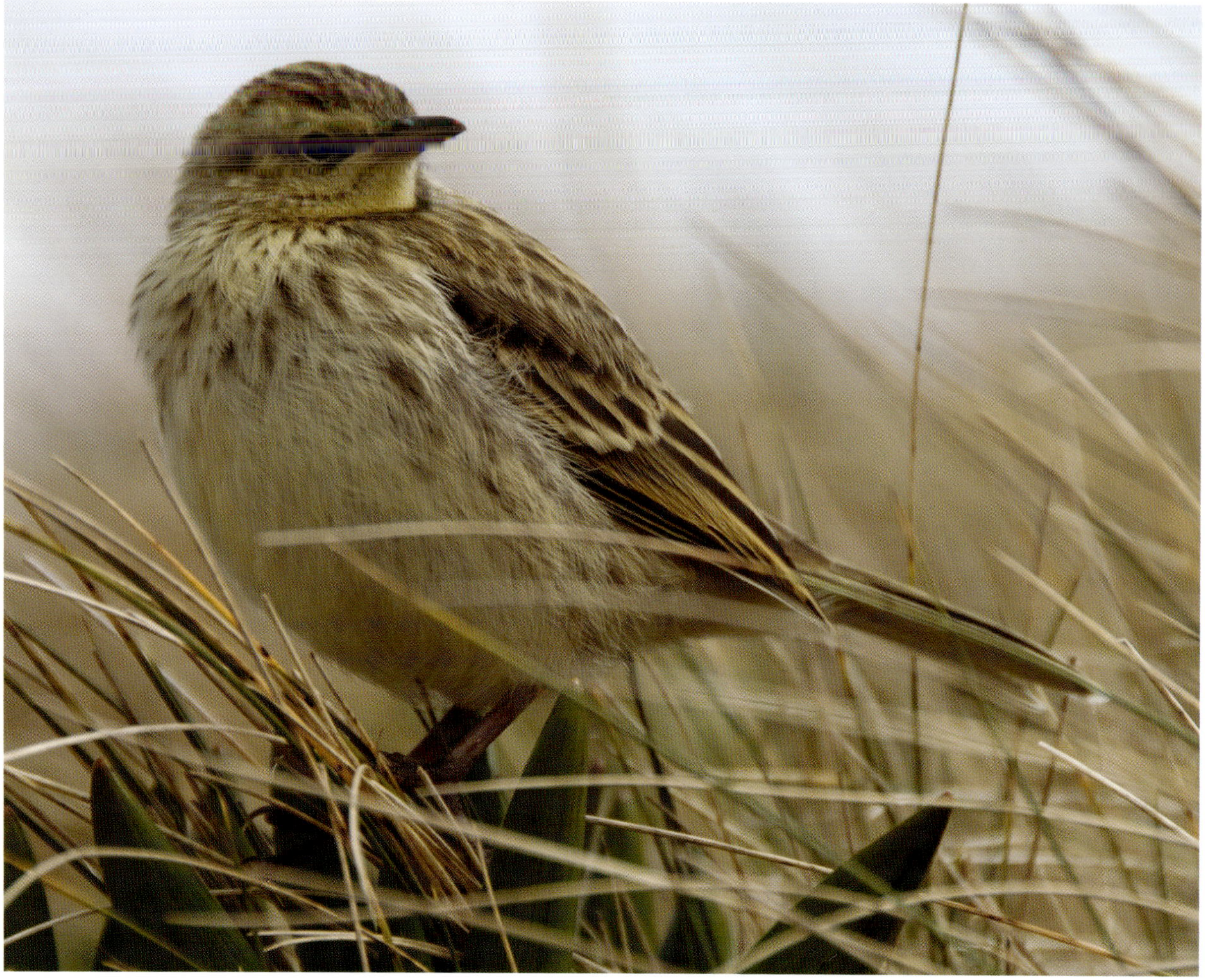

AARON RUSS

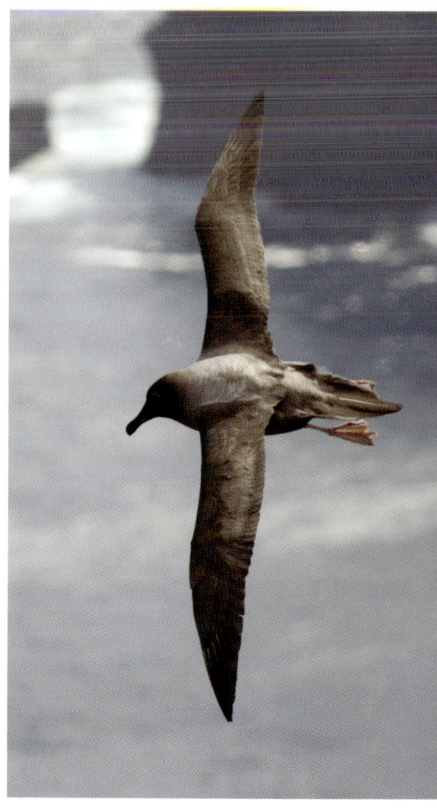

CAMPBELL ISLAND BIRDS (clockwise from top left) New Zealand Pipit, Light-mantled Sooty Albatross, Rockhopper Penguin, Campbell Island Shag.

NATHAN RUSS

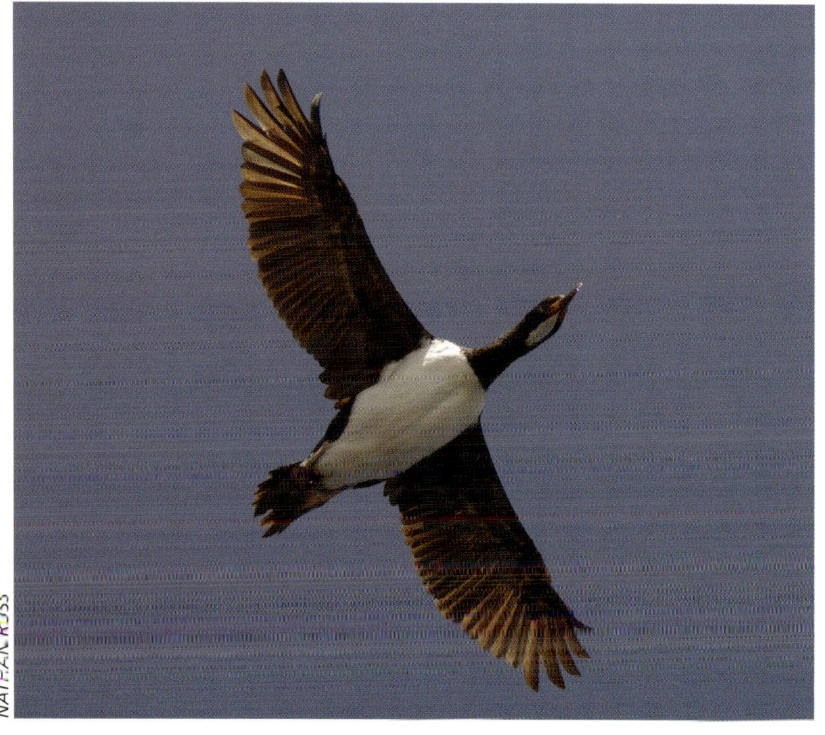

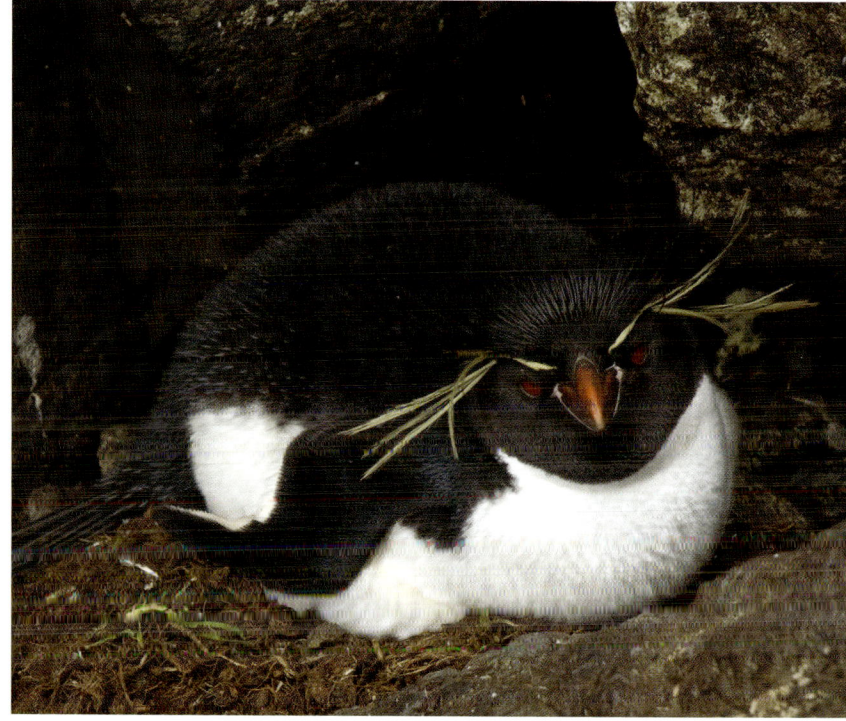

Other petrels

The breeding population of the Northern Giant Petrel (*Macronectes halli*) on Campbell Island is estimated at around 230 pairs and there is anecdotal evidence that it has been increasing. Most nests are concentrated in the southern part of the island. Breeding Grey Petrels (*Procellaria cinerea*) are concentrated around Mount Eboule area in low numbers (<100 pairs) but possibly in larger numbers on the smaller, outlying islands. Sooty Shearwater (*Puffinus griseus*) numbers have been greatly reduced on the main island due to rats but are now likely to increase significantly in their absence. Snares Cape Petrels (*Daption capense australe*) are known to breed in at least two sites in small numbers, whilst the White-chinned Petrel (*Procellaria aequinoctialis*) breeds chiefly on stacks off the main Island, with 10 000 pairs estimated to be on Monowai Island. The southern form of the Common Diving Petrel (*Pelecanoides urinatrix chathamensis*), Fairy Prions (*Pachyptila turtur*), Black-bellied Storm Petrels (*Fregetta tropica*) and Grey-backed Storm Petrels (*Garrodia nereis*) are thought to breed mainly on offshore islands, but their population on the main island has historically been inhibited by the presence of rats. White-headed Petrels (*Pterodroma lessonii*) have been recorded occasionally in the surrounding waters and it is likely this species is also breeding on some of the outlying islands.

Other seabirds

Like several of the other islands, Campbell island has an endemic shag, the Campbell Island Shag (*Phalacrocorax campbelli*), with total population of approximately 8000 birds and 1000–2000 breeding pairs. Other species breeding in small or scattered colonies include the Little Shag (*Phalacrocorax melanoleucos brevirostris*), which has been observed breeding in the region of 6 Foot Lake, Subantarctic Skua (*Catharacta lonnbergi*), Southern Black-backed Gulls (*Larus dominicanus*), Red-billed Gulls (*Larus scopulinus*) and Antarctic Terns (*Sterna vittata benthunei*).

Land birds

The endemic Campbell Island Flightless Teal (*Anas aucklandica nesiotis*) was originally wiped out from Campbell Island by the cats and rats. However, it was rediscovered by Rodney Russ in late 1975 on predator-free Dent Island. At that time the population was estimated at 30–50 birds, and following the rediscovery an active management program was initiated. Captive breeding programs and controlled wild breeding culminated in the release of 50 birds to the main island in 2004. Two further releases have occurred since this time and breeding has now been confirmed on the main island.

In 1997, a previously unknown subspecies of the Subantarctic Snipe (*Coenocorypha* sp.) was discovered on Jacquemart Island. It is difficult to estimate population numbers but there could be as few as 60 individuals. The New Zealand Pipit (*Anthus novaeseelandiae*) survives in good numbers on Dent and Jacquemart Islands and since the eradication of the rats has reestablished itself on the main island.

Self-introduced breeding birds on Campbell Island include the Grey Duck (*Anas superciliosa*), Mallard (*Anas platyrhynchos*), Skylark (*Alauda arvensis*), Song Thrush (*Turdus philomelos*), European Blackbird (*Turdus merula*), Hedge Sparrow or Dunnock (*Prunella modularis*), Goldfinch

(*Carduelis carduelis*), Redpoll (*Carduelis flammea*), House Sparrow (*Passer domesticus*), Chaffinch (*Fringilla coelebs*), Silvereye (*Zosterops lateralis*) and Yellowhammer (*Emberiza citrinella*). In recent years, more focused birdwatching trips have visited the island, and consequently the sightings of vagrants and visiting species has increased.

Marine mammals

New Zealand Fur Seals (*Arctocephalus forsteri*) are slowly recovering from their decimation in the early 1800s; however, published surveys are few and far between and the number of breeding seals on the island is unknown. Southern Elephant Seal (*Mirounga leonina*) numbers have declined dramatically since the early 1970s, and since 2001 less than five pups have been born each year. The reasons for the decrease in the elephant seal population on Campbell Island are unknown, but it could be related to such factors as shifting food resources in response to changes in oceanographic currents and fronts.

A significant number of New Zealand (Hooker's) Sea Lions (*Phocarctos hookeri*) also breed on the island, with a 2003 census estimating 385 pups were born. Female sea lions on Campbell Island tend to behave differently to those on the Auckland Islands, with many heading a long way inland to pup. For an animal that is relatively ungainly on the land, they are incredible climbers and females have been found at altitudes of several hundred metres. Historically, the sheltered bays of Campbell Island have also been the winter breeding grounds of Southern Right Whales (*Eubalaena australis*) and numbers are slowly recovering from the carnage that was exacted upon them by whalers in the 1800s.

Introduced animals

Sheep, cattle, goats and pigs were liberated on the island at various times prior to 1895 with the intention of providing sustenance to shipwrecked sailors, but none of these animals survived for very long. Cats were also brought to the island in the nineteenth century by some of the earliest visitors, but in contrast to several other Southern Ocean islands, never really established a thriving feral population. Both sheep and cattle were reintroduced after 1895, but in 1931 when the farmers abandoned the island run, about 4000 sheep and between 20–30 cattle were left unattended on the island. Sheep and cattle have subsequently been removed and the cats appear to have died out naturally.

Norway Rats (*Rattus norvegicus*) were well-established on the main island by 1874 and since then they have had a huge impact on the invertebrates and birdlife. In 2001, the Department of Conservation undertook an operation to eradicate them from the island using helicopters and poisoned bait. This logistically challenging operation was successful and in 2003 the island was declared rat free.

Terrestrial invertebrates

There are 171 known indigenous insects on Campbell Island, 30 per cent of which are considered endemic. Flies (Dipterans) dominate the insects, and beetles and moths are also common. Other invertebrates found include crustaceans, mites, collembola and spiders. In total there are thought to be over 250 species of terrestrial invertebrate, 16 of which live in the freshwater streams and creeks that flow around the island. While the terrestrial invertebrates are reasonably well-studied, detailed systematic surveys still reveal species that have not yet been described.

NEW ZEALAND (HOOKER'S) SEA LION In contrast to other islands, many females of this species on Campbell Island head inland to pup, and do not form harems on the coast. Hundreds of pups are born here each year. *AARON RUSS.*

HISTORY

Between 1805 and 1810 the hunt for more fertile sealing grounds intensified as the New Zealand mainland stocks began to diminish. In 1809, Robert Campbell and Co, one of the larger sealing companies operating out of Sydney, despatched the vessel *Perseverance*, led by Captain Frederick Hasselburgh, from Sydney on an exploratory voyage to look for exploitable stocks of seals in the Southern Ocean. On 4th January 1810, after dropping in at the Auckland Islands, the *Perseverance* discovered Campbell Island, named by Hasselburgh for the head of the firm that he worked for. Little is reported of this first visit to Campbell Island, but we do know that Hasselburgh left a small sealing gang. There is no conclusive evidence to suggest that there was any Polynesian settlement prior to this first European visit, although artefacts found on the nearby Auckland Islands provide evidence of earlier Polynesian visitors and similar visits to Campbell Island cannot be entirely ruled out.

The sealers arrive

After dropping off the gang of experienced sealers, Captain Hasselburgh returned to Sydney, where another return voyage was organised and he eventually made his way back to Campbell Island in the latter part of 1810 (after, it should be noted, his incidental discovery of Macquarie Island). Unfortunately, on this second visit, he was to met his untimely demise, drowning with two others (a young boy and a Norfolk Island woman) when a longboat capsized.

The next sealing ship to arrive at Campbell Island was the *Mary and Sally*, that landed a party in April 1811 but was blown offshore soon after and returned to Sydney empty-handed. During their stay, five of the six-man sealing party went on an exploratory trip in a longboat and never returned. The sole survivor, Henry Neale, was collected by the *Cumberland* on a sealing trip to the island in early 1812. Sealing ships visited the island regularly between 1810 and 1820, with more occasional visits after that time. On its last visit, in October 1828, the *Perseverance* was wrecked with the loss of two lives, becoming the only shipwreck known to have occurred on Campbell Island.

Captain John Balleny called at Campbell Island on 17th January 1839 on his way to Antarctica and rescued four sealers who had been marooned there. The four only had a total of 170 skins from their four years on the island, yet another example of the efficiency with which the fur seals had been despatched in previous years.

The Sir James Clark Ross Expedition

Once they left the Auckland Islands on 12th December 1840, the ships *Terror* and *Erebus*, under the command of Sir James Clark Ross, made good time and arrived at Campbell Island a few days later. During their four day stay, they conducted magnetometric measurements and made several trips on to land to investigate the wildlife. The surgeon from the *Terror* and renowned botanist, Sir Joseph Hooker, made some extended botanical forays and noted that although it was much smaller than Auckland Island, Campbell Island probably had just as many native plants. They collected some 200–300 species and identified at least 66 flowering plants. McCormick, the surgeon from the *Erebus*, noted that Campbell Island appeared to have comparatively few species of land bird.

Castaway depots, the Venus Expedition and other visitors

In 1865 the steamship *Victoria* visited Campbell Island as part of a voyage that visited most of the New Zealand subantarctic islands, establishing castaway depots and looking for shipwreck survivors. The *Amherst* followed with a similar mission in 1868. On this visit, a castaway depot was set up in Perseverance Harbour and more pigs were landed.

The French visited Campbell Island to observe the Transit of Venus across the sun in September 1874 and set up camp in what is now known as Venus Cove in Perseverance Harbour. They stayed for three and a half months and in addition to naming several prominent features, the expedition surgeon and naturalist Dr. H. Filhol made a number of important observations on the geology, flora and fauna. Unfortunately, the overcast weather of Campbell Island meant that their observations of Venus crossing the sun were not that successful. A member of the party named Duris died of typhoid fever during the stay and was buried on the island.

The *Sarah W. Hunt* visited the island with tragic consequences in 1883. Two of the ships longboats, containing most of the crew, were blown off the island in a storm, one was lost with all hands and the other made it back to the island only to find the schooner had left. The survivors were rescued in a bad state by a Government steamer soon after. Another near-disastrous mishap occurred in 1894 when the *Antarctic* attempted to stop at Campbell Island. Having recklessly taken the ship down the east coast at night, the captain tried to enter Perseverance Harbour. He finally managed it, but for three days the

There were several thousand sheep on Campbell Island in the early 1900s and they left a long lasting legacy of vegetation damage. Alexander Turnbull Library, Wellington, New Zealand. F- 2551-1/2 -MNZ

Although most seals were killed in the early 1800s, the industry continued sporadically into the early 1900s when this photograph was taken. Alexander Turnbull Library, Wellington, New Zealand. G- 100388-1/2

Whaling was an important industry for many years on Campbell Island. A wharf was set up to facilitate the movement of blubber and whalebone off the island. Alexander Turnbull Library, Wellington, New Zealand. F- 69122-1/2

Campbell Island whalers with the tools of their trade. Charlie Serle is far right (obscured), Clem Wood is left, with a lance; Albert Cook is second from right. Alexander Turnbull Library, Wellington, New Zealand. F- 52156-1/2

The first group of whalers at Campbell Island in 1909 in one of the small boats that they used to hunt the whales. Alexander Turnbull Library, Wellington, New Zealand. F- 26951-1/2

Coastwatchers on Campbell Island 1941-1945. Left to Right: H.N.J Trustrum, L.J. Stanaway, R.T. Wilson, E.W. Wilson. Alexander Turnbull Library, Wellington, New Zealand. PA1-f-169-59-08

Antarctic was hit by gale force winds and in the end it was only by hacking down the main mast that the exhausted crew saved her from being dashed against the rocks. On board the *Antarctic* on this trip was Carsten Borchgrevink, who made collections of plants and birds.

The relatively regular trips by the government steamers to Campbell Island allowed several scientific visits there throughout the 1800s and early 1900s. All of these visits contributed to the growing level of knowledge about the island, particularly the plants. These visits culminated in the 1907 expedition organised by the Philosophical Institute of Canterbury. The main aim of this expedition was to extend the magnetic survey of New Zealand and study the geology, plants and animals. The results, covering a wide range of topics, were published in a comprehensive two volume set entitled *The Subantarctic Islands of New Zealand*, edited by Professor Chilton and published in 1909.

THE FIRST PASTORAL LEASES

Despite official reports suggesting that farming was not a lucrative proposition for the New Zealand subantarctic islands, and despite the two already failed attempts to settle and farm on the Auckland Islands, the New Zealand government decided to auction a lease on Campbell Island in the late 1800s. It is likely that part of the motivation for this lease was that permanent farmers could monitor the visits of vessels and protect the ailing sealing industry. The first lease was taken up by J. Gordon in 1895. Over 350 sheep were landed in that year and living quarters, a woolshed and a store were built in what is now called Tucker Cove. For the first two years the run seemed to function sustainably, but never really looked like a profit-making enterprise. One of the biggest issues was obtaining men who would act as shepherds in the remote and inhospitable environment.

In 1900, Gordon sold the lease to W.H. Tucker and soon after 2000 sheep were freighted down from New Zealand. Obtaining men to work the runs still proved to be one of the biggest challenges and in an effort to get more ongoing employees, Tucker advertised for workers from the Shetland Islands. Four shepherds from the area arrived in 1904, but their stay did not get off to a happy start when the wife and two daughters of one of the men informed their husband and father that nothing would ever induce them to stay. While the men remained on the island for a period of time, the isolation proved too much for them and they left within a few years.

Campbell Island whalers

In an attempt to keep his pastoral leases viable, Tucker approached some whalers from the Marlborough Sounds region of mainland New Zealand. He proposed to combine managing the pastoral run and shearing sheep with shore whaling. The first party of 11 men reached Campbell Island in January 1909 basing themselves in five huts at North-west Bay and in the first winter caught 13 Southern Right Whales. They were not the only whaling party on the island; the other was based at North-east Harbour and led by H.F. Cook from the Bay of Islands. The men at North-west Bay only collected the whalebone from their catch, while the other party had the infrastructure to not only collect whalebone but also render down the blubber for oil.

The shearing and mustering usually started in October and was done by the men and dogs brought to the island for that purpose. By 1910, around 10 000 sheep were on the island and it usually took at least six months to muster and shear as many as they could. Often the men would burn the scrub areas to assist in clearing land. Due to decreasing catches of whales, the North-east Harbour party left Campbell Island in 1914 and the Marlborough Sounds whalers departed in 1916, when Tucker's lease expired.

The later farming years

Even though several thousand sheep were being shorn each year, a combination of factors contrived to turn the venture into a non-profitable enterprise and as sheep numbers fell it became more and more difficult to maintain the farm as a going concern. In 1916, Tucker sold his farm to the Campbell Island Company, owned by two Dunedin men (Matthewson and Murray). In 1921 the company had a change of shareholders and transferred its interest to the newly named Campbell Island Syndicate. The syndicate operated the farm from 1921 to 1927 under increasingly difficult circumstances. The final chapter in the history of farming on the Campbell Islands occurred when the Syndicate's license was transferred to John Warren, a shepherd on the island, in 1927. Unfortunately for Warren and his partners, flow-on effects from the Great Depression of 1929 meant that their normal resupply did not happen and the men were not rescued until 1931. Their personal effects were to remain at the farm, undisturbed until the arrival of the World War II coastwatchers 10 years later. Warren's lease had expired in 1937 and being unable to maintain the run or pay the fees, he forfeited the lease.

The coastwatchers

The potential strategic importance of the Campbell and Auckland Islands was realised early on in World War II and in response the New Zealand government sent down groups of men to be stationed on both islands. The operation was code named 'The Cape Expedition' and the first group of four men arrived at Perseverance Harbour, Campbell Island, in 1941.

They were well prepared for an uncertain future and had rations for three years. Because of the isolation and the lack of communication, their rations included luxuries like chocolate, tobacco and rum. Many of the men kept diaries and most seemed to enjoy the isolation despite the long summer hours and the harsh weather. They also contributed significantly to the knowledge of the flora and fauna and many of the Cape Expeditioners went on to become eminent scientists. Extensive surveys were carried out during their stay, and the map produced by Les Clifton in 1942 was the only one available for the next 40 years. The coastwatching era came to a close with the end of the war.

The meteorological station

During the war the coast watchers had sent back regular weather data and reports and these had proved so valuable that the New Zealand government decided to continue them after the coast watchers had been brought home. However, after a few years it became obvious that the initial site of the coastwatching hut was not appropriate for a weather station and in 1953 a new station site was chosen in Beeman Cove. The station was completed by 1957, in time for the impending International Geophysical Year. From 1957 to 1995 the Campbell Island weather station was usually manned by a staff of around 12 (including five meteorologists) that were relieved on an annual basis.

Science and management in the twentieth century

The continuous presence of people since the 1940s, first as coastwatchers and then as members of the meteorological party, contributed significantly to our knowledge of the geology, flora and fauna of the island. In fact, the information that many of these early visitors obtained was probably the primary factor in the island being declared a Nature Reserve in 1954. In addition to these contributions, there have been a number of other significant visits, collections and research projects on Campbell Island over the last 70 years.

Lance Richdale and Sir Robert Falla were early pioneers of research in the post coastwatching period on Campbell Island. In 1958, Alfred Bailey from the Denver Museum of Natural History and Kaj Westerskov spent six weeks on the island collecting flora and fauna. Several trips through the 1960s and early 1970s included studies of the feral sheep problem and culminated in the first fence line being built in 1970. Another fence line was built in 1984, dividing the island into thirds and the sheep were eventually eliminated from each section in 1970, 1984 and 1991. The scope of these expeditions throughout the 1960s and 1970s was wide and the thoroughness of their observations and collections contributed much to the current knowledge of the island. The HMNZS *Monowai* undertook a major expedition during the summer of 1984-85 to all the New Zealand subantarctic islands, combining terrestrial surveys with aerial photography to produce accurate topographical maps for the first time.

Possibly because of the existence of a manned meteorological base, the multi-disciplinary 'expedition model' of research continued on Campbell Island long after it had ceased elsewhere in the New Zealand subantarctic. Much of the research work on Campbell Island focused on the Southern Royal Albatross, and while this research continues today it is on a much reduced scale. Due to some leg bands (also known as rings) being incorrectly fitted in the past, many of the Southern Royal Albatrosses have now had their bands removed; some of these birds have been microchipped, while others were fitted with a new style of band. The current strategy is to check these birds every five years rather than on an annual basis, which has been practice since the coastwatching station was established in 1949.

Because of concerns about the impact of introduced livestock on the vegetation of the island, considerable effort has been put into describing the flora. David Given coordinated much of this work, establishing numerous photo points and producing a detailed distribution map. Norm Judd, a former Lands and Survey Ranger and leader of the 1975 expedition, has undertaken some significant historic research and was responsible for the discovery of the grave of Duris, the Frenchman who died during the 1874 Transit of Venus Expedition. He has also documented and recorded the whaling and farming activities on the island. In a shift back to the expedition style of earlier years, the New Zealand Royal Society is planning a large, multi-disciplinary science expedition to Campbell Island in 2010.

REDISCOVERY! Once thought to be extinct, the Campbell Island Teal was rediscovered on Dent Island by Rodney Russ (shown here holding a bird) in 1975. *RUSS COLLECTION*

A HISTORIC EVENT The rat eradication on Campbell Island was a turning point in the islands history. Helicopters were integral to the success of the operation. *PETE TYREE*

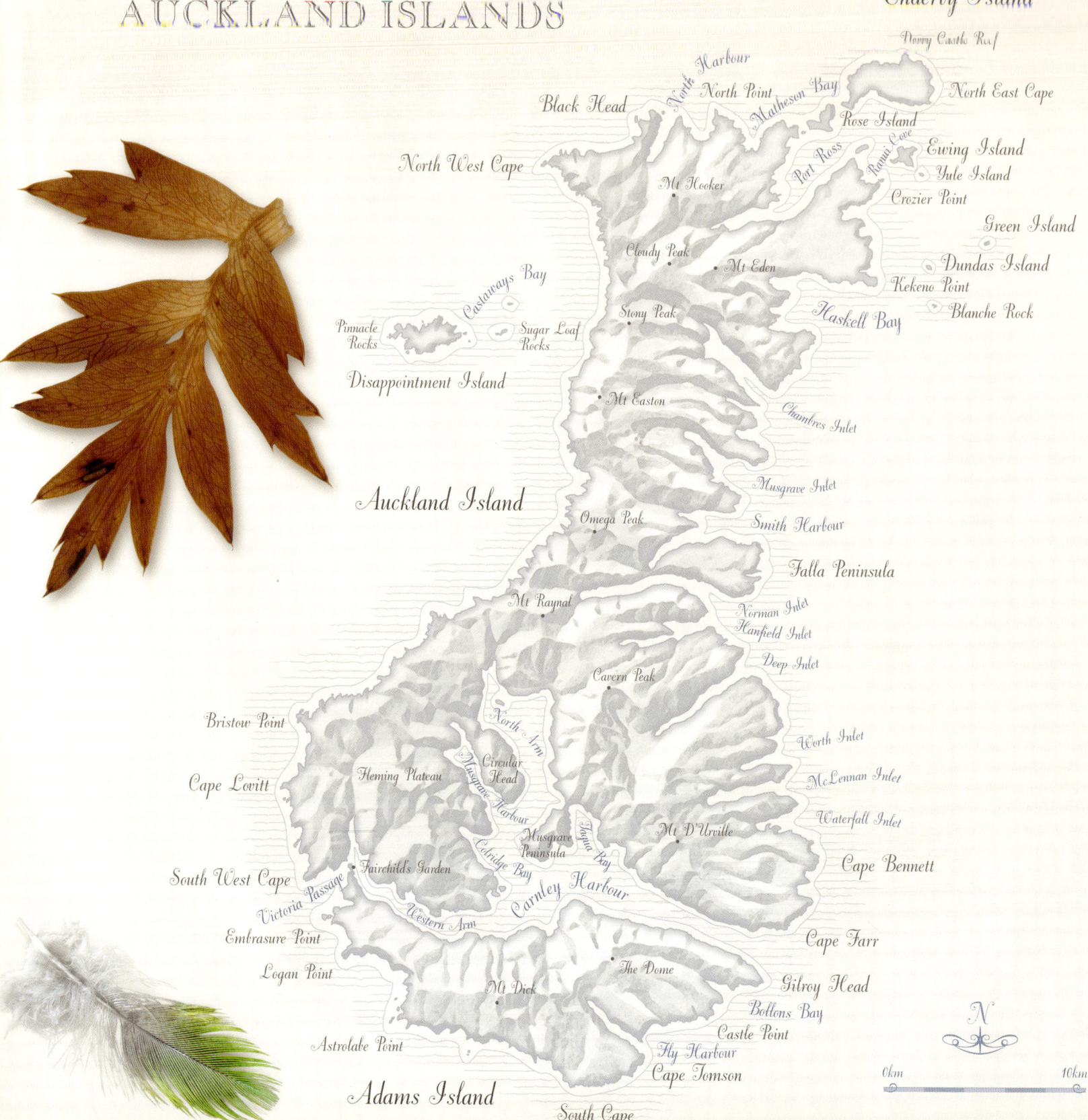

Auckland Islands

MAUNGAHUKA • 50°44'S • 166°08'E • 62 460ha • 705m a.s.l

The Auckland Island group lies approximately 450 kilometres south of New Zealand, between the Snares and Campbell Island. They are the highest and the largest of the New Zealand subantarctic islands and are one of the most biologically rich places in the Southern Ocean. In addition to diverse biological life, the group also has a rich human history, with sporadic settlement since its discovery by Europeans in 1806. It is likely that there were Polynesian visitors before this, but it is not known if they stayed for extended periods. While several of the islands in the group have been severely affected by the presence of humans and associated introduced animals and plants, Adams Island, in the south of the group, is free of introduced animals and remains one of the most pristine of all the islands in the Southern Ocean. There have been a number of successful eradication operations to remove feral animals from some smaller islands in the group, and plans are currently underway to assess the feasibility of eradicating cats and feral pigs from the main island.

Auckland Island Snipe

AUCKLAND ISLANDS This island group was formed by volcanic action between 16 and 24 million years ago. It is dominated by two large islands, and many smaller islands, the most notable being Enderby Island at the northern end.

ENDERBY ISLAND The white sand beaches of Sandy Bay, Enderby Island are unusual around volcanic islands such as these. This bay is home to the second largest aggregation of breeding New Zealand (Hooker's) Sea Lions in the world. *NATHAN RUSS.*

LEGACY OF GLACIATION This feature is a well-developed glacial cirque on Adams Island, eroded into the flat lying lava flows of the Carnley Volcano. Glacial action of this nature was relatively recent in geological terms, probably occurring in the last few hundred thousand years. *KATH WALKER*

GEOGRAPHY AND GEOLOGY

THE AUCKLAND ISLANDS consist of two large and four smaller islands and numerous small islets and rocks. Like Campbell Island, they were formed by volcanic action on the basement rock of the Campbell Plateau. The Auckland Islands are the oldest of all the volcanic islands in the New Zealand subantarctic group.

Geography

The two large islands, Auckland Island (covering *c.* 50 990 hectares) and Adams Island (10 119 hectares), dominate the group. At the northern end there are several smaller islands, most notable of which are Disappointment Island (566 hectares), Enderby Island (710 hectares) and Rose Island (75 hectares). The Auckland Island group lies on the western margin of the Campbell Plateau. To the west the ocean deepens abruptly and then rises onto the Macquarie Ridge, but north and east of the group the Auckland Island Shelf (part of the Campbell Plateau) slopes less steeply. Much of the island group is covered with a thick blanket of peat that began accumulating about 10 000 years ago. The deepest deposits are around 8–10 metres thick.

Auckland and Adams Islands are separated by Carnley Harbour, a body of water with a larger opening at the eastern end and a very small passage out to sea at the south-western end. To the south the landscape of the Auckland group is mountainous, with peaks over 600 metres, the highest being Mount Dick on Adams Island at 705 metres. The western and southern coasts are high, with precipitous cliffs, while the eastern seaboard has a much lower coastline, characerised by deep bays and inlets. Next to Carnley Harbour, the second largest bay is Port Ross in the north of the island, which provides sheltered anchorage in most weather.

Enderby Island is much smaller and lower lying than the two main islands, with a maximum elevation of 45 metres above sea level. The western end of Enderby Island is almost entirely edged by cliffs, with those to the north-west rising to over 30 metres, but those along the southern shores are around half this height as the land surface generally slopes to the south and south-east. To the east, and at Sandy Bay, the island slopes to the sea and cliffs are usually confined to headlands. Boulder beaches occur east of Derry Castle Reef and in the eastern bays. A unique, fine yellow sand beach occurs at Sandy Bay, where there is a large colony of New Zealand (Hooker's) Sea Lions (*Phocarctos hookeri*). Although much smaller, Rose Island is similar in appearance to Enderby Island and, like the larger islands, both islands are characterised by a thick blanket of peat. Because of their low height above sea level and their northerly position in the shadow of the larger island, Enderby and Rose Islands receive less rainfall and more sunshine than the two larger islands.

Origins

The Auckland Islands are the eroded remains of two basaltic shield volcanoes which erupted between 16 and 24 million years ago. The main volcanoes rest on a basement of older rocks (the Campbell Plateau) and lie next to each other on a north south axis. Over millions of years, erosion—mainly by the waves of the Southern Ocean—has taken much of these volcanoes away, although the shapes of the original volcanoes can still be made out in the vicinity of Carnley Harbour and Disappointment Island.

Carnley Harbour has been eroded into the Carnley Volcano, with its centre in the vicinity of Musgrave Peninsula. The northern Ross Volcano was centred on Disappointment Island, but its western half has been eroded away completely by the sea, leaving only Disappointment Island itself. This is made of harder rock, standing isolated around six kilometres from the main island. The youngest volcanic activity built the hills and islands in the vicinity of Port Ross.

During the ice ages of the last two million years, the Auckland Island group was almost completely ice covered at least once. Consequently, the landscape clearly reflects the influence of these huge bodies of ice. The glacier-gouged valleys contain features such as cirques, moraine-dammed lakes and hanging valleys. The lower reaches of the largest valleys have been eroded below sea level and have become the fiords that indent the entire east coast.

Geology

The volcanic formations that make up the bulk of the island rest on a continental basement of coarse-grained granite some 85–95 million years old. Known as biotite granite from one of the characteristic minerals crystallised within it, this granite is only exposed on the Musgrave Peninsula in Carnley Harbour. Overlying the granite at Carnley Harbour are small remnants of a sequence of sedimentary Cenozoic rocks. The older part of this sequence consists of conglomerate exposed in Camp Cove, and was laid down between 15 and 30 million years ago, possibly as debris flows on the flanks of a volcano. A slightly younger and very thin (15 metre) layer of marine sedimentary rocks, consisting of quartz sandstone with rare limestone, is preserved on Musgrave Peninsula, laid down around 11–15 million years ago. This layer contains rare shells of bivalves and gastropods.

The Auckland Island volcanoes erupted as many thick lava flows; between these successive flows, layers of ash and glassy volcanic rocks full of air bubbles known as scoria were laid down. Examples of this type of layering can be observed on the slopes of Adams Island and on the hills around Carnley Harbour. The nearly sheer cliffs of the western coast, unbroken in places for over 30 kilometres, are also composed of numerous and regular flows of basalt, interlayered with ash and scoria. They possibly represent the thickest and most exposed sequence of lava flows in New Zealand.

ENDERBY ISLAND COAST The cliffs of the northern Enderby Island coast are formed of black basaltic lava flows erupted from the Ross Volcano.
NATHAN RUSS.

CLIFFS OF COLUMNS This flat-lying lava flow forming an Enderby Island cliff displays a text-book example of columnar jointing. As the lava flow 'froze' or solidified from a huge puddle of molten rock, these vertical columns formed like enormous hexagonal pencils, as the lava gradually cooled and shrank. *ALEKS TERAUDS.*

Sir Charles Fleming published the first descriptions of these western cliffs and he estimated that up to 15 kilometres had been eroded away from the western coastline. He also described the two-tiered development of the cliffs, where the upper sloping part was cut back during the last period of high sea levels between the ice ages, then modified to more gentle slopes by stream erosion, until they were able to be colonised by tussock grass and other vegetation. The lower, steeper sections of the cliffs are younger again, still being actively formed by the force of the ocean, and they vary in height from 120 metres to almost 600 metres.

The distinctive vertical rock columns of Enderby Island are a result of columnar jointing during the cooling of younger lava flows on the eastern side of the Port Ross volcano. Other places where the columnar basalt rock projects above the generally smooth slopes above Port Ross are the hard volcanic plugs which have forced their way up through the underlying lava flows late in the development of the volcano. The white sand beaches and dunes at Sandy Bay on Enderby Island are unusual in this type of volcanic environment. It seems likely that the sand came from older continental rocks and was brought to its current site ahead of rising sea level at the end of the Last Glacial Maximum, some 15–18 000 years ago.

BULBINELLA ROSSII With the coast of the main Auckland Island in the background, the distinctive flowers of this species form a carpet of yellow on the western side of Enderby Island. *AARON RUSS*

FLORA

Flora on the Auckland Islands is diverse, with over 230 species of vascular plant and hundreds of species of moss and lichen. The vegetation on most of the islands has suffered heavily from the impacts of humans and associated introduced animals. Adams Island is the exception of the group, and although sporadic attempts were made to establish introduced animals, none established viable long-term populations and therefore the vegetation is largely pristine. Southern rata (*Metrosideros umbellata*) forms thick forests on the main island, Adams Island and to a lesser extent Enderby Island. The rata flowers are a feature of these islands and in a good flowering year the canopy turns a vibrant red which dominates parts of the coastal and inland landscapes.

A historic visit

When Sir James Clark Ross visited these islands in 1840 he had aboard his vessel the renowned botanist Sir Joseph Hooker, who suggested that 'perhaps no place in the course of our projected voyage in the southern ocean promised more novelty than the Auckland Islands'. He also declared that the plants he collected were 'more remarkable for their beauty and novelty than the flora of any other country'. Dr. Hooker identified five successive vegetational zones and described mosses, liverworts, lichens and a vigorous community of ferns sheltering beneath a canopy of interlaced branches. He admired the fern *Polystichum vestitum* for 'the beautiful symmetry of the crowns, with its velvety crosier-formed young leaves in the centre' and coined the term 'megaherbs' for large, broad-leaved herbaceous species. He was particularly impressed with the megaherb *Pleurophyllum speciosum*, a member of the daisy family, describing it as 'spectacularly beautiful' and an 'extremely handsome and showy species with copious large purple flowers'. He named *Bulbinella rossii* after Sir James Clark Ross and was the first to describe *Hebe benthamii*, with its bright blue flowers.

Most of the plants he collected were non-flowering and included lichens, ferns, fungi, seaweed and numerous mosses. After the Ross expedition returned to England in 1843, Hooker's studies on the Auckland and Campbell Islands were published in the first volume of *Flora Antarctica*, which remains a landmark publication to this day and which was the foundation for further studies into the botany of these islands for at least a century after its publication.

Auckland Island

The vegetation of the main Auckland Island is diverse, with its coastal communities, rata forest, *Olearia* forest, various forms of scrub, tussock grasslands, close-cropped swards and areas of grazing-induced *Bulbinella rossii*. Southern rata forest fringes the more sheltered coastline and forms dense forested stands, up to 5 metres high, throughout the island. Besides southern rata, the most common woody plants are *Dracophyllum longifolium*, *Coprosma foetidissima*, *Myrsine divaricata* and *Pseudopanax simplex*. The shrub *Hebe odora* and the glossy tree fuchsia *Fuchsia excorticata* are also woody plants found on the main island, but not on others of the group.

On the north-facing slopes of the island, continuous scrub is found either above rata forest or down to sea level on steeper, more exposed slopes. It reaches an altitude of about 130 metres and consists of five main species, including

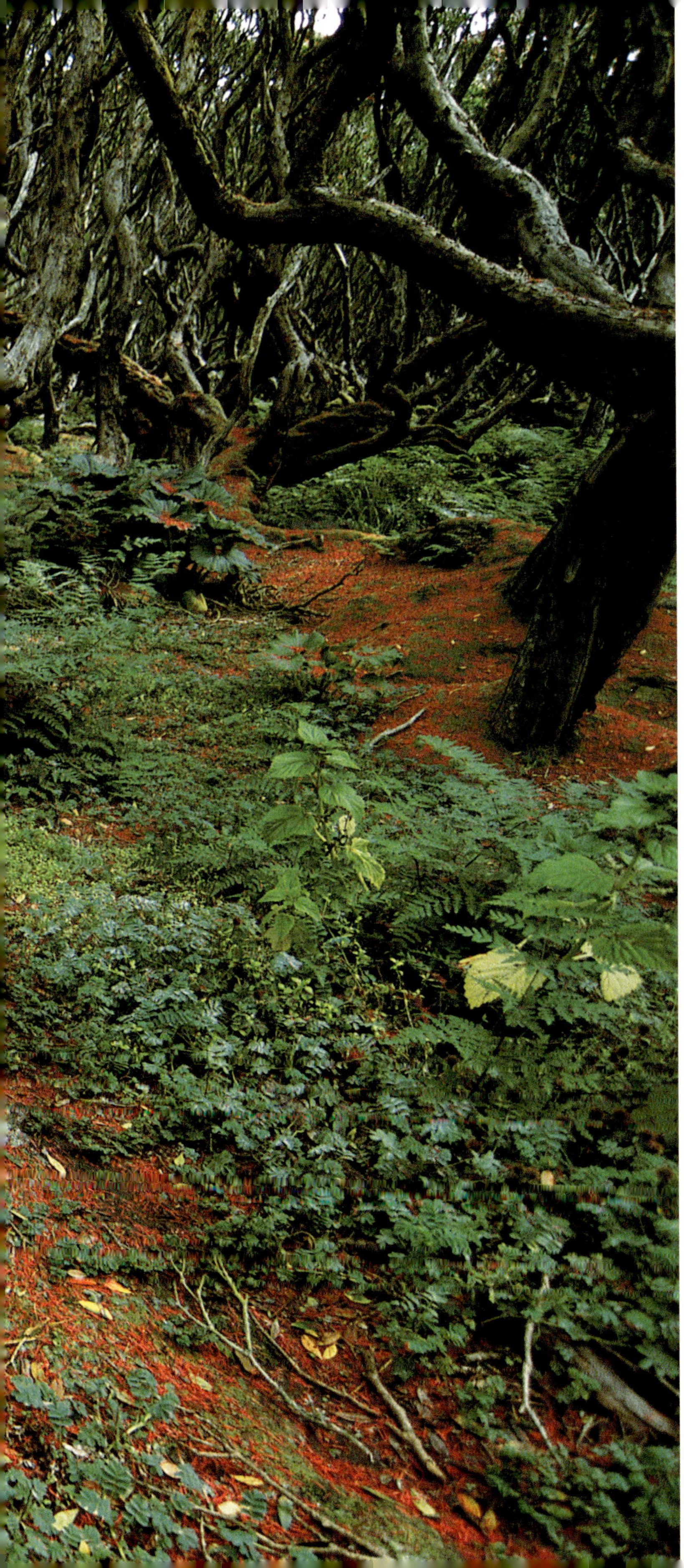

ALEKS TERAUDS

AARCN RUSS

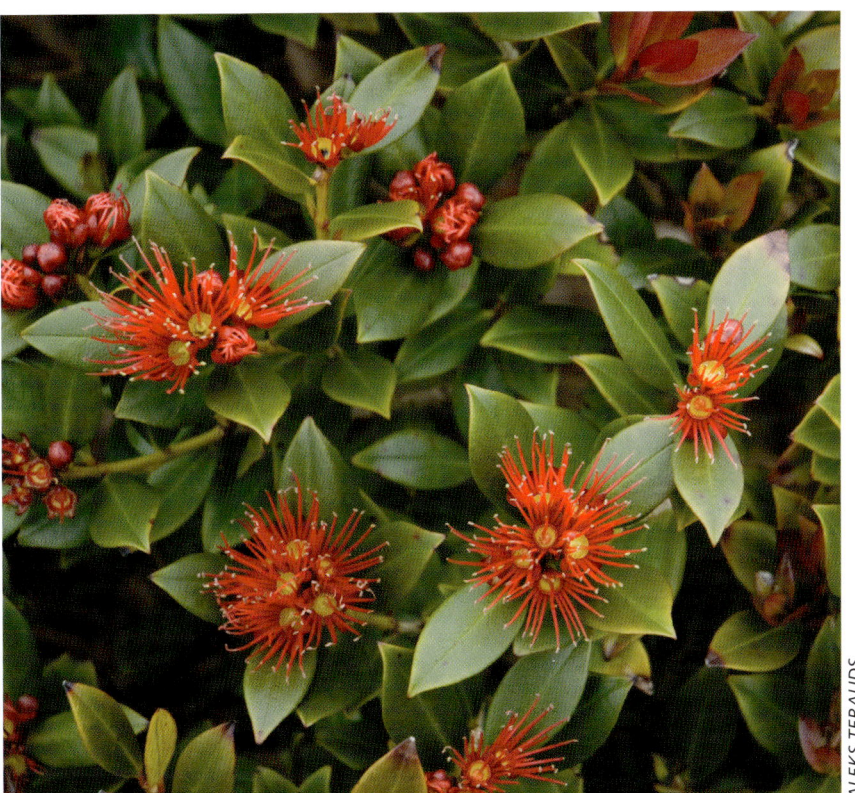

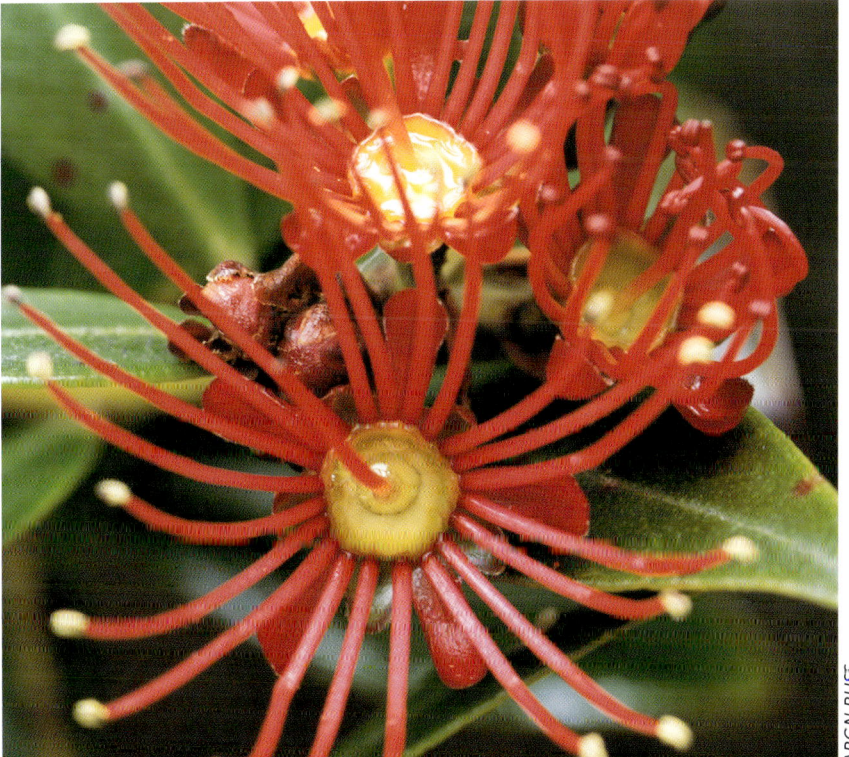

RED RATA FOREST At the right time of year, in a good flowering season, rata needles coat all the surfaces of the Enderby Island forest understorey. *RUSS COLLECTION.*

Cassinia vauvilliersii, *Coprosma ciliata* and *Coprosma cuneata*. Above this altitude is a combination of tussock grassland and scrub. Scrubland of this nature are also present in the southern valleys. 'Wind lanes' of low-lying vegetation are occasionally present within the scrub. The transition to predominantly tussock grassland, dominated by *Chionochloa antarctica*, takes place at about 200 metres, but it does grow lower in some places. This undisturbed, closed grassland is up to one metre high and supports few other species. Only in swampy patches, or where albatrosses have nested, is the grassland open enough for a greater diversity of herbs. Some of the herbs that grow in amongst the tussock include the rosette daisy *Damnamenia vernicosa*, the distinctive indigo flowered *Hebe benthamii*, and the endemic gentians *Gentiana concinna* and *G. cerina*.

Less vegetated gravel areas, or fell field, begin at about 450 metres above sea level and occur along the tops of the lateral ridges and along the main ridge of the island. The megaherb *Pleurophyllum hookeri* is the predominant plant in these areas. Other megaherbs are rare, with *Anisotome latifolia*, *Stilbocarpa polaris* and other *Pleurophyllum* species largely eliminated by pigs from all but the most inaccessible areas.

Adams Island

Adams Island has a narrow band of forest and scrub near sea level, dominated by southern rata. Tussock grassland dominates the area above the forest and scrub, with fell field at the higher altitudes. As it is free from the impacts of introduced animals, Adams Island supports vegetation in near-pristine condition. Fairchild's Garden, at the north-west tip of Adams Island, is remarkable for its diversity of megaherbs. Large, coastal megaherb species like *Stilbocarpa polaris* and *Anisotome latifolia* are mixed with species like *Pleurophyllum speciosum* and *Bulbinella rossii*. All three species of *Pleurophyllum* grow on Adams Island. *P. criniferum* grows in boggy environments, from sea level to an altitude of 400 metres, while *P. hookeri* is found from 200–640 metres above sea level, usually on exposed ridges and occasionally in swampy situations. Apart from those growing in Fairchild's Garden, *P. speciosum* is mainly confined to a belt between 460–640 metres and favours rock slides on south-facing slopes.

Enderby and Rose Islands

A belt of southern rata forest and scrub lies along the south and east sides of both islands. There is a narrow strip of dead trees surrounding much of the living forest. Within the living forest there is sparse undergrowth of *Myrsine divaricata* and scattered *Dracophyllum longifolium*, with patches of ferns, mosses and liverworts on the forest floor. In areas where the rata is more stunted, other scrub species like *Cassinia vauvilliersii* become more common. The common fern on the forest floor is *Histiopteris incisa*, while *Polystichum vestitum* and *Blechnum capense* occur sporadically in the undergrowth. On Enderby Island, Macquarie Island cabbage (*Stilbocarpa polaris*) has become abundant in some areas, particularly underneath the rata canopy on the fringes of the forest.

Away from the forest, *Myrsine divaricata* forms closely-packed wind-trimmed hedges that cover several acres in places. *Oreobolus pecinatus* and *Cassinia vauvilliersii* form a moorland that covers a broad belt in the centre of Enderby Island. Tussock grassland dominates the lower-

AUCKLAND ISLAND SCRUB Thick forest, composed largely of rata, *Dracophyllum*, *Coprosma* and *Myrsine* covers much of the Auckland Islands. The light grey covering in the tops of the trees are lichens, which thrive in the damp climate of the island. *AARON RUSS*.

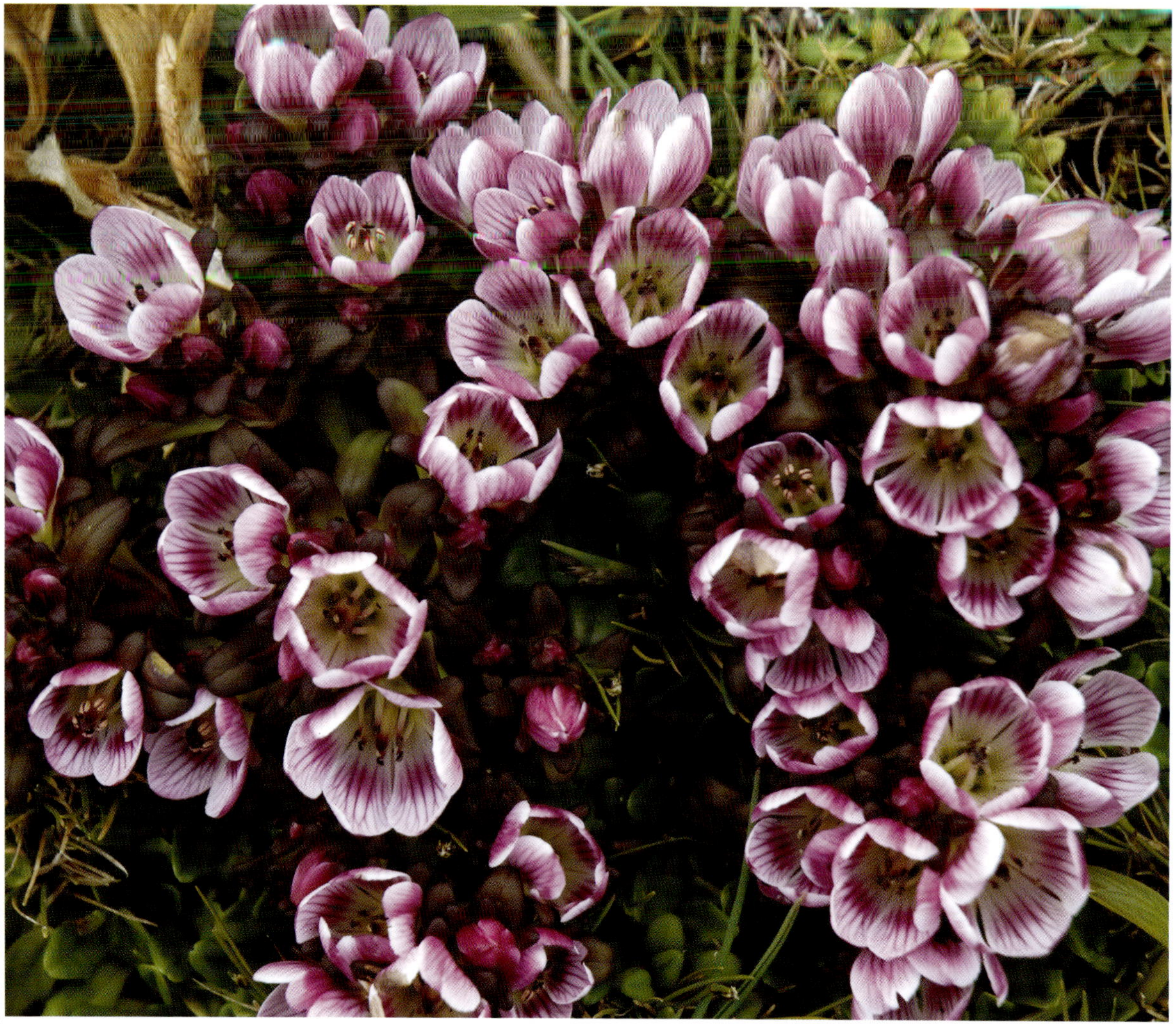

ALEKS TERAUDS

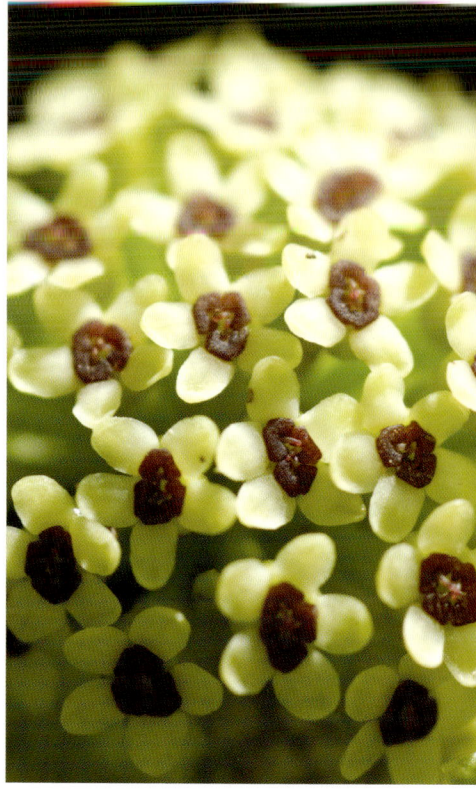

AUCKLAND ISLAND FLOWERS
(clockwise from top left) *Gentiana cerina*, Macquarie Island cabbage (*Stilbocarpis polaris*), The liverwort *Marchantia berteroana*, *Myosotis captita*

AARON RUSS

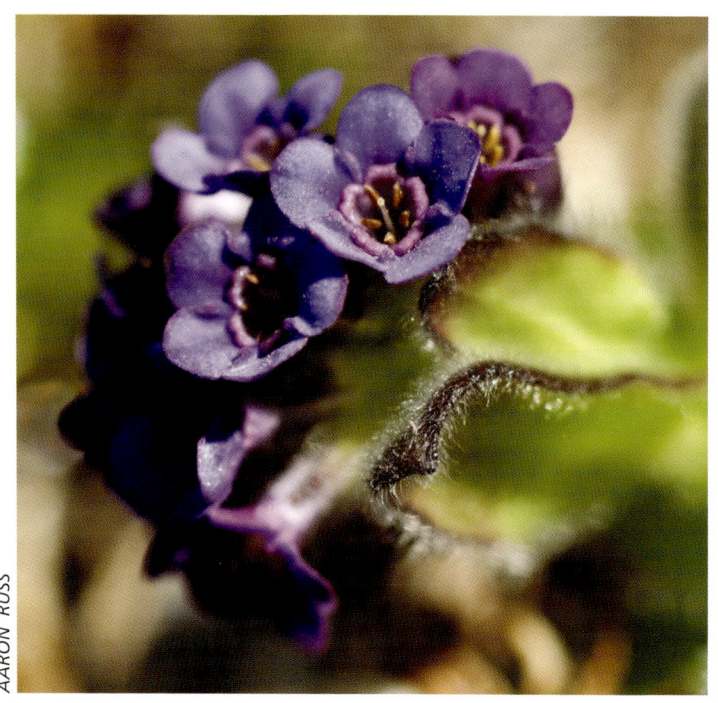

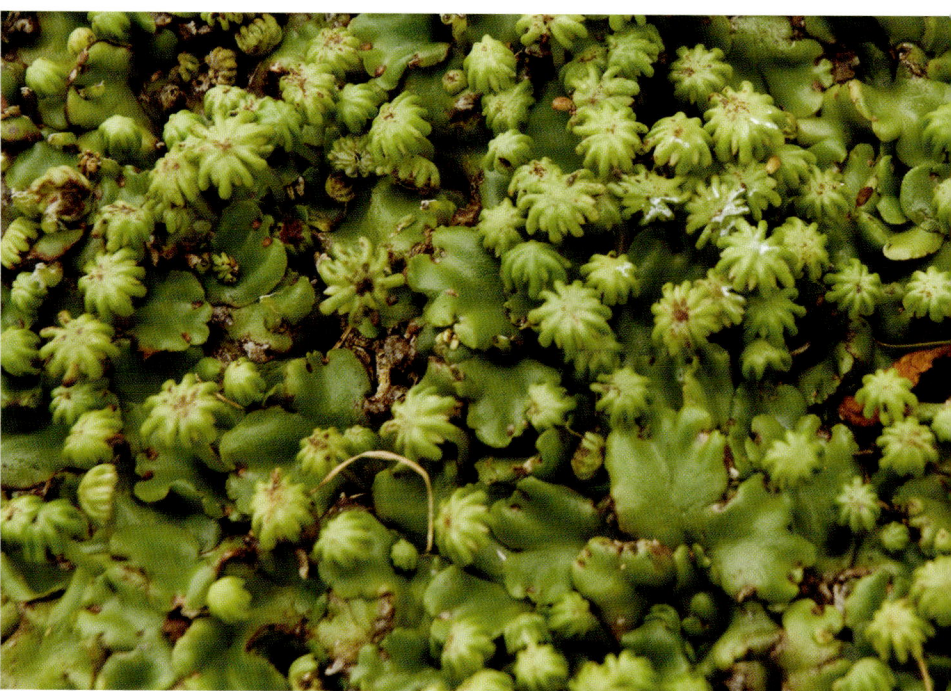

lying, more exposed areas, with *Chionochloa antarctica* and *Poa litorosa* being the most common species. Tall sedges, like *Carex appressa* and *C. trifida,* grow in amongst the tussocks in some of the wetter areas.

Since the eradication of mice, rabbits and cattle, megaherbs have become much more common on Enderby Island. Extensive meadows of *Bulbinella rossii* form a beautiful yellow carpet throughout much of the north and west of the island during November and December. *Anisotome latifolia*, previously restricted to inaccessible locations, has made a comeback, with large individuals growing in groups, particularly in the north of the island. The tree daisy *Olearia lyallii*, is reasonably common on Ewing Island and in Erebus Cove and Laurie Harbour. In recent years it has been spreading rapidly at the latter two locations. Only a few scattered plants occur on Enderby and Rose Islands. It is not known exactly when this species arrived at the Auckland Islands and there is debate as to whether it was a natural introduction, or brought to the islands by humans.

Disappointment Island

Reaching an altitude of 318 metres, Disappointment Island is covered in grassland, giant megaherbs and small areas of shrub land containing species common on the main island. Like Adams Island, this island is free from introduced species, and as such the vegetation assemblages are largely pristine.

Human and animal impacts

When Sir James Clark Ross first visited these islands he noted that the pigs, brought ashore by Bristow some 33 years earlier, were numerous and that their main food consisted of the Macquarie Island cabbage and the megaherb *Pleurophyllum criniferum,* which were both abundant at the time. Today, these fields of megaherbs have almost disappeared from the main Auckland Island. The few isolated plants that remain are largely restricted to small, inaccessible areas that pigs have been unable to reach. The vegetation of Enderby and Rose Islands has also been severely affected by feral animals, but since their eradication the vegetation has recovered considerably.

In addition to bringing the introduced animals, humans also had other impacts on the islands. The extensive stands of dead rata on Auckland and Enderby Islands are a testament to the widespread burning that was conducted, not only by farmers but also by members of the castaway depot resupply visits and shipwrecked sailors. The burning also undoubtedly had long-term effects on the tussock grass, which was nearly eliminated during the early twentieth century and for a time restricted to inaccessible areas.

Marine plants

Like most of the other Southern Ocean islands, the Auckland Islands are also rich in marine plant life. Again, a dominant and obvious member of the kelp community is the Antarctic bull kelp (*Durvillaea antarctica*), which grows around much of the coastline of the island group. Over 100 other species grow there, many of which are found on the New Zealand mainland. Brown algae dominates and although several species of the red algae are thought to be endemic, further studies of other islands may show that their distribution is more widespread.

YELLOW-EYED PENGUINS With its distincitve plumage this species is easy to identify. Unlike most other species it does not tend to nest in colonies, preferring a more solitary existence. *NATHAN RUSS*

FAUNA

The fauna of the Auckland Islands was first described by Dr McCormick (ship's surgeon for the *Erebus*) on the Sir James Clark Ross Expedition in 1840. He observed that all the birds were clearly of New Zealand origin, and noted seven or eight species of land bird. He also described (and shot for his collection) a species of saltwater duck or merganser (*Mergus australis*). This species is now extinct, probably from predation by cats, which have been on the Auckland Islands since the early 1800s. The Auckland Islands are the breeding ground for some of the rarest endemic birds in the world and are home to literally hundreds of thousands of albatrosses and other, smaller petrels. Due to these large resident populations, large mixed feeding flocks are often observed in the late afternoon in the offshore waters.

Penguins

Although located in relatively northerly latitudes, the Auckland Islands still support moderate populations of penguins. The Yellow-eyed Penguin (*Megadyptes antipodes*), one of the world's rarest penguins, is found in loose concentrations on the main island, but in higher numbers on Enderby and Rose Islands. They differ from most of the other penguins in that they breed in solitude, making cryptic nesting sites in the forest or shrub areas. On Enderby Island the population was monitored between 1987 and 1990 and was estimated to be around 470 breeding pairs. Eggs are laid in late September, hatch in November and chicks generally fledge during February.

The Rockhopper Penguin (*Eudyptes chrysocome*) population is small, and as with other islands in the region the population has declined, but colonies still exist on both coasts of the main island, Adams Island and Disappointment Island. Solitary Erect Crested Penguins (*Eudyptes sclateri*) have occasionally been observed amongst Rockhopper Penguin colonies. King Penguins (*Aptenodytes patagonicus*) have also been sporadically seen ashore.

Albatrosses

The Auckland Islands are the world's main breeding ground for the White-capped Albatross (*Thalassarche steadii*), with an estimated population of around 116 000 breeding pairs according to a 2006 census. Over 90 per cent of these birds breed on Disappointment Island. The other main colony is at South-west Cape on the main island, where around 6000 pairs were breeding in 2006. Other albatrosses breeding on the group are the Gibson's Wandering Albatross (*Diomedea gibsoni*), with an estimated breeding population of over 7000 breeding pairs. Over 70 per cent of this species breeds on Adams Island, where they are untroubled by feral animals such as pigs and cats. Around 60 pairs of Southern Royal Albatross (*Diomedea epomophora*) breed on Enderby and Adams Islands, but this population is relatively insignificant when compared to the main population on Campbell Island, which comprises over 8000 breeding pairs. Light-mantled Sooty Albatross (*Phoebetria palpebrata*) breed mostly in the south of the main island, with an estimated population of 5000 breeding pairs. Black-browed Albatross (*Thalassarche melanophrys*) and Buller's Albatross (*Thalassarche bulleri*) are often observed at sea, around the islands.

OTHER PETRELS

The Northern Giant Petrel (*Macronectes halli*) is a common breeder on most of the islands of the group and is also regularly observed in the surrounding waters. Other tubenoses that breed on the Auckland Islands include large numbers of the White-headed Petrel (*Pterodroma lessonii*), White-chinned Petrel (*Procellaria aequinoctialis*), Antarctic Prion (*Pachyptila desolata*) and Sooty Shearwater (*Puffinus griseus*). Smaller populations of Snares Cape Petrel (*Daption capense australe*), Grey-backed Storm Petrel (*Garrodia nereis*), White-faced Storm Petrel (*Pelagodroma marina maoriana*) and Black-bellied Storm Petrel (*Pachyptila belcheri*) breed on the Auckland Islands; however, the location and size of only a few colonies are known. Even less is known about breeding populations of the Subantarctic Little Shearwater (*Puffinus assimilis elegans*) and the southern subspecies of the Common Diving Petrel (*Pelecanoides urinatrix chathamensis*), but they are known to be present. The South Georgian Diving Petrel (*Pelecanoides georgicus*) has been recorded breeding on Enderby and Dundas Islands.

OTHER SEABIRDS

An example of one of the rare endemic birds is the Auckland Island Shag (*Phalacrocorax colensoi*), which breeds throughout the entire island group. There are thought to be less than 1000 breeding pairs in the entire world population, with most concentrated in colonies around Enderby Island. Subantarctic (Brown) Skuas (*Catharacta lonnbergi*) are found in scattered numbers throughout the group, while moderate numbers of the Southern Black-backed Gull (*Larus dominicanus*) and Red-billed Gull (*Larus scopulinus*) are also breeding. White-fronted Terns (*Sterna striata*) and Antarctic Terns (*Sterna vittata bethunei*) breed in small colonies throughout the group.

LAND BIRDS

The flightless Auckland Island Teal (*Anas aucklandica*) now appears to be recovering on the predator-free islets, with breeding reported on most smaller islands of the group and on Adams Island. The Auckland Island Snipe (*Coenocorypha aucklandica*) breeds on most offshore islands of the group and has made a spectacular recovery on Enderby Island following the removal of the rabbits and mice. The Auckland Island Rail (*Rallus pectoralis muelleri*) breeds on Adams and Disappointment Islands. Little is known about their breeding numbers, but a study by Kath Walker and Graeme Elliott, on Adams Island in 1989, found two active nests and they estimated that there were hundreds of birds in the population.

Other common breeding land birds include the Banded Dotterel (*Charadrius bicinctus*), which breeds on Enderby Island, and the Red-crowned Parakeet (*Cyanoramphus novaezelandiae*), which is predominantly found on the larger offshore islands, feeding on seeds and invertebrates amongst the herbs and grasses. The Yellow-crowned Parakeet (*Cyanoramphus auriceps*) is more common on the main Auckland Island, where it mainly breeds in rata forest. The local subspecies of the New Zealand Pipit (*Anthus novaeseelandiae aucklandicus*) is commonly seen around coastal areas, while the Long-tailed Cuckoo (*Eudynamys taitensis*) and Welcome Swallow (*Hirundo tahitica neoxena*) also breed in small numbers.

AUCKLAND ISLAND TEAL The highest number of breeding pairs of this species are on Enderby Island, where they inhabit fresh water bodies and occasionally the intertidal zone. Unfortunately due to cats and pigs it is no longer present on the main Auckland Island. *NATHAN RUSS*

Grey Ducks (*Anas superciliosa*) and New Zealand Falcons (*Falco novaeseelandiae*) breed in small numbers concentrated at the southern end of the main island and Enderby Island. Silvereye (*Zosterops lateralis*) and Auckland Island Tomtit (*Petroica macrocephala marrineri*) are common throughout the group. The Bellbird (*Anthornis melanura*) is probably the most numerous of the bush birds, while Tui (*Prosthemadera novaeseelandiae*) are also present throughout the group in good numbers. Several species of migratory wader visit the islands and a variety of self-introduced, non-native species have also established breeding populations.

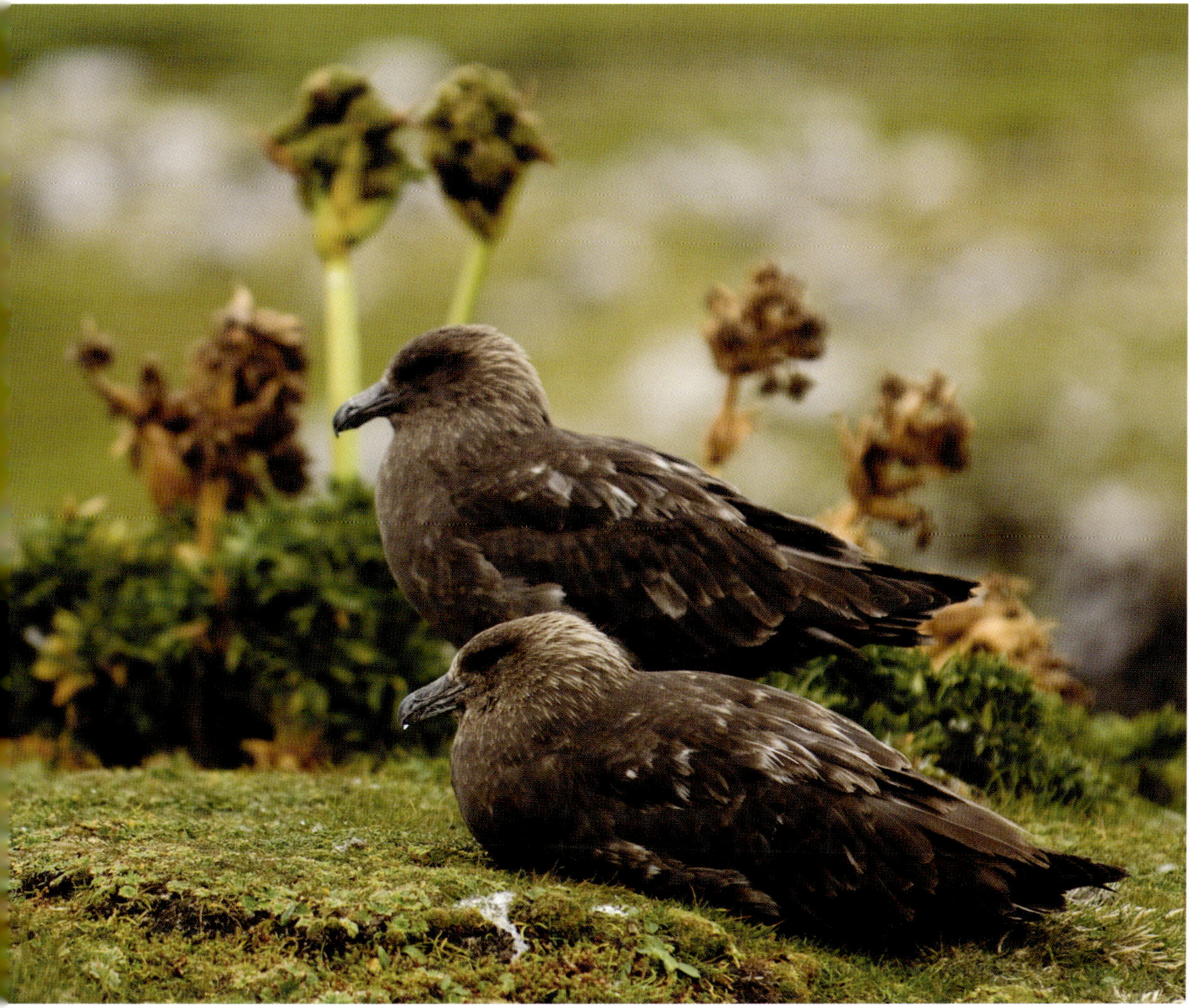

AARON RUSS

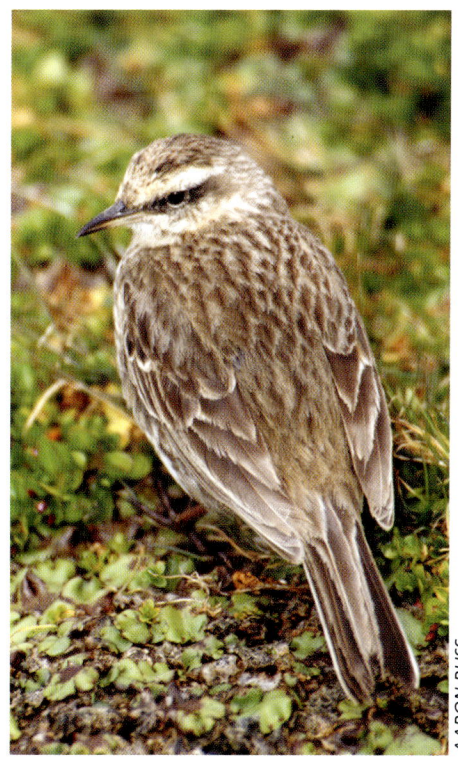

AUCKLAND ISLAND BIRDS (clockwise from top left) Red-crowned Parakeet, Auckland Island Tomtit, Subantarctic Skuas, New Zealand Pipit, Auckland Island Shag, Banded Dotterel, Auckland Island Snipe.

AARON RUSS

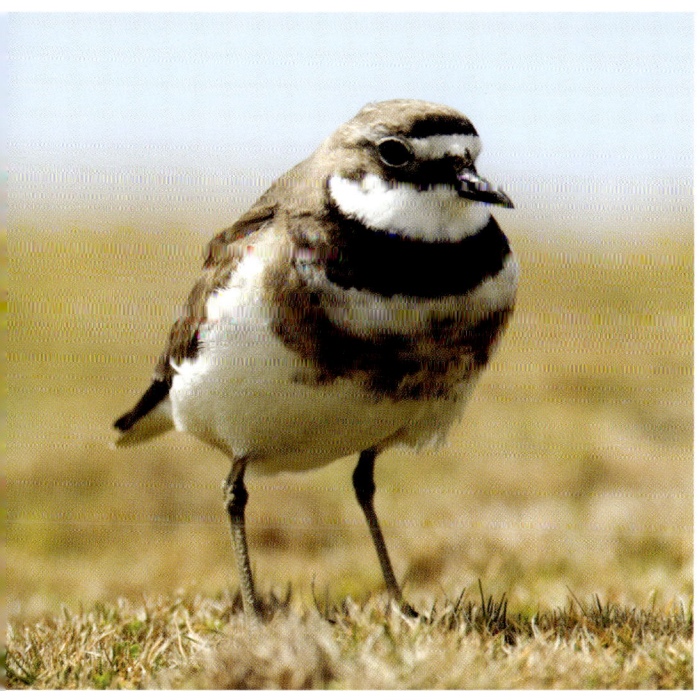

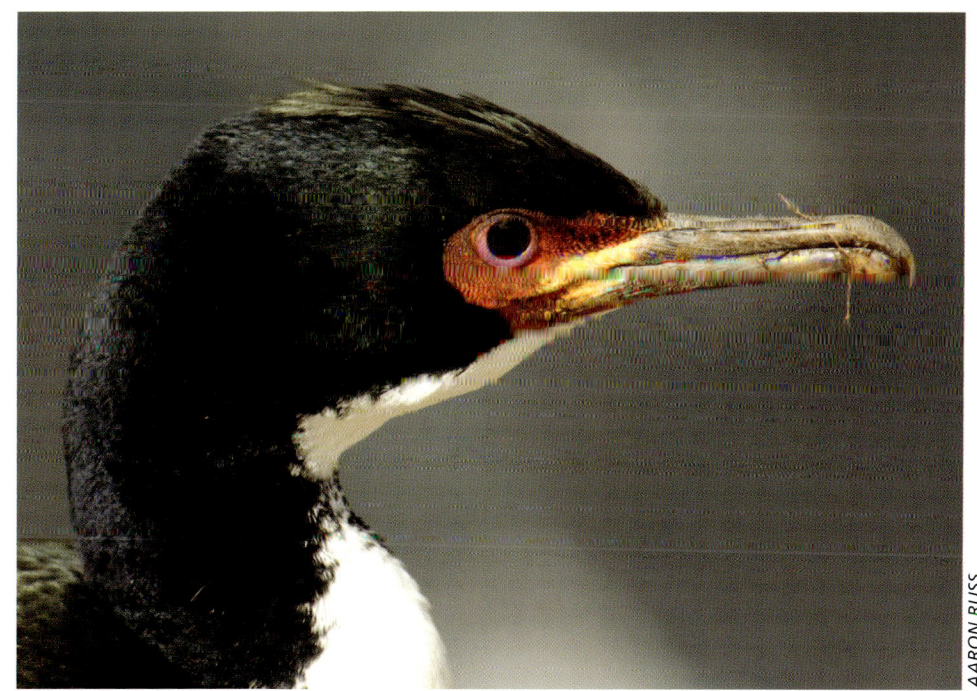

HAREM ON THE BEACH New Zealand (Hooker's) Sea Lion bulls hold harems of females on the beach at Enderby Island. Harems such as these ensure that the female can have the pup and look after it, safe from the advances of other males. *ALEKS TERAUDS*.

Marine mammals

As in other places, the New Zealand Fur Seal (*Arctocephalus forsteri*) is slowly recovering after an extended period of exploitation in the 1800s. The main population is found on the west coast of the main island, with seals also hauling out on Derry Castle Reef after the breeding season. The Auckland Islands are the main breeding ground for the New Zealand (Hooker's) Sea Lion (*Phocarctos hookeri*), with nearly 90 per cent of the global population breeding on Dundas, Enderby and Figure of Eight Islands. There are around 2000–3000 pups born each year, with the majority of those born on Dundas Island. Pup production and pup survival has varied considerably over the last few years, which may be attributable to interactions with fisheries and bacterial infections. Occasionally, Southern Elephant Seals (*Mirounga leonina*) haul out around the Auckland Island coast and they have sometimes been recorded breeding on Dundas Island.

Another marine mammal of note that is found around the Auckland Islands is the Southern Right Whale (*Eubalaena australis*). Hunted almost to extinction last century, species numbers have now increased and up to 90 individuals have been observed in the sheltered waters of Port Ross during recent winter breeding seasons.

Introduced animals

There have been a whole host of introduced animals brought onto the Auckland Islands during the last 200 years. Today, only pigs, cats and mice remain and their range is restricted to the main Auckland Island. Pigs, first liberated in 1807, have had a huge impact on the island, changing the face of the landscape dramatically.

FERAL PIG First introduced to the islands in the early 1800s, feral pigs have become a serious problem on Auckland Island, wiping out most of the accessible megaherbs and predating on the seabirds. *ALEKS TERAUDS.*

By 1880 they were widespread over the entire main island where they can still be found today. They have virtually eliminated the large-leaved megaherb species in all but the most inaccessible places and they have also had a considerable negative impact on the breeding seabirds. Cats are also likely to have had a huge impact on both breeding seabirds and land birds and are thought to have caused the localised extinction of the saltwater duck, which used to inhabit this island group.

Terrestrial invertebrates

Over 240 insects and a multitude of other invertebrates have been documented on the Auckland Islands. Like other islands of the region, the group has a high level of endemism, with 12 of the 45 species of moth considered endemic. In total, 64 insect species are found there and nowhere else. The mice are likely to have had a significant impact on the invertebrate fauna on the main island and consequently, the mouse-free Adams and Disappointment Islands have a more diverse and complete invertebrate community.

HISTORY

Although there is evidence that the Auckland Islands were discovered and visited by Polynesians over 500 years ago, little is known about the extent or purpose of these early visits. The first European to visit the islands, on 18th August 1806, was Abraham Bristow, commander of the southern whaler *Ocean*, during its third voyage around the world. Bristow named the islands after Lord Auckland, who was a friend of his father. On discovery, Bristow noted that the place 'abounds with seals' and sorrowfully observed that due to the state of his ship he could not 'examine further the resources the island had to offer'. Captain Bristow again landed in 1807, this time in the ship *Sarah*, another ship owned by the Enderby Whaling Firm. On the later voyage, Bristow landed some pigs (the first to be put on the island) and formally claimed the island group 'in the name of the Crown'.

The sealing era

Soon after their discovery, sealing gangs began to visit the Auckland Islands, their motivation fuelled by Sydney merchants who had heard of the vast numbers of seals that congregated there. When the *Commerce*, skippered by Captain Sirone, visited the islands in 1808, there were already gangs present and it was only by enticing the established parties aboard and plying them with drugged rum that he managed to make a landing with several men.

Other sealers continued to work the Auckland Islands over the next decade, including gangs from the American schooner *Yankee*, which was regarded as one of the finest sealing ships of the time because of her ability to travel from the Auckland Islands to Sydney in the space of just 12 days. Other ships that worked the Auckland Islands over this time period included the *Henry* (which took 12 000 skins from there in 1823), the *Queen Charlotte*, the *Wellington*, the *Elizabeth and Mary*, the *Samuel* and the *Sally*. The latter ship arrived at the Auckland Islands in November 1825 and two days later 'six men were drowned when two boats were lost in untoward circumstances'. Over the relatively short period of exploitation, thousands of skins were taken and seals had been largely eliminated from the Auckland Islands by the end of the 1820s.

The age of exploration

The early to mid 1800s saw a significant increase in the number of ships exploring the Southern Ocean and Antarctica. Many of these ships stopped in at the New Zealand subantarctic islands, and the Auckland Islands—being on a major shipping route—received more than its fair share of these visitors. Captain B. Morrell, in the American schooner *Antarctic*, anchored in Carnley Harbour in December 1829 and although the crew's explorations were extensive, they did not see a single fur seal and not more than 20 sea lions.

The first real scientific investigations of the island began towards the end of the sealing era with the French Antarctic Expedition of 1840, under the command of Admiral Dumont D'urville in the *L'astrolabe* and *Zelee*. There were two naturalists aboard and in addition to extensive collections of plants and seaweeds, astronomical and weather readings were also made during their eight-day stay. At around the same time, Auckland Island was also visited by the United States Exploring Expedition, under Commodore Wilkes.

The Sir James Clark Ross Expedition

This legendary and landmark voyage left Hobart on 12th November and the Auckland Islands were first sighted on 19th November 1840. The majority of the three-week stay was spent anchored in the harbour known as Sarah's Bosom, which we now know as Port Ross. One of the main aims of the voyage was to take magnetometric measurements, looking both at the level of magnetic variation of true north and the magnetic dip. The crew also spent time exploring the island, and the notes and observations of plants and animals by Hooker and McCormick were some of the most detailed of the time.

The Sir James Clark Ross Expedition released a number of introduced animals to the northern end of Auckland Island 'to increase the stock of useful animals' as Ross himself put it. No thought was given to upsetting the natural ecosystem; however, the legacy of these introductions would be with the island for many years to come. These introductions were not the only impacts of this expedition; in order to make getting around easier, the men tried to make paths by using fire and consequently set hundreds of acres alight.

The Maori and Moriori arrive

Around two years after the Sir James Clark Ross Expedition left the shores of Auckland Island, the first people to try and establish a permanent settlement on the islands arrived. In 1842, the Ngāti Mutunga chief Matioro, with around 30 of his tribe members and 30 Moriori slaves (representing around 8 per cent of the surviving population), left the Chatham Islands in the brig *Hannah*. They arrived in October 1842 and were

Scenes like these were relatively common at Port Ross at the northern end of the Auckland Island as men hunted seals for their skins. State Library of Victoria. IAN03/03/68/1

The Erebus *and the* Terror *were the two ships of the landmark expedition led by Sir James Clark Ross from 1839 to 1842.*

During the French Antarctic Expedition of 1840, Dumont D'urville anchored his ships at Port Ross to collect supplies. Alexander Turnbull Library, Wellington, New Zealand. C-036-007

reportedly aghast at the nature of the islands that were to be their new home. Matioro established his *pa* on top of Crozier Point, opposite Ewing Island, and built a number of huts. They planted flax and potatoes and intended to supplement their diet with pigs, fish, birds and seals. Unfortunately, the pigs were tough and tasted of fish, the fish they caught were full of worms and the potatoes grew poorly. Little is known of the lives of these people over the next six years, but one of the Moriori women, who survived to tell her story, described it as one of the harshest experiences of her life. There was considerable internal stress amongst the party and over the ensuing years they split up into smaller groups, some moving to nearby Enderby Island.

The Enderby settlement

In 1847, Charles Enderby, a member of the well-known whaling firm of the same name, sought to reestablish the Southern Whale Fishery and consequently obtained a grant from the Crown assigning Auckland Island to his company. Whaling had already been carried out with some success at the Auckland Islands for several years, mainly by American-owned ships. A settlement, under the command of Enderby, was duly established at Port Ross in December 1849, with much optimism and initial enthusiasm. On arrival, the group was extremely surprised to see the Maori inhabitants and it is likely that the surprise was mutual. Enderby called the Maori and Moriori together and informed them that that he was the 'Lord of the Island' and claimed all the land and their pigs. The claim was not disputed, compensation was paid and the Maori appeared to integrate well into the new settlement. There was little tension between the two groups, with most trouble caused by infighting amongst the Maoris. Their initial impression of the island left the Europeans as dismayed as the Maoris had been, but they set to and built a settlement named 'Hardwicke'.

Although at its peak the settlement contained over 300 people (including Maori, Moriori and visiting seamen), the climate and poor results of the whale fishery was less than encouraging. In addition, the wet peaty soil was not suitable for growing vegetables of any type with success and the settlement was abandoned less than three years after its establishment. Today, little trace of it remains, but a small cemetery is maintained by the Department of Conservation as a Heritage Site. Within a few years of the Europeans abandoning the settlement, the Maori inhabitants started to move away, either to Stewart Island or back to the Chatham Islands.

Shipwrecks

The unsuccessful nature of these settlements discouraged others from trying anything similar for many years and the most common inhabitants of the islands from 1860 to 1910 were probably shipwrecked sailors and castaways. The Auckland Islands lay across a major shipping route and its location, in conjunction with the fog that often shrouded its coastline, resulted in several ships coming to grief on its shores. Over this time there were eight definite wrecks and at least two other likely ones.

One of the more notable was the wreck of the *Grafton* in 1864. With only five men aboard, en route from Campbell Island, the captain anchored in North Arm of Carnley Harbour, where the ship was struck by a violent

Port Ross, at the northern end of the Auckland Islands was the site of the Enderby settlement in the mid 1800s. National Library of Australia. pic-an2964154

The General Grant is thought to have come to grief on the west coast of the Auckland Islands. Alexander Turnbull Library, Wellington, New Zealand. PUBL-0033-1868-376-1

Survivors from the General Grant also built huts with grass on the walls and roof to provide shelter from the elements. State Library of Victoria. H85.88/27

Crew of Hinemoa on an expedition to the Auckland Islands showing the frame of a boat used by the survivors of the Dundonald shipwreck. Alexander Turnbull Library, Wellington, New Zealand. PA1-q-228-09-3

The castaways from the Dundonald shipwreck made and lived in these grass huts on Disappointment Island. Alexander Turnbull Library, Wellington, New Zealand. F-1317-1/2-MNZ

Dr. Leonard Cockayne studying a large tussock grass on Ewing Island in November 1907. Alexander Turnbull Library, Wellington, New Zealand. PA1-q-228-16-1

Provision depots such as these were set up on most of the islands to help survivors of shipwrecks. Alexander Turnbull Library, Wellington, New Zealand. F-2539-1/2-MNZ

Members of the German Transit of Venus Expedition to the Auckland Islands, 1874. State Library of Victoria. H85.88/9

Members of the landmark Philosophical Society of Canterbury expedition to the Auckland Islands in 1907. Alexander Turnbull Library, Wellington, New Zealand. PA1-q-228-01

Remains and the figurehead from the wreck of the Derry Castle on Enderby Island. Alexander Turnbull Library, Wellington, New Zealand. G-38208-1/2

storm and driven onto the rocks. For eighteen months the party eked out a hard existence at their small settlement called 'Epigwait'. Three of the party made a miraculous journey in an open boat, built from the remains of their wreck, to Stewart Island and all were eventually rescued. Once at the Auckland Islands, their rescuers conducted further searches and in one of the abandoned huts at Port Ross they found the body of another shipwrecked sailor, likely to be from the *Invercauld*, which was wrecked on the north coast of the Auckland Islands in 1864.

Another notable wreck on Auckland Island was the *General Grant*, which sailed from Melbourne for London in May 1866. The cargo of the *General Grant* was rumoured to contain a quantity of gold bullion. Consequently, there have been several treasure hunting expeditions since its wreck, all unsuccessful to date. Another, more recent wreck of note was the *Dundonald*, which met an untimely fate on the shores of Disappointment Island in 1907. The survivors lived for several months in extreme hardship before building a small coracle and making their way to the main island, where they were sustained by castaway depots until their rescue in November 1907.

In addition to those mentioned above, other ships known to come to grief on or around the Auckland Islands include the *Minerva* in 1864, the *Derry Castle* in 1887, the *Compadre* in 1891 and the *Anjou* in 1905.

Castaway depots and scientists

In response to the hardship and suffering of the castaways from earlier shipwrecks, ships were despatched by provincial governments in 1865 (the *Victoria*) and 1868 (the *Amherst*) to establish castaway depots and look for survivors of shipwrecks. On the latter voyage, the government representative was Henry Armstrong and although his regard for the natural environment would have been frowned on today (for example, he commonly torched tussock grass to alert any potential castaways to his presence), his official report contained valuable information about the islands he visited. Depots were set up at several places on the Auckland Islands and in years to come proved to be of great service. Eventually, the duty of erecting and resupplying depots for castaways was taken over by the New Zealand government and the regular voyages of this service allowed several scientific visits to the islands. Important early scientific collections made possible by the government steamers include those made by Andreas Reischek in 1888, Leonard Cockayne in 1903 and W. Benham and E.R. Waite in 1907.

Expeditions to the Auckland Islands independent of the government steamers were rare. However, the German Transit of Venus Expedition, which stayed on the island from 15th October 1874 to 6th March 1875, was an exception. The expeditioners set up a base in Terror Cove, Port Ross, and from all accounts the group did not have a pleasant time, describing the weather as 'the most wretched imaginable'. The officers of the *Discovery* landed on the island in 1904 and also made some valuable scientific collections during their time ashore. Perhaps the most significant expedition, towards the end of this era, was that organised by the Philosophical Institute of Canterbury, a significant undertaking that landed a party in Carnley Harbour for nearly two weeks.

The end of farming

Despite the publicity surrounding the failed Enderby Settlement, farming was again attempted on the Auckland Islands in the latter half of the 1800s. This venture only lasted three years, with the farmers resorting to raiding the castaway depots to survive. After its failure, the New Zealand government did not grant another lease until 1895, when W.J. Moffett landed 9 cattle and 20 sheep on Enderby Island.

His lease, and three others that were offered on the Auckland Islands, was taken over by George Fleming, a Southland farmer, in 1900. He built a homestead and sheds at Carnley Harbour and landed some 2000 sheep, most of which died within a few years. The lease on the main island was re-let to the Moffett family in 1910, however they did little serious farming after this time. In the same year, Adams Island was declared the first Flora and Fauna Reserve of the subantarctic region and in 1934, when the Moffetts' lease expired, the whole Auckland Island group was gazetted as a protected reserve.

The coastwatchers

In 1939, with a world war imminent, the German cargo steamer *Erlangen* left Dunedin under the cover of darkness and made its way to Carnley Harbour, Auckland Island. Here she stayed for five weeks while the Chinese crew and German officers cut over 200 tonne of rata to fuel the coal-fired burners for their intended voyage across the Pacific Ocean.

This incident highlighted the importance of the Auckland Islands as a potential enemy base and the New Zealand government quickly took action. Under the code name 'The Cape Expedition', small coastwatching parties of three to five men were established at Port Ross and Carnley Harbour. The first volunteers landed in 1941 and were provisioned for a potential stay of three years. The men did very long hours in the summer months and with few ships sighted it must have been difficult to maintain motivation. Nevertheless, the men seemed to enjoy their isolation and several conducted valuable research on the island while they were there, producing several published reports on a variety of topics. As the coastwatching became less necessary, the scientific work became the primary focus of the Cape Expeditions.

After the coastwatchers

Directly after the war the coastwatching stations were abandoned and there was a period of inactivity that saw almost no visits to the Auckland Islands for around nine years. In 1954, the New Zealand Department of Scientific and Industrial Research (DSIR) and the Dominion Museum organised two expeditions, followed by others in 1962 and 1966. The 1966 expedition comprised 15 scientists who divided into two groups—one based at Port Ross in the north, led by Sir Robert Falla, and the other on Adams Island led by Eric Godley. The New Zealand Oceanographic Institute also made several visits, in 1963, 1964 and 1973. In the summer of 1972–73 a New Zealand Lands and Survey expedition was undertaken with the ambitious purpose of establishing a set of baseline knowledge from the Auckland Islands that could be used as a reference for future research and management. In addition to the comprehensive work that was conducted by the 28-member team, collections of flora and fauna were also made for scientists from other institutions.

AUCKLAND ISLAND EXPEDITION 1972-73 In 1972, an expedition to the Auckland Islands was organised by the New Zealand Department of Lands and Survey. It was a landmark expedition in the history of research on the island. *RUSS COLLECTION.*

Recent research and management

The 1972–73 expedition marked the end of an era in Auckland Island research, with multi-disciplinary expeditions abandoned in favour of a more specific project-based model. Small teams would visit the islands to research or manage one species, with defined goals and objectives. The longest running project on the Auckland Islands is the New Zealand Sea Lion research, which was started in 1975 by Martin Cawthorn. It continues to this day, with annual expeditions to Enderby Island.

Scientists Kath Walker and Graeme Elliott first visited the Auckland Islands in 1989 to study the Auckland Island Rail on Adams Island. During that visit they also counted the Gibson's Wandering Albatross, marking the beginning of a long-term study into this species. The project has run continuously since its inception in 1991, only missing one year due to transport difficulties. Funding for this project has been problematic and often these researchers have funded aspects of the research themselves. Recent results suggest that there could be a decline in the survival of individuals of this species and future monitoring of the population is critical. Recently, the New Zealand Ministry of Fisheries has made funds available for monitoring of the White-capped Albatross using both ground and aerial census methods.

The majority of projects undertaken since the 1972–73 expedition have focused on management issues. Feral goats were removed from the Hooker Hills in 1992, cattle were removed from Enderby Island in 1990 and rabbits were eradicated from Enderby and Rose Islands in the same year. The rabbit poisoning operation on Enderby Island also removed the mice. Recent management projects have focused on learning more about the feral pigs and cats on the main Auckland Islands, with a view to eradicating them. A funding application has been lodged with the government, but no decision has been made to date.

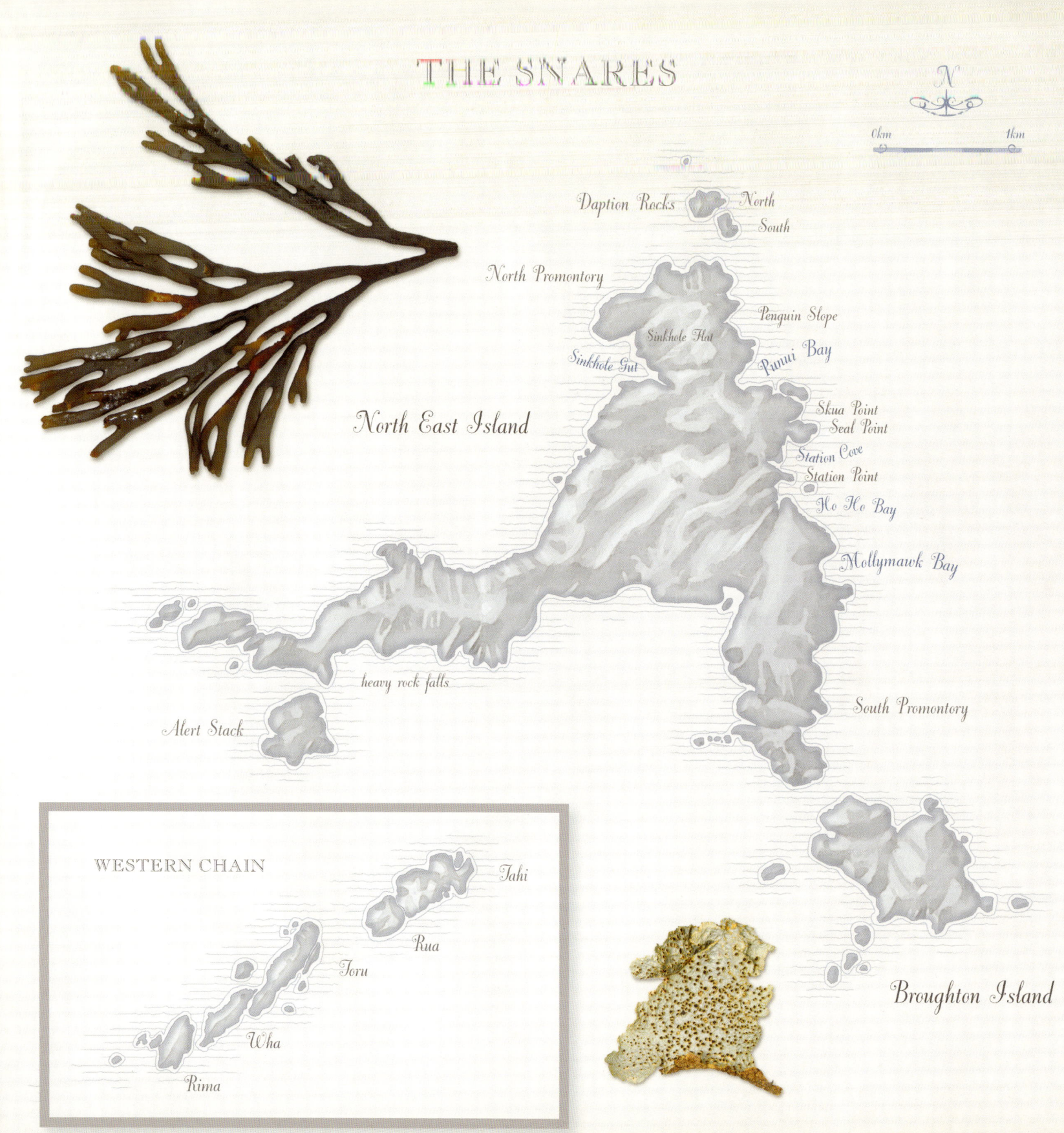

THE SNARES

48°02'S • 179°55'W • 330ha • 150m a.s.l

The Snares are situated approximately 209 kilometres south-west of New Zealand and consist of two main islands and several large rocks. Due to their proximity to New Zealand, they were one of the first island groups to be discovered by Europeans. Like many of the other islands of the region, once discovered The Snares were used as a base by fur sealers, who proceeded to kill most of the fur seals and sea lions living there over a relatively short space of time. However, following the sealing era there were few visits and no populations of introduced animals have become established. Today, the main island is literally teeming with wildlife, from the dense daisy-tree forests to the thousands of seabirds that breed there. In fact, The Snares represent a unique oceanic sanctuary, largely untouched by the presence of humans and their associated impacts. In recognition of their unique status, the New Zealand government strictly controls access to the islands and only researchers who can demonstrate a tangible conservation outcome for the islands are permitted to land on their shores.

Black Tomtit

THE SNARES Although The Snares are a relatively small group of islands, their value as a oceanic wildlife sanctuary is significant. These islands are home to literally millions of seabirds, there are no introduced animals and very few introduced plants.

THE SNARES COAST The granite which forms these cliffs on The Snares solidified in a batholith deep in the crust around 100 million years ago, and shows typical angular fracturing and jointing, similar to the Bounty Islands granites. *AARON RUSS.*

GEOGRAPHY AND GEOLOGY

LIKE THE BOUNTY Islands, The Snares are an eroded remnant of a raised section of the Campbell Plateau, dating back to over 100 million years, when this section of the continental crust was formed. The effects of long-term marine erosion are clearly seen in the shape of the islands, with angular stacks and weathered, smooth granite commonplace.

GEOGRAPHY

The main island of The Snares, known as North-east Island, is by far the largest of the group, with an area of 280 hectares. Broughton Island, the second largest of the group, lies a few kilometres off South Promontory on the main island and covers an area of just under 50 hectares. Alert Stack is the next biggest island, positioned just off the south-western tip of the main island. A group of jagged, teeth-like stacks lie further offshore, four and a half kilometres to the south-west of the main island. This group, known as the Western Chain, has five main features, named for the Maori numbers one to five (Tahi, Rua, Toru, Wha, Rima). In general, all the islands are low-lying, with the highest point on North-east Island at 150 metres.

Most of the surface of the main island is a plateau sloping gently to the east, ringed by steep cliffs that form most of the coastline. The effects of vigorous marine erosion are clearly visible on these cliffs. The surface of the island is almost entirely covered with peat, to an average depth of about 2 metres, but reaching 7 metres in places. The peat tends to be thin or absent on the steeper slopes, on exposed rock and in some of the well-established penguin colonies. Mineral soils are rare and only found as a thin layer between the base granite and the peat.

ORIGINS

When large intrusions of granite magma are forced upwards into the Earth's crust and then cool, they form a 'batholith', or dome, deep under the surface of the Earth. The relatively slow cooling of these batholiths results in a coarse-grained granite. This process occurred throughout the Campbell Plateau, to the south of New Zealand, between 90 and 150 million years ago, and the granites of the Bounty Islands, Auckland Islands and The Snares are all tiny fragments of batholiths. Southern Stewart Island, directly south of New Zealand, is a much larger example of the eroded remnants of a batholith. The rocks that occur on both The Snares and Stewart Island are very similar, supporting the hypothesis that they are of similar origin. The summit platform of The Snares is thought to be a relict wave-cut platform, formed by marine erosion during higher interglacial sea levels.

GEOLOGY

The main rock on The Snares is a coarse, even-grained granite, similar in age to the Auckland Islands granite (94–97 million years). Its name, muscovite granite, comes from one of the main constituent minerals, muscovite or white mica, that is present throughout it. It is almost white in colour and weathers to a pink or even reddish tint. The crystalline nature of the muscovite, feldspar and quartz that make up the granite can be seen in most cliff and rock platform exposures. Occasionally, the underlying granite protrudes through the peat layers in domes, providing stark contrast to their heavily vegetated surroundings. On the islets of the Western Chain, fragments of schist are caught up in the granite and are also very similar to schist from nearby Stewart Island.

THE WESTERN CHAIN The islets of the Western Chain of The Snares, like the main island, are formed of strongly jointed muscovite granite. Only on Rua islet have different rocks (small fragments of mica schist) been found. *ALEKS TERAUDS.*

FOREST ON THE SNARES The dark green leaves of the *Brachyglottis* are in stark contrast to the light grey-green leaves of the *Olearia*. The two species form a dense forest covering most of the main island. *ALEKS TERAUDS.*

FLORA

Compared to some of the other, larger islands, The Snares have relatively few plant species; only the windswept and inhospitable Bounty Islands have less. There are 22 species of vascular plant, two of which are endemic to the island group. Mosses and liverworts are more diverse, with 77 species recorded. There are 45 species of lichen and at least six species of fungi. While indigenous plant species are few, the climate, soil and resident bird populations have created well-defined plant communities. The first botanical collections were made by Thomas Kirk in 1890, and in 1907 the Philosophical Institute of Canterbury Expedition significantly increased knowledge of plant species on The Snares. Following the establishment of a field station in 1961, botanists have been able to make regular visits to the island.

Forest

Due to its northerly location and relatively hospitable climate, The Snares are one of the few Southern Ocean islands that are forested. This forest, which forms a canopy of up to 10 metres tall in places but more commonly 6 or 7 metres, is composed primarily of the tree daisy *Olearia lyalli*. It covers the greater part of the island, extending in places to the margin of the cliffs and occupying the gullies and most sheltered slopes. These trees often have gnarled and convoluted trunks, sometimes lying prostrate for over half their length. Often growing amongst the *Olearia* is another tree daisy, *Brachyglottis stewartiae*. The darker green of the *Brachyglottis* patches stand out against the distinctive glaucous *Olearia* leaves, creating a mosaic of green, particularly around Boat Harbour and Ho Ho Bay.

STILBOCARPA ROBUSTA Closely related to the Macquarie Island cabbage, this species is one of only two megaherbs on The Snares. *ALEKS TERAUDS.*

In many places the undergrowth is sparse, primarily due to the activities of the small and medium-sized petrels and shearwaters that occupy these areas in large numbers. The ferns *Polystichum vestitum*, *Asplenium obtusatum* and *Blechnum durum* are prominent under patches of the canopy and also occur in the more sheltered gullies. Megaherbs, particularly *Stilbocarpa robusta*, are also common components of the understorey in places.

Herbs

The two largest herbaceous plants of The Snares are known as megaherbs—large-leafed plants that are unique to the Southern Ocean islands. *Stilbocarpa robusta* is closely related to the Macquarie Island cabbage

(*Stilbocarpa polaris*), which also grows on Auckland, Macquarie, Antipodes and Campbell Islands. *S. robusta* is differentiated from its close relative by a darker green, shinier leaf, but in shape and size they are similar. On The Snares it grows to over 1.5 metres in height and tends to be larger in open and/or bird-manured areas. The other megaherb, *Anisotome acutifolia*, is endemic to The Snares and grows to a height of 1 metre. It is not common and only known from three places on the main island. Cook's scurvy grass (*Lepidium oleraceum*), which is actually a cress, also grows on The Snares, being predominant on cliff tops and often associated with the feeding sites of the Subantarctic (Brown) Skua (*Catharacta lonnbergi*).

Tussock meadows

The main tussock grassland formation is composed of *Poa tennantiana*, which covers nearly 20 per cent of the surface area of the main island. Few other species tend to be associated with the *Poa tennantiana* tussockland, but isolated individuals of *Stilbocarpa robusta* grow sporadically amongst it, often occupying the hollows and sheltered places, or occasionally in broader patches mixed with *Asplenium* and *Blechnum* ferns. The shorter, silver tussock *Poa astonii* is more common in exposed areas, covering just over 10 per cent of the main island. The two species of *Poa* grow quite differently, with *P. astonii* developing a distinct, often unstable pedestal up to 50 centimetres high, which in combination with associated shearwater burrows can make moving through these areas extremely difficult. The two tussock species rarely grow together and there is usually quite a sharp boundary between adjacent stands.

Coastal communities

The coastal margins of the forest, particularly near the edge of cliffs, is often occupied by *Hebe elliptica* shrubland. The bright green leaves and white flowers of this species are another distinctive feature of the island's vegetation and it reaches a height of 1.5 metres, colonising slips and sometimes forming dense, near-impenetrable stands. This community appears to have increased over the past 20 years. Vivid green cushions of *Colobanthus muscoides* occur on many of the rocky areas, and rock crevices are often filled with the semi-succulent creeper *Crassula moschata*, which also forms bright green mats on the adjacent wet, peaty ground where the cress *Callitriche antarctica* occurs. Along the coast, turf dominated by *C. moschata* and the small rush *Isolepis cernua* is also common, often forming on rocks where there is very little soil. Both *Crassula* sp. and *Callitriche* sp. are common colonisers of the nutrient-rich soils of abandoned penguin colonies.

Introduced (alien) plants

Even though there are records of plants like cocksfoot (*Dactylis glomerata*) and rye grass (*Lolium perenne*), amongst others, being introduced to The Snares, today the only non-native species surviving are the chickweed *Stellaria media* and the annual meadow grass *Poa annua*. These species are most common around Boat Harbour and Station Cove. Potatoes were once grown by a group of abandoned sealers and for a time they thrived; however, once the men were rescued from the island, the fields of potatoes were eventually overtaken by native vegetation.

ALBATROSSES IN THE FOREST The Snares is one of the few places in the world where albatrosses nest in the forest. These Buller's Albatross chicks are just a few weeks off fledging. *AARON RUSS.*

Broughton Island

Broughton Island, the largest of the other smaller islands that make up the group, also has *Olearia* forest, but in contrast to the main island this only covers around 10 per cent of its surface. However, together with the other tree daisy, combined forest covers around 25 per cent of the island. The other main components of the ground cover on Broughton include *Poa tennantiana* and *Stilbocarpa robusta,* both covering around 20 per cent of the island respectively. Nearly 30 per cent of the island is unvegetated.

Marine plants

Due to its close proximity to New Zealand, the marine algal community of The Snares has many species in common with the South Island of New Zealand. Of the 114 species recorded, only 32 are not recorded from any other Southern Ocean island group. The Antarctic bull kelp (*Durvillaea antarctica*) is the most distinctive member of the seaweed community, its large fronds forming an extensive intertidal fringe, grading in colour from mustard yellow to dark green-black depending on the level of exposure to sunlight.

SNARES CRESTED PENGUINS The Snares are the only place that this species breeds. Individuals come ashore in spring and make their was up steep cliffs and through forest to get to their breeding colonies. *AARON RUSS.*

FAUNA

The Snares are free of introduced predators and for this reason they have a large number of breeding birds. The islands are especially well-known for the endemic Snares Crested Penguin (*Eudyptes robustus*), large colonies of the southern race of Buller's Albatross (*Thalassarche bulleri*) and millions of Sooty Shearwaters (*Puffinus griseus*). The lack of terrestrial predators has also allowed the land birds to develop thriving populations. There are small populations of New Zealand (Hooker's) Sea Lions (*Phocarctos hookeri*) and New Zealand Fur Seals (*Arctocephalus forsteri*) and seal populations are slowly recovering from their decimation at the hands of the sealers in the early 1800s. Through extensive work by John Warham, Paul Sagar and co-workers, the breeding populations of many species of seabird on The Snares are relatively well-known. A comprehensive summary of the known data on birds of The Snares was published by Colin Miskelly and colleagues in 2001.

Penguins

Closely related to the Erect Crested Penguin (*Eudyptes sclateri*) of the Antipodes and Bounty Islands and the Fiordland Penguin (*Eudyptes pachyrhynchus*) from southern New Zealand, the Snares Crested Penguin only breeds on The Snares island group. Superficially they are difficult to tell apart from their closely related cousins, but their size and pink gape help to distinguish them. Snares Crested Penguins come ashore on the rocky coastline and make their way up into the *Olearia* forests, covering distances of up to 900 metres. In the mid to late 1980s, just over 20 000 pairs of this species were estimated to be breeding throughout the group. Eggs are laid in spring and most chicks fledge during January and February. Although other species are occasionally observed, most are only present in small numbers during the moult and have not been recorded breeding.

Albatrosses

The Snares are a major breeding ground for the southern race of the Buller's Albatross. These are amongst the smallest albatrosses in the world and are distinguished from other species by their small size, grey head and broad yellow colouring on upper and lower bill. This annually breeding species returns to the islands from early December, with most eggs laid in January and the vast majority of fledglings and adults leaving by September or October. They differ from almost every other small albatross species in the timing of their breeding, raising their chicks through winter rather than the summer months. Population estimates from 2002 put the numbers at 8700 breeding pairs, which is almost double the size of the population estimated to breed there in 1969. The increase is in contrast to many other albatross populations around the world and has been attributed to their diets being supplemented by discards from fishing vessels.

The other main species of albatross that breeds around The Snares is the Salvin's Albatross (*Thalassarche salvini*). Although the majority of the New Zealand population breeds on the Bounty Islands, there is a colony on Toru and Rima islets in the Western Chain with an estimated breeding population of around 1000 breeding pairs. Very small numbers of Black-browed Albatross (*Thalassarche melanophrys*) and Chatham Albatross (*T. eremita*) have also occasionally been recorded breeding on the Western Chain.

SOOTY SHEARWATERS Home to over a million breeding pairs, the surface of The Snares is riddled with the burrows of this species. Each morning in summer thousands of birds leave the island to go and forage in the waters of the Southern Ocean. *AARON RUSS*

Other petrels

The breeding populations of some of the smaller petrels are very large. The main island is absolutely riddled with shearwater burrows, with the Sooty Shearwater breeding population once estimated as high as 2.7 million pairs. Estimates from 1996 to 2000 suggest that burrow numbers have dropped by about 37 per cent, or around one million pairs, since the early 1970s. Sooty Shearwaters are notoriously difficult to census, with deep burrows that have multiple entrances. However, there is little doubt that the population has declined over this time period. This species makes a large migration to the northern hemisphere in the non-breeding season. Significant declines, linked to changing oceanic temperatures, have also been documented in the migrating population as they move past the coast of North America.

The second most common breeding bird on The Snares is the southern subspecies of the Common Diving Petrel (*Pelecanoides urinatrix chathamensis*), with a breeding population estimated in the hundreds of thousands of pairs. The Mottled Petrel (*Pterodroma inexpectata*) is also known to breed on The Snares in populations numbering tens of thousands of birds. The Snares Cape Petrel (*Daption capense australe*), which is a subspecies of the Cape Petrel (*Daption capense*) and has less white on its upperwing than its closely related congener, also breeds on the main island, associated stacks and the Western Chain. The total breeding population is unknown but is thought to be in the vicinity of several thousand breeding pairs. Less is known about the prion breeding populations, but Broad-billed Prions (*Pachyptila vittata*), Fairy Prions (*Pachyptila turtur*) and Fulmar Prions (*Pachyptila crassirostris*) are known to occur, the latter largely restricted to the Western Chain.

BULLER'S ALBATROSS With its grey head and brightly coloured bill this species is one of the most striking of all the albatross species. *AARON RUSS.*

Other seabirds

Subantarctic Skuas (*Catharacta lonnbergi*) breed in scattered numbers throughout the islands of the group. Often this species will form a cooperative breeding unit composed of two to five birds. Red-billed Gulls (*Larus scopulinus*) and Antarctic Terns (*Sterna vittata bethunei*) also breed in small and scattered colonies throughout the group.

Land birds

As it is free of land-based predators, terrestrial birdlife has thrived on The Snares. There are several endemic subspecies, including the Black Tomtit (*Petroica macrocephala dannefaerdi*), which is differentiated from

BIRDS AND INVERTEBRATES (clockwise from top left) Snares Tomtit, Snares Island Snipe, Snares Fernbird, weevil, land slug. *AARON RUSS*

its close relative on the Auckland Islands by the absence of any white plumage. There is also the Snares Fernbird (*Bowdleria punctata caudata*) and the Snares Island Snipe (*Coenocorypha aucklandica huegli*). The Snares Fernbird is found in good numbers and often observed close to the coast, foraging around the roots of the *Olearia* trees or under the leaves of the cabbage. A small number of Grey Ducks (*Anas superciliosa*) breed only where appropriate aquatic habitat has formed. Silvereye (*Zosterops lateralis*) commonly breed over the whole island.

Some introduced European species also found on mainland New Zealand have extended their range to breed on The Snares, including Mallard (*Anas platyrhynchos*), Song Thrush (*Turdus philomelos*), Blackbird (*T. merula*), Redpoll (*Carduelis flammea*) and European Starling (*Sturnus vulgaris*).

Non-breeding birds

Non-breeding visitors include species such as the Erect Crested Penguin (usually observed moulting) and the Northern Giant Petrel (*Macronectes halli*), which is frequently seen ashore though no breeding is confirmed. Sightings of migrant waders usually involve small numbers of individuals, such as Eastern Bar-tailed Godwit (*Limosa lapponica*), Sharp-tailed Sandpiper (*Calidris acuminata*) and Greenshank (*Tringa nebularia*).

In recent years, regular and extended visits have increased the number of sightings, especially of migrants and stragglers. Several species of penguin, at least three species of shag, and a diverse range of landbirds have been found in varying numbers.

Seals

New Zealand Fur Seals (*Arctocephalus forsteri*) are the main species of seal breeding on the island. After being decimated in the early 1800s, this species was almost entirely absent for the next 100 years. Numbers slowly increased during the twentieth century and in 1970 just over 1000 animals were counted in a census by M. Crawley and G. Wilson. Since this time, the breeding range within the island group has expanded, with some sites that were previously only used as haul-outs developing into breeding colonies. A census in 1997 found 188 pups, which is likely to be considerably less than the pre-exploitation levels. New Zealand (Hooker's) Sea Lions (*Phocarctos hookeri*) are a regular visitor to The Snares, but to date only a few pups have been recorded there.

Terrestrial invertebrates

The first collection of terrestrial invertebrates on The Snares was made in 1907 by G. Hudson as part of the Philosophical Institute of Canterbury Expedition. While only 14 species were found during the five hours of sampling, it was noted that the terrestrial invertebrates were likely to be rich and diverse. Since that first survey, a further 105 species of insect and a host of other invertebrates, including land snails and worms, have been identified. Of the 119 species of insect, 41 are considered endemic to the island group. One of the worms grows to a length of 20 centimetres and several species of beetle and moth represent the southernmost limit of their populations.

EMERGING FROM THE KELP Although there are few records of New Zealand (Hooker's) Sea Lions breeding on The Snares, it is a popular haul out site for young males. *ALEKS TERAUDS*.

HISTORY

LIKE MANY of the Southern Ocean islands, The Snares were discovered quite by accident, during a voyage led by Captain George Vancouver in 1791. This voyage left England with the aim of exploring the north-west coast of America and the Pacific, with instructions to only briefly visit New Zealand en route. After leaving Dusky Bay, Fiordland in late November, the *Discovery* and the *Chatham* headed south around southern New Zealand, en route for Tahiti. They encountered a storm that forced them to part company and took them quite a way offshore. Both vessels came across The Snares independently, but almost simultaneously on 23rd November. Captain George Vancouver in the *Discovery* saw them first at 11 a.m., noting that 'they were composed of a cluster of seven craggy islands' and named them 'The Snares'. Lieutenant Broughton on the *Chatham* sighted the islands at 2 p.m., noting 'a cluster of small islets and rocks'. He called them Knights Island. It was only when the two ships met up on 30th December that they were able to compare notes and decided that as Vancouver's sighting was made first, they would retain the name The Snares.

EARLY VISITORS AND SEALERS

The first two ships to visit the islands following their discovery did not land. The first was the *Brittania* in 1792, when Captain William Raven named them Sunday Islands, not realising they had already been discovered. The next near approach was made by Captain Amasa Delano. After skirmishing with Australian sealing gangs already established on the Bass Strait islands, Captain Delano took his American ships, the *Perseverance* and the *Pilgrim*, across to the southern New Zealand islands and sighted The Snares on 3rd November 1804. Due to the strong westerly blowing at the time, he could not investigate the islands as well as he would have liked, but noted that the islands appeared to offer little safe shelter for anchorage and did not appear to be that productive in terms of wildlife.

In 1810, the schooner *Adventure* was sealing in the area and, falling short of provisions, Captain Keith gave his crew a choice of going ashore on The Snares or starving aboard, for there were not enough supplies to keep them all alive in the short term. Four men were put ashore, reportedly against their will. They took with them a few potatoes, some rice and an iron pot. They managed to cultivate the potatoes and with these and the odd bird and seal they managed to survive there for some seven years until they were rescued by the American whaler, the *Enterprise*, in 1817. Captain Coffin of the *Enterprise* described the men as being in somewhat of a wretched state and also described how well the potatoes had spread, apparently covering half of one side of the island. The men had managed to build five houses and had 1300 dried seal skins when the *Enterprise* found them.

There is little doubt that many sealing parties landed on The Snares between 1817 and 1830. After finding that there were no fur seals to be found at the Auckland Islands, Captain B. Morrell in the American schooner *Antarctic* arrived at The Snares in 1830 to continue his search for sealing grounds. In his own words, Captain Morrell 'searched The Snares in vain for fur-seal with which they formerly abounded. The population was extinct, cut off, root and branch by the sealers of Van Diemens Land, Sidney, etc.' This exploration of The Snares effectively marked the end of the sealing industry.

Castaway depots and scientists

At the end of the sealing era, there were few recorded visits to The Snares. It was proposed as a suitable site for a lighthouse in the late 1800s and a report for the New Zealand government in 1894 suggested that The Snares might be suitable for a farming venture. Neither the lighthouse or the farming eventuated and consequently The Snares today remain one of the more pristine or 'natural' islands in the Southern Ocean.

The first castaway depot was set up on The Snares during the voyage of the *Amherst* in 1865. This was the first visit in many years and the government representative, Henry Armstrong, showed a surprising lack of regard for the pristine environment that he found. The men on this expedition caused chaos by walking through and stoving in hundreds of shearwater burrows, kicking penguins out of their way as they moved around and setting fire to the grass in an attempt to attract the attention of any castaways that may have been on the islands. Several subsequent visits were made in ensuing years, but the lack of good harbour made landings by scientists less common than on some of the larger subantarctic islands.

The first naturalist to land on The Snares was the Austrian Andreas Reischek on the government resupply ship the *Stella*, in 1888. His notes on the visit reveal a similar disregard for the wildlife, shooting numerous birds and killing many penguins for museum collections. This party also released two goats on the island—one of the few times that feral animals were let loose on The Snares. Some tree and grass seeds were also sown. The botanist Thomas Kirk and his companion Frederick Chapman landed on The Snares in 1890 and made some of the first

Captain George Vancouver discovered The Snares in 1791. He was on an exploratory voyage in his ship Discovery *(shown below)*

Sailors painting the castaway food depot at Station Point, North-east Islands, The Snares in 1905. Alexander Turnbull Library, Wellington, New Zealand. F- 2415-1/2

Andreas Reischek was the first naturalist to visit The Snares in 1888 and he was the first to collect and describe many of the plants and animals. Alexander Turnbull Library. F- 300-1/4 -MNZ

known botanical collections. The Snares were also visited on the outward journey of the 1907 expedition by the Philosophical Institute of Canterbury and although the visit was relatively short, it still contributed significantly to the current knowledge of the geology, flora and fauna of the region. The end of the government resupply ships in 1928 marked the end of further visits to The Snares for some 20 years.

Post-war research and management

The first post-war scientific visit to The Snares was led by renowned naturalist and scientist Sir Robert Falla and included Robert C. Murphy from the American Museum of Natural History. They stayed on the island for nearly two weeks in the early summer of 1947. A month later, The Snares were visited by albatross biologist Lance Richdale. Following these two visits, The Snares were not visited again until the late 1950s, when the University of Canterbury began its long association with the island. In 1961, soon after this new era of field work began, The Snares were declared a reserved area.

The University of Canterbury Zoology Department maintained a field station on The Snares from the late 1950s until 1987. The project was initially overseen by Professor George Knox, and later Drs John Warham and Don Horning. An ambitious aim of the research was to catalogue every species that occurred on the island and the nature of the work led to a large number of students undertaking postgraduate research there. Several of the students from this period are now very active in Southern Ocean research and conservation. The university funded the research through grants from a number of sources and the RNZ Navy and local fishermen provided the transport. The research was scaled down towards the end of the 1970s but picked up again in 1982-83 when the Lands and Survey Department, who then administered the island as a Nature Reserve, invited or encouraged the university to work on the island in an attempt to keep an eye on the local fishermen. There is only one place where fishing boats can safely moor at the island and there were real (and genuine) concerns that rats could get ashore from these fishing boats if they had mooring lines connected to the shore.

The Lands and Survey Department eventually prohibited the use of mooring lines, believing that the researchers on shore would act as a deterrent to boats mooring. This arrangement continued until 1987, when the Department of Conservation was formed. The management of these islands came under the Southland Conservancy and the newly appointed Conservator terminated this agreement and shortly afterwards gave permission for three boats to use mooring lines.

In 1990, albatross by-catch had become a global issue and there were real concerns over the number of albatross that were being caught by long-line fishing vessels. Paul Sagar, a graduate of the University of Canterbury who had worked on The Snares in the 1970s and who was then working for the National Institute of Water and Atmospheric Research (NIWA), tried to get funding to study the breeding biology and foraging ecology of the Buller's Albatross on The Snares. The Department of Conservation finally offered logistical support in 1992 and the programme has been funded at varying levels to the present day. More recently, the New Zealand Ministry

ALBATROSS RESEARCHERS Aaron Russ and Paul Sagar hold an albatross chick in preparation for banding. *RUSS COLLECTION*

of Fisheries has announced a three-year project on the population dynamics and foraging ecology of the Salvin's Albatross, due to continuing concerns that fishing activities may be impacting on this species.

Sooty Shearwaters, which breed in such abundance on The Snares, have also been the subject of extensive research in the last decade. These birds are taken as a traditional food from several small islands around Stewart Island and as there had been no study to assess the impact on the population, there were questions as to whether it was sustainable. In an attempt to investigate the sustainability of the harvest, the New Zealand government provided funds to the local Maori people, who contracted the University of Otago to undertake a ten-year study. As The Snares are free of harvesting, they were used as a control site for this study, which was completed in 2005.

The Snares remains one of the most pristine of all the islands south of Australia and New Zealand, testament to the relatively small footprint that people have left there over the last 200 years.

MACQUARIE ISLAND

North Head
Hasselborough Bay
Handspike Point
ANARE Station
Halfmoon Bay
Buckles Bay
Nuggets Point
Mt Elder
Bauer Bay
Mawsons Point
Cormorant Point
Sandy Bay
Brothers Point
Aurora Point
Soucek Bay
Prion Lake
Green Gorge
Mt Waite
Double Point
Davis Bay
Sandell Bay
Saddle Point
Major Lake
Cape Toutcher
Rockhopper Point
Waterfall Bay
Mt Hamilton
Mt Fletcher
Lusitania Bay
Precarious Point
Cape Star
Carrick Bay
Caroline Cove
Waterfall Lake
Caroline Point
South West Point
Hurd Point

0km — 5km

MACQUARIE ISLAND

54°38'S • 158°52'E • 12788ha • 433m a.s.l

Macquarie Island is the southernmost of all the island groups in the Galapagos of the Antarctic. Located approximately 1500 kilometres to the south-east of Tasmania, Australia, and a similar distance from New Zealand, it is the only subantarctic island in this part of the world that is under Australian jurisdiction. Macquarie Island was discovered in 1810, as ships ventured further afield looking for fresh sealing grounds, and in just over a decade all the fur seals had been killed. Humans continued to exploit the natural resources of the island following the fur seal era with both elephant seals and penguins killed for the oil from their blubber layers. Today, the island is a World Heritage Area and considered one of the most important natural wildlife havens of Australia. Literally millions of penguins come ashore to breed here during the summer months and the island is also home to a multitude of breeding seabirds and thousands of elephant seals.

Macquarie Island Shag

MACQUARIE ISLAND Lying approximately 1500 km south-east of Australia and a similar distance from New Zealand, this island is the only one of the wild islands south of New Zealand that is an Australian territory.

MACQUARIE ISLAND STATION The Isthmus at the northern end of Macquarie Island has always been the site of most human habitation. Today the main station has enough accommodation and infrastructure to support 40 people, as well as workshops and equipment for maintenance and building programs. *ALEKS TERAUDS.*

GEOGRAPHY AND GEOLOGY

MACQUARIE ISLAND is one of the more remote of the wild islands south of New Zealand, with the closest land mass being the Auckland Islands some 600 kilometres to the north-east. It is literally a speck in the Southern Ocean and the jagged rocks and bays of the west coast are testament to thousands of years of pounding by Southern Ocean waves. It is the only exposed portion of the vast Macquarie Ridge Complex, which stretches from New Zealand far into the Southern Ocean, and it lies just to the north of the Antarctic Convergence, more commonly known today as the Polar Front.

GEOGRAPHY

The Macquarie Island group is made up of the main island and two smaller groups of islets at the northern and southern ends. Bishop and Clerk islets lie 33 kilometres off the southern end of the main island. The larger of these two islets only covers a few hectares and supports several species of breeding seabird. These low-lying islets are extremely exposed and support very little vegetation, with only a few lichens and a cushion plant growing there. Judge and Clerk islets are smaller still and lie 14 kilometres off the northern end of the main island. Due to their wave-washed nature, no flora or fauna lives or breeds on these islets.

The main island is long and narrow, being 34 kilometres long and 5 kilometres across at its widest point. It lies on a north-south axis and covers an area of 12 788 hectares. Around much of the island, steep coastal slopes rise from the ocean to an undulating plateau region. Most of Macquarie Island consists of this plateau—a windswept region that ranges from around 200 metres to just over 400 metres above sea level. There are numerous mountains, lakes and tarns, with the highest point being Mount Hamilton at 433 metres above sea level. One of the few areas where the plateau drops to sea level is the Isthmus, at the northern end of the island. This low-lying piece of land, which has been the main site of human settlement since the island's discovery, separates the main island from the small landform known as North Head.

The escarpments falls away sharply from much of the plateau, particularly on the west and south coasts. The east coast is not as steep as the west coast and in some places the plateau slopes gently down to the coastal fringe. These often wet and boggy coastal terraces vary in extent and are also known as 'the featherbed' for their springy nature underfoot.

ORIGINS

Millions of years before its emergence, the rocks that make up Macquarie Island were formed by tremendous forces as the Australian/Indian and Pacific tectonic plates moved apart, forcing lava into the ocean. Over millions of years these tectonic plates stopped moving apart and eventually reversed their direction of movement and started to move towards each other, slowly but inexorably pushing up the ocean floor into what was to become the Macquarie Ridge Complex. This massive undersea ridge complex, similar in height to some of the world's largest exposed mountain ranges, stretches 1500 kilometres from New Zealand well into the Southern Ocean. Macquarie Island represents the only exposed portion of this undersea ridgeline and is one of the best exposed and most isolated pieces of the ocean seafloor in the world.

It is thought that Macquarie Island first emerged above the ocean around 600 000–700 000 years ago, and since that time changing sea levels and the erosive force of the ocean have created the landscapes that we see today. In addition to uplifting and erosion, the Macquarie Island landscape has also been influenced by faulting, with larger scale faults causing major features like the Isthmus at the northern end, and smaller scale faults forming the localised shape of the cliffs and some parts of the coastline. Due to its location on the edges of the Pacific continental plate, there is considerable seismic activity and small earthquakes are a relatively common occurrence.

THE FEATHERBED The extended coastal terraces of Macquarie Island are also sometimes known as the featherbed. *ALEKS TERAUDS*

Geology

The geology of Macquarie Island is unique as it represents a cross-section through the ocean crust that is in relatively pristine condition, still in the oceanic basin in which it formed and independent of any continent. In fact, the formation and subsequent geology is so unique that it was the basis for its designation as a World Heritage Area in 1997.

The rocks that make up the island have recently been dated at around 9 million years. These are almost exclusively volcanic in origin, formed as molten magma spewed out into the ocean from deep in the crust of the Earth as the plates spread apart. As this molten lava solidified, it formed several types of volcanic rocks, including the common pillow basalts. Coarser grained dolerite and gabbro is also present, formed by magma crystallising more slowly below the basalts. Pillow basalts make up much of the exposed part of the island that we see today and their shape belies the nature of their formation. As the cold deep water rapidly cooled the magma, it formed semi-spherical 'pillows' that are often observed on the surface of the island, locked together in a kind of geological jigsaw puzzle. In addition to the pillow basalts there are more continous lava flows, which were created from less vigorous volcanic activity and cooled more slowly into tabular basalt layers.

The underwater volcanic environment of Macquarie Island was also the site of associated sediment deposition. Sediments of marine origin (also known as oozes) also occur in the gaps between the volcanic rock. There are mudstones and young sandstones, pebble cobble accumulations (or breccias) and accumulations of volcanic glass interlayered with the basalts. Intrusive dolerite dykes are found in a number of locations, often in parallel groups, which are also known as sheeted dyke complexes. At the northern end of the island, coarser grained gabbro bodies, representing deeper levels of the oceanic crust, are exposed. Also exposed in the north of the island are ultramafic rocks, which formed at depths of up to 6 kilometres underground and which are rarely exposed on the surface.

MACQUARIE ISLAND 175

FLORA

The climate of Macquarie Island limits what can grow there and its relatively young age, combined with its remote location and isolation, means that comparatively few species have colonised the island from other locations. It is thought to be too cold and windy for woody plants to survive and there are no trees or shrubs. The island is dominated by megaherbs and tussock grass, with the higher windswept altitudes predominantly made up of relatively bare gravel areas known as feldmark, pocketed with hardy, low-lying species of moss, lichens and cushion plants. The southernmost orchids in Australasia grow on Macquarie Island and they are very small, rarely exceeding more than a few centimetres in height. Although several attempts were made by early visitors to cultivate non-native species, today there are only three established species that are recognised as introduced, all of which were accidental introductions. The short grass *Poa annua* is widely distributed, while the weedy herb *Cerastium fontanum* and the chickweed *Stellaria media* are widespread but rare.

Plant communities

The grasses, herbs, cushion plants, ferns and sedges that make up the majority of the tall vegetation on Macquarie Island are known as vascular plants. Since studies first began on these plants in the late 1800s, their similarities to New Zealand flora have been noted and documented. The main reason for these similarities is that the New Zealand subantarctic islands are the closest landmasses to Macquarie Island. The plants would have arrived on Macquarie Island through wind dispersal of seeds, or seed transport via birds. Vascular plants occur throughout Macquarie Island in a range of communities, the nature of which is influenced by a complex combination of factors which include: available water and drainage, the underlying geology and soil structure, aspect, exposure to weather or salt spray, altitude, and nutrient availability. The following communities are recognised today: tall tussock grassland, short grassland, fernbrake, mire, feldmark and herbfield.

Grasslands

Tall grassland is dominated by the tussock grass *Poa foliosa* and occurs on much of the coastal slopes and sheltered valleys around the island. Tussock grass grows right down to the beach margins and on the coastal stacks in places. In these regions *Poa cookii* occurs and it grows particularly well in the nutrient-rich environments around penguin colonies. Both *Poa* species are relatively slow growing and have been devastated in recent years by rabbit grazing. The short grassland usually copes much better with grazing and is dominated by smaller grasses like *Agrostis magellanica*, *Festuca contracta* and the sedges *Luzula crinita* and *Uncinia hookeri*. One of the few introduced species, annual meadow grass (*Poa annua*), forms lush green carpets around the coastal fringe and is quick to colonise nutrient-rich, disturbed sites. *Poa litorosa* also occurs but only in small isolated patches. Other grasses include the less common *Deschampsia* spp. and the salt-resistant coastal endemic *Puccinellia macquariensis*.

Herbs

Herbfields are more common in sheltered areas like valleys, coastal slopes and the raised coastal terraces. The megaherbs *Pleurophyllum hookeri* and the Macquarie Island cabbage

FLOWERING MEGAHERBS One of Macquarie Island's dominant megaherbs, *Pleurophyllum hookeri*, only flowers en masse every two or three years. *ALEKS TERAUDS*

MACQUARIE ISLAND CABBAGE Prior to the recent increases in rabbit grazing, the Macquarie Island cabbage, *Stilbocarpa polaris*, covered many of the coastal slopes, providing ideal nesting habitat for the Light-mantled Sooty Albatross. *ALEKS TERAUDS*

(*Stilbocarpa polaris*) form large, dominant stands in many places, but also grow together in co-dominant communities. The cabbage sometimes grows interspersed with the tussock grass on coastal slopes. The megaherbs have different flowering regimes; the cabbage flowers each year, while *Pleurophyllum*, which is actually part of the daisy family, only flowers once every two or three years.

Other herbaceous species are much smaller—rarely reaching over 20 centimetres in height—and most tend to flower annually. They include the brassica *Cardamine corymbosa*, the buttercup *Ranunculus crassipes*, the water-loving cress *Callitriche antarctica*, and *Montia fontana*. There are two species of herb from the genus *Epilobium*, and they seem to be able to thrive in a variety of environments. Many of these species are often amongst the first colonisers of disturbed ground, such as that caused by landslips or severe rabbit grazing.

While there are no trees or shrubs, there is one 'woody' plant, although it is so small and prostrate that to the untrained eye it would rarely be identified as such. *Coprosma perpusilla* has the distinction of being the only woody plant on the island and its small, tightly woven green leaves and distinctive red berries are relatively common in places on the coastal terraces. There are also two species of semi-woody plant, known as bidi-bidi or buzzies, that occur on Macquarie Island. *Acaena minor* has bright green spiky seed heads, while *Acaena magellanica* is more purple in colour, and they often grow together, covering large areas. On the coast, *Leptinella plumosa*, a small daisy with fine, filamentous leaves, often forms soft carpets around the periphery of some of the beach areas.

CUSHION PLANTS There are four species of cushion plant on Macquarie Island. This one, *Colobanthus muscoides*, sometimes grows in extensive homogenous stands covering several hectares. *ALEKS TERAUDS*

Cushion plants

Cushion plants are widely distributed around the island, from the coastal rock stacks to the windswept higher altitudes. Four main species grow on Macquarie Island, with three of them from the genus *Colobanthus*. The most widespread of these is *C. muscoides* which forms dense, tight cushions throughout the coastal regions. In a few places it grows in a homogenous stand covering hundreds of square metres, but it also grows on rock stacks and occasionally interspersed with tussock grass. In some coastal areas where rabbit grazing has destroyed the tussock grass, *C. muscoides* has been observed colonising the dead pedestals, making it difficult for anything else to grow. The fourth cushion plant, *Azorella macquariensis*, is most common at higher altitudes and is one of the only four plants on Macquarie Island that is considered endemic.

FERNS

The largest of the ferns, *Polystichum vestitum*, grows to a height of 1.5 metres and dominates fern communities on Macquarie Island, particularly on the east coast. Other ferns on the island are smaller and less common. These include *Blechnum penna-marina*, which grows in short grasslands, and the tiny *Grammitis poeppigiana*, which is restricted to higher altitudes. Closely related to the ferns are the filmy fern *Hymenophyllum falklandicum* and the lycopod *Huperzia australiana*, both of which are uncommon on the island.

ANIMAL IMPACTS

The native animals on Macquarie Island have a considerable impact on the plants. Penguin colonies, often containing thousands of individuals, provide high levels of nutrients to the surrounding environment, often resulting in lush growth of the surrounding *Poa* tussock grasses. Seals also change the vegetation when they come ashore, both by destroying plants and by creating wallows—high-nutrient, boggy areas where some plant species thrive.

Introduced animals have a far more negative effect on the vegetation. Mice and rats cache and graze on seeds and also influence the dispersal of many species. The effect of rabbits on the vascular plants of the island has been dramatic, particularly in more recent years. The vegetation has developed and evolved without rabbits and as a result many species are extremely vulnerable to grazing damage. The megaherbs and tussock grasses are extremely palatable to rabbits and they have severely grazed hundreds of hectares, resulting in many areas now being completely devoid of vegetation.

BRYOPHYTES, LICHENS AND FUNGI

Mosses, liverworts and lichens are abundant on Macquarie Island and they occur in all areas, from the saltwater drenched rocky coastlines to the exposed, high altitude feldmark.

Some species of lichen have the ability to tolerate a high salt load and survive close to the intertidal zone. One or two species of moss are also able to withstand these harsh environments and can survive the occasional inundation of salt water. In many of the coastal areas there is a complex interaction between vascular plants, mosses and lichens. Nowhere is this seen more clearly than in the mires of the featherbed, where lichens, liverworts and mosses are common. *Sphagnum* moss occurs in isolated patches and changes in its distribution and abundance have been used as an indication of changing climate.

Beneath the dense tussocks of the coastal slopes, mosses and liverworts are common, thriving in the sheltered, wet environment. Many moss species preferentially colonise the wet, peaty soils, where there is very little competition from other plants. Mosses and liverworts also dominate in the barren feldmark regions, where they might make up as much as 70 per cent of the total vegetation cover. In these regions they often occur in terraces formed by frost heave in the gravel beds, or occupy niches in the rocky outcrops that are characteristic of these areas.

While there have been several studies on the fungi of Macquarie Island, many species remain undescribed. There are literally hundreds of species of different shapes and sizes which flourish in the cold, damp conditions, from slime moulds that colonise the litter under megaherbs to the larger mushrooms that pop up through the

RABBIT DAMAGE Between 1994 and 2005 rabbit numbers are thought to have increased 10-fold on Macquarie Island. Consequently, increased grazing pressure has resulted in the devastation of many areas, and a significant decrease in the vegetation cover. *ALEKS TERAUDS*

featherbed. Many of the fungi also grow symbiotically with vascular plants, living on or in the root systems and assisting in nutrient acquisition.

Marine plants

Kelp, a large brown algae, is the largest of the marine flora and it dominates the upper intertidal zone, below the red algal zone, in the form of Antarctic bull kelp (*Durvillaea antarctica*). Further offshore from this zone, another large form of brown algae, *Macrocystis pyriphera*, forms extensive floating beds in waters up to 30 metres deep. All of the algae, but particularly some of the larger forms, provide extensive habitat for a whole range of invertebrates, sheltering them from UV, wind and wave actions and giving them protection from predators. Red and green algae also occurs around the coastline and are often found in the numerous intertidal pools that are common features of the coast.

GREY-HEADED ALBATROSSES On the slopes of Petrel Peak, two young Grey-headed Albatrosses gather around a nesting bird. There are less than 100 pairs of this species breeding on Macquarie Island each year. *ALEKS TERAUDS*

FAUNA

Given the lack of dry land in the region, Macquarie Island is an important land base and breeding ground for a diverse and abundant range of wildlife living in the surrounding waters of the Southern Ocean. Penguins, albatrosses, petrels and seals all need dry land in order to breed and hundreds of thousands of individuals move out of the ocean and onto the shores of Macquarie Island each year. Most of this movement occurs in the spring and summer months, and the sheer presence of such a massive influx brings with it a cacophony of sights, sounds and smells that threaten to overwhelm the senses. While there are no native land mammals, Macquarie Island has House Mice (*Mus musculus*), Black (Ship) Rats (*Rattus rattus*) and European Rabbits (*Oryctolagus cuniculus*), a legacy of sealers and other early visitors to the island. Another legacy of these early visitors and the animals they brought with them was the extinction of the only two native land birds, the Macquarie Island parakeet (*Cyanoramphus novaezelandiae erythrotis*) and the endemic subspecies of the Pacific Banded Rail (*Rallus philippensis macquariensis*).

Penguins

Four species of penguin breed on Macquarie Island. The largest is the striking King Penguin (*Aptenodytes patagonicus*), standing just over a metre tall, with bright yellow/orange colouring at the base of the neck, sides of the head and bill. It is the only penguin that has a presence on Macquarie Island all year round and it was nearly wiped out in the late 1800s by the penguin oiling industry. There are thought to be between 300 000 to 400 000 pairs breeding on Macquarie Island today.

The second largest penguin on the island is the Gentoo Penguin (*Pygoscelis papua*). Their distinctive orange feet and bill, together with the white blaze on the sides of their heads, make them easy to identify. They form small colonies on the island, nesting on and around the grassy coastal flats and occasionally the lower reaches of the coastal slopes. The total breeding population on Macquarie Island is around 5000 pairs.

There are also two species of crested penguin. The Royal Penguin (*Eudyptes schlegeli*) only breeds on Macquarie Island and it forms large colonies, with the total population estimated at around 800 000 breeding pairs. In addition to forming colonies on the coast, this species also breeds in plateau colonies, traveling long distances up to altitudes of 200 metres. Rockhopper Penguins (*Eudyptes chrysocome*) are the smallest of the penguins on Macquarie Island and they primarily nest on the coast or on the coastal slopes. Being the smallest penguin, they are the most vulnerable to predators like the Subantarctic (Brown) Skua (*Catharacta lonnbergi*) and therefore they often nest in cryptic locations, making population estimates difficult. There are likely to be hundreds of thousands of breeding pairs on the island but little is known about their population trends.

Albatross

Four species of albatross breed on the island and all are found at other locations around the world. A very small population of the Wandering albatross (*Diomedea exulans*) breeds here, with fewer than fifteen pairs breeding each year and a total population likely to number less than 100 individuals. They are the largest of all the albatrosses,

KING PENGUIN COLONY At Lusitania Bay, King Penguins congregate in their largest colony on Macquarie Island. This species was nearly wiped out during the penguin oiling industry, but since it's cessation numbers have increased to pre-exploitation levels. *ALEKS TERAUDS*

MACQUARIE ISLAND BIRDS (clockwise from top left) Royal Penguin, Gentoo Penguin and chicks, Rockhopper Penguin, Southern Giant Petrel chick. *ALEKS TERAUDS*

with a wingspan of over 3 metres, and have the ability to travel vast distances across the ocean in search of food. They mainly nest in the south-western corner of the island, with a few pairs on the north-western featherbed.

Black-browed Albatrosses (*Thalassarche melanophrys*) and Grey-headed Albatross (*Thalassarche chrysostoma*) also have small breeding populations in the south-west of the main island, with around 40 and 70 breeding pairs respectively each year. Black-browed Albatrosses also breed on Bishop and Clerk islets to the south, with over 100 breeding pairs utilising the small amount of soil that is present to build their nests. Light-mantled Sooty Albatrosses (*Phoebetria palpebrata*) are the most common albatross on the island, with around 1000–1500 pairs breeding around the coastal slopes each year. They are distinctive because of their dark plumage and mesmerising courtship flights, where birds fly together in almost perfect synchrony.

Other petrels

Both species of giant petrel breed on Macquarie Island. Breeding numbers of the Northern Giant Petrel (*Macronectes halli*) have been increasing steadily over the last 15 years and nearly 2000 breeding pairs nest around the coastal periphery each year. The Southern Giant Petrel (*Macronectes giganteus*) population is slightly bigger, with just over 2000 breeding pairs. While superficially similar in appearance, their breeding ecology is quite different, with Southern Giant Petrels forming colonies that might contain over 100 pairs.

Antarctic Prions (*Pachyptila desolata*) are probably the most numerous and widespread of the smaller petrels, with around 50 000 pairs estimated to breed in small burrows around the island. White-headed Petrels (*Pterodroma lessonii*) also occur in reasonable numbers, with somewhere between 5000 and 8000 breeding pairs. Sooty shearwaters (*Puffinus griseus*), Blue Petrels (*Halobaena caerulea*) and Grey Petrels (*Procellaria cinerea*) also breed on the island.

Many of the smaller petrels benefited from the recent eradication of cats; however, populations are still being negatively affected by the presence of rats and habitat degradation due to rabbit grazing. Consequently, small species like the Blue Petrel are mainly restricted to offshore stacks that are free from introduced animals. Cape Petrels (*Daption capense*), Fairy Prions (*Pachyptila turtur*), Common Diving Petrels (*Pelacanoides urinatrix*), Fulmar Prions (*Pachyptila crassirostris*) and Soft-plumage Petrels (*Pterodroma mollis*) have also been recorded breeding, albeit in low numbers.

Other birds

In addition to the albatrosses and other petrels, several other species of birds have been described on the island. Other seabirds include the Subantarctic Skua, Southern Black-backed Gulls (*Larus dominicanus*), Macquarie Island Shags (*Leucocarbo atriceps purpurascens*) and Antarctic Terns (*Sterna vittata bethunei*). The skuas breed all over the island, from the plateau to the coastal flats, and are extremely territorial. They are voracious scavengers but also actively prey on small petrels and the eggs and chicks of albatross and penguins. Southern Black-backed Gulls breed around the coast in small numbers, with around 100–150 breeding pairs. The endemic Macquarie Island Shags breed on rock stacks around the coast in colonies ranging from just a few birds to hundreds of pairs. Antarctic Terns breed at several sites but numbers are low, with only 20–30 breeding pairs. In addition to the seabirds, there are the self-introduced Redpolls (*Carduleis flammea*) and European Starlings (*Sturnus vulgaris*) breeding on the island and two species of duck; Mallards (*Anas platyrhynchos*) and Grey Ducks (*Anas superciliosa*).

Marine mammals

Three species of fur seal breed on Macquarie Island but numbers are still lower than they would have been prior to the arrival of man. Today, both Subantarctic Fur Seals (*Arctocephalus tropicalis*) and Antarctic Fur Seals (*Arctocephalus gazella*) breed in small numbers. The two species are known to hybridise, but most of the 200 or so pups born each year are Antarctic Fur Seals. New Zealand Fur Seal (*Arctocephalus forsteri*) females are not usually observed on the island but several hundred sub-adult and adult males come ashore in the summer months.

Southern Elephant Seals (*Mirounga leonina*) breed in large numbers, with males coming ashore in August. In the vicinity of 20 000 pups are born each year on the island. The largest and strongest males hold harems of up to several hundred females. These bulls, knows as beachmasters, spend most of the summer months protecting the females from the advances of other males and then, once the pups have weaned, service the females. Fierce fights between rival males are common as younger bulls attempt to gain control of a harem. Females usually come ashore several days before giving birth to the pups in September and October.

New Zealand (Hooker's) Sea Lions (*Phocarctos hookeri*) come ashore in low numbers each year, but no breeding has been recorded. A small number of Leopard Seals (*Hydrurga leptonyx*) also come ashore, but most tend to be in poor condition. Macquarie Island is also an important feeding ground for Killer Whales (*Orcinus orca*) and they are most commonly observed in the summer months, taking advantage of the large numbers of young elephant seals entering the water. They also prey on the penguins and smaller fur seals.

Introduced animals

Non-native animals have been introduced to Macquarie Island throughout its human history, both accidentally and on purpose. Wild animals like European Rabbits and Stewart Island Wekas (*Gallirallus australis scotti*) were introduced as a food source and several attempts were made to establish domesticated animals like sheep, cattle, goats and chickens. The wekas were eradicated in the 1980s, but the rabbit numbers are booming and wreaking havoc throughout the island, particularly on the coastal slopes. Myxoma virus was used successfully as a control agent between 1978 and the early 1990s, but since that time numbers have increased exponentially and there are now thought to be over 100 000 rabbits on the island. Plans are underway for a major eradication operation, due to start in 2010, targeting both rabbits and the rodents, which were inadvertently brought to the island in the 1800s.

Cats and dogs were brought to the island in the early days of settlement, and while the dogs were eventually killed or died out, cats quickly established a feral population, feeding on the multitude of small petrels that were breeding all over the island. A targeted eradication operation by the Tasmanian Parks and Wildlife Service began in the 1990s and in 2000 the last cat was shot.

SOUTHERN ELEPHANT SEAL The most abundant species of seal on Macquarie Island is the Southern Elephant Seal with nearly 20 000 pups born each year This sub adult male will need to wait a few years before it reaches the size and weight needed to hold and protect its own harem. *NATHAN RUSS*

Terrestrial invertebrates

Terrestrial invertebrates, including insects, are common on Macquarie Island, although not as abundant or diverse as some of the New Zealand islands. Flies are the most abundant group, with 11 species recorded from the island. There are over 50 species of lice, which mainly live parasitically on the seabirds. In addition to the flies and lice, there are beetles, fleas and moths. Other terrestrial invertebrates that have been recorded include over 20 species of springtail, 2 terrestrial crustaceans, 7 species of spider and over 100 species of mites and ticks. Worms are also well-represented, with at least 15 species of earthworm identified, three of which are considered endemic and five of which are probably introduced.

HISTORY

Macquarie Island was discovered accidentally in 1810 when the sealing ship *Perseverance*, captained by Frederick Hasselburgh, was blown off course en route to Campbell Island. Excited by the high numbers of fur seals reported on its shores, several ships travelled to Macquarie Island soon after news of the discovery was made public. In addition to the *Perseverance*, other ships that made their way down to Macquarie Island in the first year to take advantage of the fur seal bonanza included the American brig *Aurora*, the brig *Star*, the schooner *Unity*, the *Elizabeth and Mary* and the *Sydney Cove*.

Fur sealing

Cargo records suggest that literally hundreds of thousands of individuals were killed by the fur sealers in the first 11 years following discovery and the population was effectively wiped out by 1821. Researchers have not yet been able to ascertain the main species that was present at that time. It seems likely that Subantarctic Fur Seals were the most common species, but it is possible that we will never really know for sure. Reports of the time describe the indiscriminate killing of seals, with males, females and even young pups slaughtered in an ongoing and sustained massacre that is difficult to comprehend today. Even though the industry only lasted just over a decade, its legacy was long-lasting and fur seals were not recorded breeding on the island again until the 1950s.

From elephant seals to penguins

Following the collapse of the fur seal industry, the sealers turned their attention to the abundant Southern Elephant Seals. They targeted the large males, stunning the sleeping individuals with a blow to the nose and finishing them off with a knife or spear. The blubber was then cut off in chunks, put in a boiler (also known as a trypot) and heated by a fire underneath, also fuelled by blubber. The oil was siphoned off, poured into barrels and eventually shipped to markets in New South Wales or Britain. Several hundred kilograms of oil could be obtained from a single bull elephant seal.

Those working in this industry lived in squalor, occupying small dark huts covered on the inside with elephant seal skins and tussock grass on the outside. A fire, fuelled by the blubber, was kept burning continuously for warmth, staining everything inside the huts black with soot. The main food was elephant seal flippers and penguins, supplemented with the odd parakeet and eggs from the penguins, petrels and albatrosses. The men were poorly provisioned with fresh food and if it were not for the Macquarie Island cabbage, it is likely many of them would have succumbed to scurvy.

The elephant seal industry continued up until the 1850s and thousands of seals were killed during this time period. After a brief human hiatus between 1850 and 1870, it resumed again, often occurring in conjunction with the burgeoning penguin oil industry. King Penguins were the initial main target of this industry but as they become scarcer, Royal Penguins were also targeted. Hundreds of thousands of penguins were packed into large metal vats known as digesters and boiled down for the oil that was contained in their blubber layer. A New Zealand entrepreneur, Joseph Hatch, was one of the main players in this industry and he held a license to conduct this business until the early 1900s.

Shipwrecks

Throughout the island's recent history, shipwrecks have been relatively common, by far the majority occurring on the east coat, when ships were caught out by an unexpected easterly gale. Some of the first to come to grief on the island included the *Campbell Macquarie* in 1813 and the *Betsey*, which was abandoned soon after leaving the island in 1815. Another early shipwreck was the *Caroline*, one of the few to be recorded in the south of the island and for which Caroline Cove is named. Following the *Caroline*, the next recorded shipwreck on the island was the *Lord Nelson*, which floundered on a reef off Handspike Point in 1830. In 1849, the *Countess Cimento* was wrecked near the Nuggets in the north-east of the island.

Nearly 30 years later, the *Bencleugh* arrived at Macquarie Island in the winter of 1877. It was hit by a tremendous easterly storm while at anchor and was driven ashore. Several men were injured and one died. The survivors were shipwrecked for four months, living off the land, until they were rescued by another sealing vessel. About the same time as the *Bencleugh*, a schooner called the *Eagle* was caught in a gale and wrecked on the west coast. The surviving party of nine men and one woman lived in what became known as Eagle Cave for almost two years. Tragically, the day before being rescued the woman died, and to this day the details of her death are unknown.

In 1891, the *Kakanui* was chartered by the New Zealand government to rescue some of Hatch's men, who had run out of food. Her suitability for the voyage was questionable and although she was successfully used to collect most of the sealers, once she left Lusitania Bay she was never heard of again, lost with all hands. The next

Otto Bauer, the head man of the Macquarie Island oiling industry at the time, points out the best landing. State Library of NSW. Home and Away-36117

The remains of the wreck of the Gratitude *sticks up out of the sand at the Nuggets Beach, with Royal Penguins looking on.* National Library of Australia. vn3121458

recorded shipwreck was in late 1898 when the captain of the *Gratitude* left his run too late in the face of deteriorating weather and despite the best efforts of her crew, the ship was eventually driven ashore near the Nuggets by a strong easterly gale. The *Jessie Niccol* also came to grief on the east coast of the island in the early 1900s and the captain, cook and chief mate lost their lives when they refused to abandon their sinking ship. The last ship involved with the sealing industry to come to grief was the *Clyde*, which was wrecked in Buckles Bay on the shores of the Isthmus, near where the main station stands today.

More recent shipping casualties include the Australian government resupply ship the *Endeavour*, which was lost with all hands en route back to Australia in 1914, and the *Nella Dan*, another Australian government resupply ship, blown aground in Buckles Bay while unloading fuel in an easterly gale in 1987.

Early scientific expeditions

Although exploitation of the natural resources was the main aim of most voyages to Macquarie Island in the first 100 years following its discovery, there were several visitors that contributed to the general and scientific knowledge of the island. A Russian expedition led by Admiral Bellinghausen arrived on the island in 1821 and was probably the first to visit the island for scientific research. Some members of the early sealing parties, most notably Thomas Raine, also made notes and observations on the flora and fauna. An American expedition led by Lieutenant Charles Wilkes visited the island in 1840, although they only visited the island briefly. Several researchers from New Zealand universities,

Staff of the 1914 Macquarie Island expedition. National Library of Australia. vn3119274

At the southern end of the Isthmus, this hut was one of the few buildings on Macquarie Island in the early 1900s. National Library of Australia. vn3122716

In 1948, a permanent presence on the island was established for the first time. Much equipment and supplies were needed to set up the station. National Library of Australia. vn2765887

including J. Scott, A. Hamilton and J. Burton, visited in the 1880s and 1890s and collected many valuable plant and animal specimens. Several ships that were taking part in expeditions to Antarctica also stopped at Macquarie Island. Captain Scott visited the island in the *Discovery* in 1901 and Captain Davis visited in the *Nimrod* in 1909 at the close of Shackleton's Antarctic Expedition.

A landmark expedition

In 1911, a party of five was dropped on the shores of Macquarie Island by Sir Douglas Mawson on his way down to east Antarctica. One of the main aims of this party was to establish a communications base that would facilitate communication between Mawson's party in Antarctica and Australia. The five men successfully set up a base and wireless hut and stayed on the island for the next two and a half years. This was a landmark expedition in the history of Macquarie Island and the discoveries and observations made by these men underpinned much of the further research that was to follow in the twentieth century. The island was declared a Nature Reserve in 1933 and this heralded a new era of science and conservation on the island.

Research and management

In 1948 the Australian government established the Australian National Antarctic Research Expeditions (ANARE) station on the Isthmus. This station has been permanently manned since this time, with up to 40 people stationed there over summer and around a dozen people over winter. For the first decade, only men were allowed to stay on the island and the first women visited the island for overnight stays in 1959. It was not until 1976 that the first female overwintered. Today, both men and women live and work on the island, and while the ratio is not usually 50:50, it is much more balanced than during the early years.

Field huts were established around the island and research on numerous aspects has been carried out. In the early days of the ANARE station, the focus tended to be more on the physical sciences, with meteorologists, physicists and geologists dominating the scientific teams. Eventually, biological sciences were elevated to a similar priority and biologists became regular members of overwintering teams. Today, many aspects of the island have been studied, with more recent research tending to focus on areas that can provide a direct conservation benefit to the island.

The island is now a World Heritage Area, a Biosphere Reserve and an Australian Nature Reserve. Much of the management in recent years has focused on removal of the feral pests, and the eradication of the wekas and then the cats has considerably lessened the impact of introduced animals on the native birds. However, over the last ten years the impact of rabbits has dramatically changed the face of the landscape, with major negative impacts. It is encouraging that the Australian and Tasmanian governments have agreed to fund the eradication of rabbits and rodents from the island and the planning for this ambitious project is well underway. The eradication of these feral pests from Macquarie Island is a huge task, and if successful will remove the last of the introduced mammals from the island and finally give it a fighting chance of returning to a pristine and natural state.

THE FUTURE

It is clear to all who have had even the most fleeting contact with these island groups that they are a special part of the world we live in; that they represent unique wilderness areas with incredible biodiversity, which must be preserved and maintained. Nevertheless, all of the island groups described in this book are threatened in some way, whether it be from humans and their actions or more natural causes. At an ecosystem level, humans are the biggest threat that any of the islands face, particularly in the short term. In the longer term, it is possible that changes in global climate will alter the face of the islands as we know them today. However, by far the biggest changes, both positive and negative, are likely to come from the actions of people. Advocacy through tourism, active management by governments and promotion of conservation ideals are all effective methods of ensuring that these places are properly managed and conserved, not just for today, but for the foreseeable future.

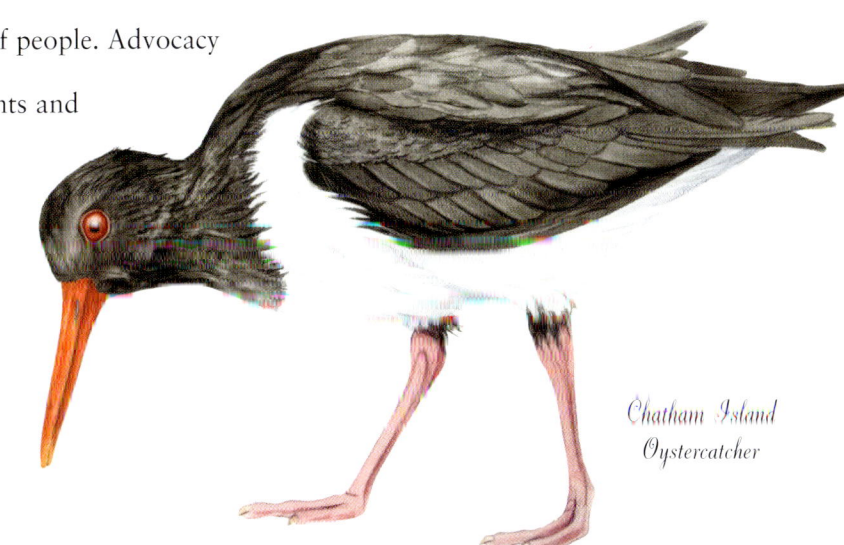

Chatham Island Oystercatcher

A DAY IN PARADISE On Enderby Island, visitors under permit from the New Zealand Department of Conservation can walk around much of the coastline, allowing them ample opportunity to see most of the natural wonders the island has to offer. *ALEKS TERAUDS*

TOURISM

Tourism to the Southern Ocean islands south of New Zealand is not a new phenomenon, but with a growing interest in wilderness and wildlife travel, the number of people wanting to visit these islands is increasing, almost on an annual basis. Inevitably, there are concerns over the possible negative impacts from increased visitation.

History of tourism

The first tourists to the Southern Ocean islands south of New Zealand traveled on the government steamships that periodically checked and resupplied the castaway depots from the 1880s to the 1920s. Passengers could also travel to the Chatham Islands on board the small coastal ships that serviced those islands, but as visits were infrequent, their holidays were sometimes (unintentionally) extended. When a regular air service between New Zealand and the Chatham's became operational, travel to and from these islands became a little easier, but not always more predictable.

After the government steamers were withdrawn from resupplying the New Zealand islands in the 1920s, there was a period of about 50 years when tourist visits were virtually impossible. One of the first to break the tourism drought was the American travel company Lindblad Travel, who visited the subantarctic islands in conjunction with tourist expeditions to Antarctica in the 1970s. Society Expeditions also began taking ships to these islands around that time and continued into the 1980s.

In 1988, New Zealand based Southern Heritage Tours (now Heritage Expeditions), owned by Rodney and Shirley Russ, advertised an expedition to the Auckland Islands on board the research vessel *Acheron*. This marked the beginning of cruises to the subantarctic islands of the region.

CAMPBELL ISLAND WALKERS With Beeman Hill and Mount Honey in the background, tourists reach the top of the boardwalk at the Col Lyall Saddle. With unique opportunities to see Southern Royal Albatrosses, this is one of the highlights for many who visit the wild islands south of New Zealand. *NATHAN RUSS.*

Around the same time, Southern Heritage Tours also advertised a series of tours to the Chatham Islands, which were amongst the first scheduled tours to these islands. While Heritage Expeditions no longer offers dedicated Chatham Island tours, a number of New Zealand tour companies do and people can visit the island in a style of their choosing. With a more reliable air service, hotels, motels, lodges and even a rental car agency on the Chatham Islands, it is now a relatively easy destination to reach and explore. The smaller, offshore islands of this group remain as difficult to visit as they always were; the majority are either privately owned or are nature reserves, with special permission or permits needed for people to go ashore.

A turning point

The summer of 1989–90 was a watershed for subantarctic tourism in the Australasian region. That summer, New Zealand hosted the International Council for Bird Preservation (ICBP) and the International Ornithological Congress (IOC) conferences. Organisers chartered the vessel *Frontier Spirit* (now trading as *Bremen* and operated by Hapag-Lloyd) and promoted a post-conference subantarctic island cruise, which proved to be extremely popular. In the same season, American-based Society Expeditions, hoping to piggyback on the interest generated by these conferences, also promoted two subantarctic cruises.

Tourism management

Faced with this unprecedented demand, the New Zealand Department of Conservation, which was responsible for managing the islands, drew up the first Subantarctic Island Tourism Guidelines. These were based largely on a model developed for tourism in the Galapagos Islands. The guidelines set a limit of 600 visitors per year. The Tasmanian Parks and Wildlife Service, faced with similar pressure for visits to Macquarie Island, wrote similar guidelines and adopted the same figure, but with one major difference—their policy was '600 visitors or four ship visits'. Even though it was eventually removed, for the first few years of tourism to the island the latter clause often made it difficult for small ship operators to obtain permits.

Under these guidelines, companies wanting to conduct tourist expeditions to the subantarctic had to apply for permits, which were issued by the New Zealand government on an annual basis. Often, delays in issuing permits meant that operators were left in the difficult position of not knowing whether a planned and advertised expedition actually had the necessary permits. This problem was solved in 1998 with the introduction of the Subantarctic Conservation Management Strategy (CMS), which allowed for the issuing of five-year concessions and the allocation of permits for the purpose of tourism. The CMS also incorporated the earlier Subantarctic Tourism Guidelines.

The CMS limited tourist landings to the Auckland and Campbell Islands. Three sites (two in the Auckland Islands and one on Campbell Island) were designated as 'large sites' capable of taking 550 visitors each year, with the other 50 held for research and management purposes. Other landing sites on both islands were defined as 'small sites' capable of taking 150 visitors per year.

The CMS also required that all visits to the New Zealand islands should carry a New Zealand Government Observer on board. Originally, government or university

SANDY BAY Tourists to Macquarie Island are only permitted to land at Sandy Bay (shown here) and the Isthmus, where the main station stands. *NATHAN RUSS.*

employees with subantarctic knowledge or experience had been taken as lecturers and guides, and this was considered acceptable. Under the CMS, it became mandatory to have an independent observer on board; these observers were given statutory powers to report to the Department of Conservation on matters of compliance and impact.

The Tasmanian Parks and Wildlife Service adopted a similar approach to tourism on Macquarie Island. Two sites have been nominated on the island—Sandy Bay and Buckles Bay—where visitors are allowed to come ashore. No government observers are required for visits to Macquarie Island, but all visits are preceded by a mandatory on board briefing by the Macquarie Island Ranger-in-charge and visits are supervised by the rangers based on the island. Recently, a new Macquarie Island Management Plan was published by the Tasmanian Parks and Wildlife Service and this incorporates the tourism guidelines.

The changing face of tourism

Tourism has changed significantly since the original guidelines were drawn up, particularly in the New Zealand region. When the original guidelines were drawn up, with the exception of two fledgling New Zealand companies, tourism was limited to a small number of international companies offering worldwide itineraries. These itineraries varied from year to year and it was rare that the same itineraries were offered in two consecutive years. Consequently, the New Zealand subantarctic islands that were visited changed each year and the number of tourists landing on them was variable and difficult to predict.

When Communism collapsed in Russia in 1992, many vessels suitable for expedition cruising became available for lease or purchase and the number of companies offering expedition cruising increased significantly, particularly in polar regions. This increase coincided with an exponential growth in the popularity of 'cruising' and

THE FUTURE

a growing interest in ecotourism. The demand for ecotourism has not abated since this time and there is an increasing demand for visits to the subantarctic islands south of New Zealand. The islands lie as stepping stones to the Antarctic, and with an increase in Antarctic tourism and overcrowding becoming an issue in the Antarctic Peninsula, more and more operators are looking at opportunities in the Ross Sea. Heritage Expeditions has promoted the subantarctic islands as a destination and they are becoming increasingly popular for what they have to offer and not just because they happen to be on the way to Antarctica.

At the time of writing, a review of the CMS is imminent and tourist operators wait to see how a revised version will deal with the changing nature of the industry. Officially, tourism to the subantarctic is sanctioned by the respective governments, but not everybody agrees that it is a proper use of these magnificent nature reserves. Some argue that they should be left completely alone. Others suggest that by allowing people to visit these islands, it creates ambassadors and advocates for their conservation. For instance, recently over 100 letters were sent to the Australian and Tasmanian governments by people who had visited Macquarie Island, urging them to fund a proposal to eradicate rabbits and rodents on the island. There is little doubt that these letters—many of them from international visitors—helped to convince the federal government something needed to be done. Had these people been unable to visit Macquarie Island, it is doubtful that even a handful would have been interested in the issue.

THE PENGUIN SLIDE Snares Crested Penguins ascend and descend these steep and slippery cliffs on a daily basis, never failing to astound visitors that are fortunate enough to see them. *AARON RUSS.*

A FINAL WORD

It is rather ironic, as more of the world becomes accessible and we talk about a global village, that these islands are in some ways more remote today than they were when they were first discovered. While it is true that we know more about them than ever, how much do we really understand about the interrelationship between them and the ocean in which they occur? Collectively, these islands are an integral part of what is perhaps one of the largest and complex ecosystems in the world—the Southern Ocean or subantarctic ecosystem. The world is only now waking up to just how important this vast ecosystem is as a barometer of the health of the globe and as such it is important that these islands are managed in an international context as well as at the regional level which we have described here.

Much of the current research on these islands is focused on restorative management— removing introduced predators and plants with the aim of giving the islands a chance to return to as natural a state as possible. There is often a considerable financial cost to these projects, and it is not always easy to convince governments of the value or necessity of the required investment. Fortunately, both the Australian and New Zealand governments have been proactive in this regard and there have been some significant results, with eradications of introduced animals on Campbell, Enderby and Macquarie Islands. Another major operation, to eradicate rabbits and rodents, is planned for Macquarie Island, while the feasibility of eradicating pigs and cats on the main Auckland Island is under investigation. Even so, more could be done if the resources were made available.

A major challenge facing government decision makers in the future is to develop strategies and management plans beyond the restorative stage. It is not always enough to simply 'clean up the islands and lock them away'. Some of the pressures these islands will face in the future are predictable. Wilderness and nature tourism will grow and so will the associated demands on accessibility. Simply denying access does not seem to be a feasible solution in most cases, particularly as the value of advocacy and increasing awareness has already been demonstrated on numerous occasions. Nevertheless, in the face of increasing demand, providing a meaningful wilderness experience and a range of activities will also be challenging. Clearly, there are risks with tourism of this nature and impacts need to be monitored and managed.

Less predictable than the burgeoning tourist industry in the region, is the potential exploitation of natural resources. Oil is known to exist in the vicinity of some of these islands; just how much is unknown, but the ancient sedimentary rock strata of the Campbell Plateau has the potential to hold vast reserves of natural resources. With rising demand and price increases, it will be interesting to see how the government and the relevant legislation holds up under the inevitable pressure of exploration companies.

Exploitation of other natural living resources is also an issue in the region. Several fishing industries already operate under permit from the respective governments. These include a Patagonian Toothfish (*Dissostichus eleginoides*) industry around Macquarie Island and a large squid fishery around the Auckland Islands. While the government can regulate these industries within their territorial waters (within 200 nautical miles of land), there is little that can be done to stop exploitation of natural resources beyond these limits. Most of the birds and seals

ALBATROSS RESEARCH On seldom visited Adams Island in the Auckland Island group a researcher makes his way back to the hut after a day of working with the albatrosses. The convoluted inlets and bays of Carnley Harbour and the main Auckland Island can be seen in the background. *KATH WALKER.*

that breed on these islands spend the majority of their lives outside the political boundaries that offer this protection and as such are vulnerable to by-catch issues and competition for food resources. In a world of diminishing natural resources and increasing technology to harvest those resources, governments need to consider carefully the management strategies for these industries.

It is impossible to predict every possible scenario or situation that may affect these islands and the wildlife that inhabits them. Nevertheless, it is critical that governments ensure both funding and opportunities are available for research so that any necessary responses can be immediate and informed. Only then will the remarkable wildlife and natural values of these islands have a chance of surviving, in a world where biodiversity is decreasing at an alarming, and unsustainable rate.

PITT ISLAND CIRCA 1970 The author, Rodney Russ (centre) with former Wildlife Service Senior Fauna Conservation Officer, Brian Bell (left) and Wildlife Trainee, Les Scown, inspecting a proposed fenceline for the Southern Glory Block Reserve on Pitt Island. NEW ZEALAND ARCHIVES AANS 8131 W5154 92

BIBLIOGRAPHY

Introduction

1. Michaux, B. and Leschen, R.A.B. (2005) East meets west: biogeology of the Campbell Plateau. *Biological Journal of the Linnean Society,* **86**:95-115.

2. Chown, S.L.C., Rodrigues, A.S.L., Gremmen, N.J.M. and Gaston, K.J. (2001) World Heritage status and conservation of Southern Ocean islands. *Conservation Biology,* **15**:550-557.

3. Adams, C.J. and Cullen, D.J. (1978) Potassium-argon ages of granites and metasediments from Bounty Islands area, southwest Pacific Ocean. *Journal of the Royal Society of New Zealand,* **8**:127-132.

4. Adams, C.J. (1981) Migration of late Cenozoic volcanism in the South Island of New Zealand and in the Campbell Plateau. *Nature,* **294**:153-155.

5. Adams, C.J., Morris, P.A. and Beggs, J.M. (1979) Age and correlation of volcanic rocks of Campbell Island and metamorphic basement of the Campbell Plateau, southwest Pacific. *New Zealand Journal of Geology and Geophysics,* **22**:679-691.

6. Quilty, P.G. (2007) Origin and evolution of the sub-antarctic islands: the foundation. *Papers and Proceedings of the Royal Society of Tasmania,* **141**:35-58.

7. Cook, R.A., Sutherland, R. and Zhu, H. (1999) Cretaceous-Cenozoic geology and petroleum systems of the Great Southern Basin, New Zealand. *Institute of Geological and Nuclear Sciences Monograph,* **20**:1-190.

8. Ross, C.S.J.C. (1847) *A Voyage of Discovery and Research in the Southern and Antarctic Regions. Volume 1: August '39-April '41.* David and Charles Reprints (1969). Great Britain.

9. Rintoul, S.R. (2000) Southern Ocean currents and climate. *Papers and Proceedings of the Royal Society of Tasmania,* **133**:41-50.

10. Selkirk, P.M., Seppelt, R.D. and Selkirk, D.R. (1990) *Subantarctic Macquarie Island Environment and Biology.* Cambridge University Press, Cambridge.

11. Peat, N. (2003) *Subantarctic New Zealand A Rare Heritage.* New Zealand Department of Conservation, Invercargill.

12. Pendlebury, S.F. and Barnes-Keoghan, I.P. (2007) Climate and climate change in the sub-Antarctic. *Papers and Proceedings of the Royal Society of Tasmania,* **141**:67-81.

13. Smith, V.R. (1993) Climate change and ecosystem functioning: a focus for subantarctic research in the 1990s. *South African Journal of Science,* **89**:69-71.

Chatham Islands

1. New Zealand Department of Conservation (Ed) (1996) *The Chatham Islands – Heritage and Conservation.* Canterbury University Press. Christchurch.

2. Miskelly, C. (Ed) (1999) Chatham Islands Heritage and Conservation. Canterbury University Press / New Zealand Department of Conservation, Christchurch.

3. Wills Johnson, T.M.K. (1996) Introduction. In: New Zealand Department of Conservation (Ed) *The Chatham Islands - Heritage and Conservation.* Canterbury University Press, Christchurch. pp 11-20.

4. Atkinson, I. (1996) Major Habitats. In: New Zealand Department of Conservation (Ed) *The Chatham Islands - Heritage and Conservation,* Canterbury University Press, Christchurch. pp 49-61.

5. King, M. and Morrison, R. (1990) *A Land Apart: The Chatham Islands of New Zealand.* Random Century, Auckland.

6. Campbell, H. (1996) Geology. In: New Zealand Department of Conservation (Ed) *The Chatham Islands - Heritage and Conservation,* Canterbury University Press, Christchurch. pp 34-48.

7. McGlone, M.S. (2002) The late quaternary peat, vegetation and climate history of the southern oceanic islands of New Zealand. *Quaternary Science Reviews,* **21**:683-707.

8. Larter, R.D., Cunningham, A.P., Barker, P.F., Gohl, K. and Nitsche, F.O. (2002) Tectonic evolution of the Pacific margin of Antarctica 1. Late Cretaceous tectonic reconstructions. *Journal of Geophysical Research-Solid Earth,* **107**: 2345, doi: 10.1029/2000JB000052

9. Campbell, H.J., Andrews, P.B., Beu, A.G., Maxwell, P.A., Edwards, A.R., Laird, M.G., Hornibrook, N.D., Mildenhall, D.C., Watters, W.A., Buckeridge, J.S., Lee, D.E., Strong, C.P., Wilson, G.J. and Hayward, B.W. (1993) Cretaceous-Cenozoic geology and biostratigraphy of the Chatham Islands, New Zealand. *Institute of Geological and Nuclear Sciences Monograph,* **2**:1-269.

10. Stillwell, J.D., Consoli, C.P., Sutherland, D., Salisbury, S., Rich, T.H., Vickers-Rich, P.A., Currie, P.J. and Wilson, G.J. (2006) Dinosaur sanctuary on the Chatham Islands, southwest Pacific: first record of theropods from the K-T boundary Takatika Grit. *Palaeogeography Palaeoclimatology Palaeoecology,* **230**:243-250.

11. Wood, R.A. and Herzer, R.H. (1993) The Chatham Rise, New Zealand, In: Balance, P.F. (Ed) *South Pacific Sedimentary Basins.* Elsevier, Auckland. pp 329-349.

12. Forsyth, P.J., Barell, D.J.A. and Jongens, R. (2008) *Geology of the Christchurch Area 1:250000 geological map 16.* Institute of the Geological and Nuclear Sciences, Lower Hutt.

13. Given, D. (1996) Flora. In: New Zealand Department of Conservation (Ed) *The Chatham Islands - Heritage and Conservation*, Canterbury University Press, Christchurch. pp 80-92.

14. Walls, G., Baird, A., de Lange, P. and Sawyer, J. (2003) *Threatened Plants of the Chatham Islands*. New Zealand Department of Conservation, Wellington.

15. Parsons, M.J. (1985) New Zealand seaweed flora and its relationships. *New Zealand Journal of Marine and Freshwater Research*, **19**:131-138.

16. Schiel, D. (1996) Marine Life. In: New Zealand Department of Conservation (Ed) *The Chatham Islands - Heritage and Conservation*, Canterbury University Press, Christchurch. pp 62-73.

17. Schiel, D.R., Andrew, N.L. and Foster, M.S. (1995) The structure of subtidal algal and invertebrate assemblages at the Chatham Islands, New Zealand. *Marine Biology*, **123**:355-367.

18. Aikman, H. and Miskelly, C.M. (2004) *Birds of the Chatham Islands*. Department of Conservation, Wellington.

19. Crockett, D. (1994) Rediscovery of the Chatham Island Taiko *Pterodroma magentae*. *Notornis*, **41**(S):49-60.

20. Imber, M.J. (1993) Seabirds recorded at the Chatham Islands 1960 to May 1993. *Notornis*, **41**(S):97-108.

21. Bell, M. and Bell, D. (2003) The recolonisation of Mangere Island by New Zealand White-faced Storm Petrels (*Pelagodroma marina maoriana*). *Notornis*, **50**:43-44.

22. West, J.A. and Nilsson, R.T. (1994) Habitat use and burrow densities of burrow-nesting seabirds on South-east Island, Chatham Islands. *Notornis*, **41**(S):27-40.

23. Bell, M. and Bell, D. (2000) Census of the three shag species in the Chatham Islands. *Notornis*, **47**:148-153.

24. Bester, A.J. and Charteris, M. (2005) The second census of Chatham Island Shag and Pitt Island Shag - are numbers declining? *Notornis*, **52**:6-10.

25. Dugdale, J. and Emberson, R. (1996) Insects. In: New Zealand Department of Conservation (Ed) *The Chatham Islands - Heritage and Conservation*, Canterbury University Press, Christchurch. pp 93-98.

26. King, M. (1996) Historic Sites. In: New Zealand Department of Conservation (Ed) *The Chatham Islands - Heritage and Conservation*, Canterbury University Press, Christchurch. pp 21-33.

27. Richards, R. (1982) *Whaling and Sealing on the Chatham Islands*. Roebuck Society (Publication Number 21), Canberra.

28. Richards, R. (1972) A population distribution map of the Moriories of Chatham Island, circa 1790. *Journal of the Polynesian Society.* **81**.

Bounty Islands

1. Taylor, R. (2006) *Straight through from London The Antipodes and Bounty Islands, New Zealand*. Heritage Expeditions New Zealand Ltd, Christchurch.

2. Speight, R. (1909) Physiography and geology of the Auckland, Bounty and Antipodes Islands. In: Chilton, C. (Ed) *The Subantarctic Islands of New Zealand Volume 2*. Philosophical Institute of Canterbury, Wellington. pp 705-744.

3. Beggs, J.M., Challis, G.A. and Cook, R.A. (1990) Basement geology of the Campbell Plateau - implications for correlation of the Campbell Magnetic Anomaly System. *New Zealand Journal of Geology and Geophysics*, **33**:401-404.

4. Carter, R.M., Carter, L. and Davy, B. (1994) Seismic stratigraphy of the Bounty Trough, south-west Pacific-Ocean. *Marine and Petroleum Geology*, **11**:79-93.

5. Adams, C.J. (2008) Geochronology of Paleozoic terranes at the Pacific Ocean margin of Zealandia. *Gondwana Research*, **13**:250-258.

6. Fraser, C. (1986) *Beyond the Roaring Forties New Zealand's Subantarctic Islands*. Government Printing Office, Wellington.

7. Peat, N. (2003) Department of Conservation, Invercargill.

8. Wardle, P. (1991) *Vegetation of New Zealand*. Cambridge University Press, Cambridge.

9. Amey, J., Lord, J.M. and de Lange, P. (2007) First record of a vascular plant from the Bounty Islands: *Lepidium oleraceum* (nau, Cook's scurvy grass) (Brassicaceae). *New Zealand Journal of Botany*, **45**:87-90.

10. Nelson, W.A. (1999) *Marginariella parsonsii* (Seirococcaceae, Phaeophyta), a new species from the Bounty and Antipodes Islands, southern New Zealand. *New Zealand Journal of Botany*, **37**:732-735.

11. Taylor, G.A. (2000) Action Plan for Seabird Conservation in New Zealand, Part A - Threatened Seabirds. *Threatened Species Publication No. 16*. New Zealand Department of Conservation, Biodiversity Recovery Unit, Wellington.

12. Robertson, C.J.R. and van Tets, G.F. (1982) The status of birds at the Bounty Islands. *Notornis*, **29**:311-336.

13. Taylor, R.H. (1982) New Zealand Fur Seals at the Bounty Islands. *New Zealand Journal of Marine and Freshwater Research*, **16**:1-9.

14. Taylor, R.H. (1996) Distribution, abundance and pup production of the New Zealand Fur Seal (*Arctocephalus forsteri* Lesson) at the Bounty Islands. *Science for Conservation Series*, **32**. New Zealand Department of Conservation, Wellington.

15. Williams, G.R. (1982) Species-area and similar relationships between insects and vascular plants of the southern outlying islands of New Zealand. *New Zealand Journal of Ecology*, **5**:86-96.

16. Marris, J.W.M. (2000) The beetle (Coleoptera) fauna of the Antipodes Islands, with comments on the impact of mice; and an annotated checklist of the insect and arachnid fauna. *Journal of the Royal Society of New Zealand*, **30**:169-195.

17. Patrick, B. (1994) Antipodes Island Lepidoptera. *Journal of the Royal Society of New Zealand*, **24**:91-116.

18. Smithers, C.N. (1999) *Sandrapsocus clarki*, an unusual new genus and species of Elipsocidae (Insecta : Psocoptera) from the Bounty Islands. *Journal of the Royal Society of New Zealand*, **29**:159-164.

19. McNab, R. (1907) *Murihiku and the Southern Islands*. William Smith, Invercargill.

20. Richards, R. (1982) Roebuck Society (Publication Number 21), Canberra.

21. Chilton, C. (1909) The subantarctic islands of New Zealand and the history of their scientific investigation. In: Chilton, C. (Ed) *The Subantarctic Islands of New Zealand Vol 1*. Philosophical Institute of Canterbury: Wellington. pp xiv-xxxv.

22. Suter, H. (1909) The mollusca of the subantarctic islands of New Zealand. In: Chilton, C. (Ed) *The Subantarctic Islands of New Zealand Vol 1*. Philosophical Institute of Canterbury: Wellington. p. 1-57.

23. Clark, G., Booth, A. and Amey, J. (1998) *The* Totorore *expedition to the Bounty Islands, New Zealand, October 1997 to January 1998*. New Zealand Department of Conservation (Unpublished Report), Invercargill.

Antipodes Islands

1. Taylor, R. (2006) Heritage Expeditions New Zealand Ltd, Christchurch.

2. Peat, N. (2003) Department of Conservation, Invercargill.

3. Fraser, C. (1986) Government Printing Office, Wellington.

4. Tulloch, A.J., Ireland, T., Parkinson, D. and Turnbull, I.M. (2003) *Nature of eastern Campbell Plateau basement: age and character of granite exolith from a late Cenozoic lava flow on Antipodes Island*. Geological Society of New Zealand (Miscellaneous Publication), Dunedin.

5. Gamble, J.A. and Adams, C.J. (1990) Antipodes Islands. In: LeMasurier, W.E. and Thompson, J.W. (Eds) *Volcanoes of the Antarctic Plate and Southern Oceans*. American Geophysical Union (Antarctic Research Series 48), pp 400-403.

6. Quilty, P.G. (2007) *Papers and Proceedings of the Royal Society of Tasmania*, **14**:35-58.

7. Cullen, D.J. (1969) Quaternary volcanism at Antipodes Islands - its bearing on structural interpretation of the southwest Pacific. *Journal of Geophysical Research*, **74**:4213-4220.

8. Gamble, J.A., Morris, P.A. and Adams, C.J. (1986) The geology, petrology and geochemistry of Cenozoic volcanic rocks from the Campbell Plateau and Chatham Rise. In: Smith, I.E.M (Ed) *Late Cenozoic Volcanism in New Zealand*. Royal Society of New Zealand (Bulletin 23). pp 344-365.

9. Panter, K.S., Blusztajn, J., Hart, S.R., Kyle, P.R., Esser, R. and McIntosh, W.C. (2006) The origin of HIMU in the SW Pacific: evidence from intraplate volcanism in southern New Zealand and subantarctic islands. *Journal of Petrology*, **47**:1673-1704.

10. Speight, R. (1909) In: Chilton, C. (Ed) *The Subantarctic Islands of New Zealand Volume 2*. Philosophical Institute of Canterbury, Wellington. pp 705-744.

11. Godley, E.J. (1989) The flora of Antipodes Island. *New Zealand Journal of Botany*, **27**:531-563.

12. Cockayne, L. (1904) A botanical excursion during midwinter to the southern islands of New Zealand. *Transactions of the New Zealand Institute*, **36**:225-330.

13. Cheeseman, T.F. (1909) On the systematic botany of the islands to the south of New Zealand. In: Chilton, C. (Ed) *The Subantarctic Islands of New Zealand Volume 2*. Philosophical Institute of Canterbury, Wellington. pp 389-471.

14. Cockayne, L. (1909) The ecological botany of the subantarctic islands of New Zealand. In: Chilton, C. (Ed) *The Subantarctic Islands of New Zealand Volume 1*. Philosophical Institute of Canterbury, Wellington. pp 182-235.

15. Wardle, P. (1991) Cambridge University Press, Cambridge.

16. Hay, C.H., Adams, N.M. and Parsons, M.J. (1985) Marine algae of the southern islands of New Zealand. *National Museum of New Zealand, Miscellaneous Series* **11**.

17. Nelson, W.A. (1999) *New Zealand Journal of Botany*, 37:137-145.

18. Parsons, M.J. (1985) *New Zealand Journal of Marine and Freshwater Research*, 19:131-138.

19. Walker, K. and Elliott, G. (2002) *Monitoring Antipodean wandering albatross, 1995/96*. New Zealand Department of Conservation (*DOC Science Internal Series*), Wellington.

20. Tennyson, A., Imber, M. and Taylor, R. (1998) Numbers of Black-browed mollymawks (*Diomedea m. melanophrys*) and White-capped mollymawks (*D. cauta steadi*) at the Antipodes Islands in 1994-95 and their population trends in the New Zealand region. *Notornis*, 45:157-166.

21. Tennyson, A., Taylor, R., Taylor, G., Imber, M. and Green, T. (2002) Unusual bird records from the Antipodes Islands in 1978-1995, with a summary of other species recorded at the group. *Notornis*, 49:241-245.

22. Bell, E.A. (2002) *Grey petrels (Procellaria cinerea) on Antipodes Island, New Zealand: research feasibility, April to June 2001*. New Zealand Department of Conservation (unpublished report), Wellington.

23. Imber, M.J. (1983) The lesser petrels of Antipodes Islands, with notes from Prince Edward and Gough Islands. *Notornis*, 30:283-298.

24. Wiltshire, A.J. and Hamilton, S. (2003) Population estimate for Northern Giant Petrels (*Macronectes halli*) on Antipodes Island, New Zealand. *Notornis*, 50:128-132.

25. Imber, M.J., Bell, B.D. and Bell, E.A. (2005) Antipodes Island birds in Autumn 2001. *Notornis*, 52:125-132.

26. Warham, J. and Bell, B.D. (1979) The birds of the Antipodes Islands, New Zealand. *Notornis*, 26:121-169.

27. Taylor, G.A. (2000) *Threatened Species Publication No. 16*. New Zealand Department of Conservation, Biodiversity Recovery Unit, Wellington.

28. Sagar, P.M., Murdoch, R., Sagar, M.W. and Thompson, D.R. (2005) Rockhopper penguin (*Eudyptes chrysocome filholi*) foraging at Antipodes Islands. *Notornis*, 52:75-80.

29. Greene, T.C. (1999) Aspects of the ecology of Antipodes Island Parakeet (*Cyanoramphus unicolor*) and Reischek's Parakeet (*C. novaezelandiae hochstetteri*) on Antipodes Island, October - November 1995. *Notornis*, 46:301-310.

30. Taylor, R.H. (1975) Some ideas on speciation in New Zealand parakeets. *Notornis*, 22:110-121.

31. Taylor, R.H. (1985) Status, habits and conservation of *Cyanoramphus* parakeets in the New Zealand region. In: Moors, P.J. (Ed) *Conservation of island birds - Case studies for the management of threatened species*. Cambridge International Council for Bird Preservation (Technical Publication No. 3). Cambridge. pp 195-211

32. Taylor, R.H. (1992) Fur seals on the Antipodes Islands. *Journal of the Royal Society of New Zealand*, 22:109-122.

33. Marris, J.W.M. (2000) *Journal of the Royal Society of New Zealand*, 30:169-195.

34. Patrick, B. (1994) *Journal of the Royal Society of New Zealand*, 24:91-116.

35. McNab, R. (1907) William Smith, Invercargill.

36. Chilton, C. (1909) In: Chilton, C. (Ed) *The Subantarctic Islands of New Zealand Volume 1*. Philosophical Institute of Canterbury, Wellington. pp xiv-xxxv.

37. Murphy, R.C. (1938) *Birds collected during the Whitney South Sea Expedition*. The American Museum of Natural History, New York.

CAMPBELL ISLAND

1. Peat, N. (2003) Department of Conservation, Invercargill.

2. Morris, P.A. and Gamble, J.A. (1990) Campbell Island. In: LeMasurier, W.E. and Thompson, J.W. (Eds) *Volcanoes of the Antarctic Plate and Southern Oceans*. American Geophysical Union (Antarctic Research Series 48). pp 474-475.

3. McGlone, M.S. (2002) *Quaternary Science Reviews*, 21:683-707.

4. Hollis, C.J., Beu, A.G., Raine, J.I., Strong, C.P., Turnbull, I.M., Waghorn, D.B. and Wilson, G.J. (1997) Integrated biostratigraphy of Cretaceaous-Paleogene strata on Campbell Island, southwest Pacific. *Institute of Geological and Nuclear Sciences Report 97/25*. pp 1-47.

5. Quilty, P.G. (2007) *Papers and Proceedings of the Royal Society of Tasmania*, 14:35-58.

7. Adams, C.J., Morris, P.A. and Beggs, J.M. (1979) *New Zealand Journal of Geology and Geophysics*, 22:679-691.

8. Fraser, C. (1986) Government Printing Office, Wellington.

9. Marshall, P. (1909) The geology of Campbell Island and the Snares. In: Chilton, C. (Ed) *The Subantarctic Islands of New Zealand Volume 2*. Philosophical Institute of Canterbury, Wellington. pp 680-704.

10. Hooker, J.D. (1847) *The Botany of the Antarctic Voyage of H.M. Discovery ships* Erebus *and* Terror *in the years 1839-1843, under the command of Captain Sir James Clark Ross, Vol 1: Flora Antarctica. Pt 1: Botany of Lord Auckland's Group and Campbell's Island*. Reeve, London.

11. Ross, C.S.J.C. (1847) David and Charles Reprints (1969), Great Britain.

12. Kirk, T. (1891) On the botany of the Antarctic Islands. *Reports of the Australian Association for the Advancement of Science*, 3:213.

13. Cockayne, L. (1904) *Transactions of the New Zealand Institute*, 36:225-330.

14. Cockayne, L. (1909) In: Chilton, C. (Ed) *The Subantarctic Islands of New Zealand Volume 1*. Philosophical Institute of Canterbury, Wellington. pp 182-235

15. Cheeseman, T.F. (1909) In: Chilton, C. (Ed) *The Subantarctic Islands of New Zealand Volume 2*. Philosophical Institute of Canterbury, Wellington. pp. 389-471.

16. Godley, E.J. (1969) Additions and corrections to the flora of the Auckland and Campbell Islands. *New Zealand Journal of Botany*, 7:336-348.

17. Meurk, C.D. (1982) Regeneration of sub-Antarctic plants on Campbell Island following exclusion of sheep. *New Zealand Journal of Ecology*, 5:51-58.

18. Meurk, C.D., Foggo, M.N., Thomson, B.M., Bathurst, E.T.J. and Crompton, M.B. (1994) Ion-rich precipitation and vegetation patterns on sub-Antarctic Campbell Island. *Arctic and Alpine Research*, 26:281-289.

19. Meurk, C.D., Foggo, M.N. and Wilson, J.B. (1994) The vegetation of sub-Antarctic Campbell Island. *New Zealand Journal of Ecology*, 18:123-168.

20. McGlone, M., Wilmshurst, J. and Meurk, C. (2007) Climate, fire, farming and the recent vegetation history of subantarctic Campbell Island. *Earth and Environmental Science Transactions of the Royal Society of Edinburgh*, 98:71-84.

21. McGlone, M.S., Moar, N.T., Wardle, P. and Meurk, C.D. (1997) Late-glacial and Holocene vegetation and environment of Campbell Island, far southern New Zealand. *Holocene*, 7:1-12.

22. Moore, P.J., Scott, J.J., Joyce, L.J. and Peart, M. (1997) Southern Royal Albatross *Diomedea epomophora epomophora* census on Campbell Island, 4 January -6 February 1996, and a review of population figures. *Science and Research Series*, 101. New Zealand Department of Conservation, Wellington.

23. Taylor, G.A. (2000) *Threatened Species Publication No. 16*. New Zealand Department of Conservation, Biodiversity Recovery Unit, Wellington.

24. Moore, P.J. (2004) Abundance and population trends of mollymawks on Campbell Island. *Science for Conservation*, 242. New Zealand Department of Conservation, Wellington.

25. Waugh, S.M., Weimerskirch, H., Moore, P.J. and Sagar, P.M. (1999) Population dynamics of Black-browed and Grey-headed Albatrosses *Diomedea melanophrys* and *D. chrysostoma* at Campbell Island, New Zealand, 1942-96. *Ibis*, 141:216-225.

26. Moore, P.J. (1996) Light-mantled Sooty Albatross on Campbell Island, 1995-96: a pilot investigation. *Science for Conservation Series*, 41. New Zealand Department of Conservation, Wellington.

27. Cunningham, D.M. and Moors, P.J. (1994) The decline of Rockhopper Penguins *Eudyptes chrysocome* at Campbell Island, Southern Ocean and the influence of rising sea temperatures. *Emu*, 94:27-36.

28. Moore, P.J., Fletcher, D. and Amey, J. (2001) Population estimates of Yellow-eyed Penguins, *Megadyptes antipodes*, on Campbell Island, 1987-98. *Emu* 101:225-236.

29. Wiltshire, A.J. and Scofield, P. (2000) Population estimate of breeding Northern Giant Petrels *Macronectes halli* on Campbell Island, New Zealand. *Emu*, 100:186-191.

30. Kinsky, F.C. (1969) New and rare birds on Campbell Island. *Notornis*, 16:225-236.

31. Robertson, C.J.R. and Bell, B.D. (1984) Seabirds status and conservation in the New Zealand region. In: Croxall, J.P., Evans, P.G.H. and Schreiber, R.W. (Eds) *Status and Conservation of the Worlds Seabirds*. Cambridge International Council for Bird Preservation (Technical Publication No. 2). Cambridge. pp 573-586.

32. Judd, N. (1998) Find of the decade ? *New Zealand Geographic*, 37:8.

33. Miskelly, C.M. (2000) Historical records of snipe from Campbell Island, New Zealand. *Notornis*, 47:131-140.

34. Childerhouse, S., Gibbs, N., McAlister, G., McConkey, S., McConnell, H., McNally, N. and Sutherland, D. (2005) Distribution, abundance and growth of New Zealand sea lion *Phocarctos hookeri* pups on Campbell Island. *New Zealand Journal of Marine and Freshwater Research*, 39:889-898.

35. Gressitt, J.L. (1964) Insects of Campbell Island. *Pacific Insects Monograph*, 7:1-63.

36. Koy, M.K. and Death, R.G. (2000) Stream invertebrate communities of Campbell Island. *Hydrobiologia* 439:115-124.

37. Michaux, B. and Leschen, R.A.B. (2005) Biological Journal of the Linnean Society, **86**:95-115.

38. McNab, R. (1907) William Smith, Invercargill.

39. Chilton, C. (1909) In: Chilton,C. (Ed) *The Subantarctic Islands of New Zealand Vol 1*. Philosophical Institute of Canterbury, Wellington. pp xiv-xxxv.

40. Kerr, I.S. (1976) *Campbell Island: A History*. A.H and A.W. Reed, Wellington.

41. Kerr, I.S. and Judd, N. (1978) *Marlborough Whalers at Campbell Island. 1909-1916 recollections of J. Timms*. Department of Lands and Survey, Wellington.

42. Bailey, A.M. and Sorensen, J.H. (1962) *Subantarctic Campbell Island*. Denver Museum of Natural History (Proceedings Number 10), Denver.

Auckland Islands

1. Taylor, R.H. (1971) Influence of man on vegetation and wildlife of Enderby and Rose Islands, Auckland Islands. *New Zealand Journal of Botany*, **9**:225-268.

2. Gamble, J.A. and Adams, C.J. (1990) Auckland Islands. In: LeMasurier, W.E. and Thompson, J.W. (Eds) *Volcanoes of the Antarctic Plate and Southern Oceans*. American Geophysical Union (Antarctic Research Series 48). pp 470-473.

3. Speight, R. (1909) In: Chilton, C. (Ed) *The Subantarctic Islands of New Zealand Volume 2*. Philosophical Institute of Canterbury, Wellington. pp 705-744.

4. Peat, N. (2003) New Zealand Department of Conservation, Invercargill.

5. Ritchie, D.D. and Turnbull, I.M. (1985) Cenozoic sedimentary rocks at Carnley Harbour, Auckland Island, Campbell Plateau. *New Zealand Journal of Geology and Geophysics*, **28**:23-41.

6. Fleming, C.A. (1965) Two-storied cliffs at the Auckland Islands. *Transactions of the Royal Society of New Zealand. Geology* **3**:171-174.

7. Fleming, C.A. (1975) An outline of the geology of the Auckland Islands. In: Yaldwyn, J.C. (Ed) *Preliminary results from the Auckland Islands Expedition 1972-1973*. Department of Lands and Survey, Wellington. pp 411-415.

8. Fleming, C.A., Mildenhall, D.C. and Moar, N.T. (1976) Quaternary sediments and plant microfossils from Enderby Island, Auckland Islands. *Journal of the Royal Society of New Zealand*, **6**:433-458.

9. Fraser, C. (1986) Government Printing Office, Wellington.

10. McEwen, M. (2006) *Charles Fleming's Cape Expedition Diary, Auckland Islands, 1942-43*. McEwen Associates, Wellington.

11. McFadgen, B.G. and Yaldwyn, J.C. (1984) Holocene sand dunes on Enderby-Island, Auckland Islands. *New Zealand Journal of Geology and Geophysics*, **27**:27-33.

12. Quilty, P.G. (2007) *Papers and Proceedings of the Royal Society of Tasmania*, **14**:35-58.

13. Johnson, P.N. and Campbell, D.J. (1975) Vascular plants of the Auckland Islands. *New Zealand Journal of Botany*, **13**:665-720.

14. Meurk, C. (1982) Supplementary notes on plant distributions of the subantarctic Auckland Islands. *New Zealand Journal of Botany*, **20**:373-380.

15. Hooker, J.D. (1847) Reeve, London.

16. Ross, C.S.J.C. (1847) David and Charles Reprints (1969), Great Britain.

17. Cheeseman, T.F. (1909) In: Chilton, C. (Ed) *The Subantarctic Islands of New Zealand Volume 2*. Philosophical Institute of Canterbury, Wellington. pp 389-471.

18. Parsons, M.J. (1985) *New Zealand Journal of Marine and Freshwater Research*, **19**:131-138.

19. Baker, G.B., Jensz, K., Double, M.C., and Cunningham, R. (2007) *Data collection of demographic, distributional and trophic information on selected seabirds species to allow estimation of effects of fishing on population viability*. Report prepared for the New Zealand Ministry of Fisheries, PRO2006-01F, April 2007. Latitude 42 Environmental Consultants, Kettering, Australia. www.latitude42.com.au.

20. Walker, K. and Elliott, G. (1999) Population changes and biology of the Wandering Albatross *Diomedea exulans gibsoni* at the Auckland Islands. *Emu*, **99**:239-247.

21. Bell, B.D. (1975) Report on the birds of the Auckland Islands Expedition 1972-73, In: Yaldwyn, J.C. (Ed) *Preliminary results from the Auckland Islands Expedition 1972-1973*. Department of Lands and Survey, Wellington. pp 136-142.

22. Robertson, C.J.R. and Bell, B.D. (1984) In: Croxall, J.P., Evans, P.G.H. and Schreiber, R.W. (Eds) Cambridge International Council for Bird Preservation (Technical Publication No. 2). Cambridge. pp 573-586.

23. Moore, P.J. and McClelland, P.J. (1990) Notes on birds of the Auckland Islands, November-December 1989. *Science and Research Internal Report No. 93*. New Zealand Department of Conservation: Wellington.

24. Moore, P.J. (1992). *Notornis*, **39**:1-15.

25. Moore, P.J. and Moffat, R.D. (1992) Predation of Yellow-eyed Penguins by Hooker's Sea Lion. *Notornis*, **29**:68-69.

26. Moore, P.J. and Walker, K. (1989) Auckland Island Teal on Ewing and Adams Island, Auckland Islands, November, 1989. *Science and Research Internal Report*, **82**. New Zealand Department of Conservation, Wellington

27. Chilvers, B.L., Wilkinson, I.S. and Childerhouse, S. (2007) New Zealand Sea Lion, *Phocarctos hookeri*, pup production 1995 to 2006. *New Zealand Journal of Marine and Freshwater Research*, **41**:205-213.

28. Gales, N.J. and Fletcher, D.J. (1999) Abundance, distribution and status of the New Zealand Sea Lion, *Phocarctos hookeri*. *Wildlife Research*, **26**:35-52.

29. Challies, C.N. (1975) Feral Pigs (*Sus scrofa*) on Auckland Island: status, and effects on vegetation and nesting sea birds. *New Zealand Journal of Zoology*, **2**:479-490.

30. Anderson, A. (2003) *Prehistoric archeology in the Auckland Islands*. New Zealand Department of Conservation (Unpublished Report), Wellington.

31. Dingwall, P.R., Fraser, C., Gregory, J.G. and Robertson, C.J.R. (1999) *Enderby Settlement Diaries, Record of a British Colony at the Auckland Islands, 1849-1852*. Wild Press/Wordsell Press, Wellington

32. McLaren, F.B. (1936). *The Auckland Islands: their eventful history*. A.H. and A.W. Reed, Wellington.

33. McNab, R. (1907) William Smith, Invercargill.

34. Dunmore, J. (2007). *The Life of Dumont D'Urville. From Venus to Antarctica*. Exisle Publishing, Auckland.

35. D'Urville, D. (1955) *The Voyage of the Astrolabe-1840: An English Rendering of the Journals*. Translated by O. Wright. A.H. and A.W. Reed, Wellington.

36. King, M. (1989) *Moriori-A People Rediscovered*. Viking, Auckland

37. Eunson, K. (1974) *The Wreck of the General Grant*. AH and AW Reed, Wellington.

38. Allen, M.F. (1997) *Wake of the Invercauld*. Exisle Publishing, Auckland.

39. Eden, A.W. (1955) *Islands of Despair*. Andrew Melrose Ltd. London.

40. Raynal, F.E. (1880) *Wrecked on a Reef: Twenty months in the Auckland Isles*. Thomas Nelson and Sons, London.

41. Chilton, C. (1909) In: Chilton, C. (Ed) *The Subantarctic Islands of New Zealand Volume 1*. Philosophical Institute of Canterbury, Wellington. pp xiv-xxxv.

The Snares

1. Fleming, C.A., Reed, J.J. and Harris, W.F. (1953) The geology of the Snares Islands. *New Zealand Department of Conservation Science and Research Cape Expedition Series Bulletin*, **13**:1-41.

2. Peat, N. (2003). New Zealand Department of Conservation, Invercargill.

3. Marshall, P. (1909) In: Chilton, C. (Ed) *The Subantarctic Islands of New Zealand Volume 2*. Philosophical Institute of Canterbury, Wellington. pp 680-704.

4. Flint, E.A. and Fineran, B.A. (1969) Observations on the climate, peats and terrestrial algae of the Snares Islands. *New Zealand Journal of Science*, **12**:268-301.

5. Fraser, C. (1986). Government Printing Office, Wellington.

6. Watters, W.A. and Fleming, C.A. (1975) Petrography of rocks from the Western Chain of the Snares Islands. *New Zealand Journal of Geology and Geophysics*, **18**:491-498.

7. Cockayne, L. (1909) In: Chilton, C. (Ed) *The Subantarctic Islands of New Zealand Volume 1*. Philosophical Institute of Canterbury, Wellington. pp 182-235

8. Cheeseman, T.F. (1909) In: Chilton, C. (Ed) *The Subantarctic Islands of New Zealand Volume 2*. Philosophical Institute of Canterbury, Wellington. pp. 389-471.

9. Fineran, B.A. (1969) The flora of the Snares Islands, New Zealand. *Transactions of the Royal Society of New Zealand, Botany*, **3**:237-270.

10. Hay, C.H., Warham, J. and Fineran, B.A. (2004) The vegetation of the Snares, Islands south of New Zealand, mapped and discussed. *New Zealand Journal of Botany*, **42**:861-872.

11. Miskelly, C.M., Sagar, P.M., Tennyson, A.J.D. and Scofield, P. (2001) Birds of the Snares Islands, New Zealand. *Notornis*, **48**:1-40.

12. Warham, J. (1974) Breeding biology and behaviour of the Snares Crested Penguin. *Journal of the Royal Society of New Zealand*, **4**:63-108.

13. James, G.D. and Stahl, J.C. (2000) Diet of southern Buller's albatross (*Diomedea bulleri bulleri*) and the importance of fishery discards during chick rearing. *New Zealand Journal of Marine and Freshwater Research*, **34**:435-454.

14. Sagar, P.M., Stahl, J.C., Molloy, J., Taylor, G.A. and Tennyson, A.J.D. (1999) Population size and trends within the two populations of Southern Buller's Albatross *Diomedea bulleri bulleri*. *Biological Conservation*, **89**:11-19.

15. Miskelly, C.M. (1984) Birds of the Western Chain, Snares Islands 1982-84. *Notornis*, **31**:209-223.

16. Sagar, P.M. (1977) Birds of the Western Chain, Snares Islands, New Zealand. *Notornis* **24**:178-183.

17. Clark, G. (1996) *The Totorore expedition to the Snares Western Chain; September 1995-December 1995*. Department of Conservation (Unpublished Report), Invercargill.

18. Warham, J. and Wilson, G.J. (1982) The size of the sooty shearwater population on the Snares Islands, New Zealand. *Notornis*, **29**:23-30.

19. McKechnie, S., Fletcher, D., Moller, H., Scott, D.S., Newman, J. and Bragg, C. (2007) Estimating and correcting for bias in population assessments of sooty shearwaters. *Journal of Wildlife Management*, **71**:1325-1335.

20. Veit, R., McGowan, J., Ainley, D., Wahl, T. and Pyle, P. (1997) Apex marine predator declines ninety percent in association with changing oceanic climate. *Global Change Biology*, **3**:23-28.

21. Warham, J., Keeley, B.R., and Wilson, G.J. (1977) Breeding of the Mottled Petrel. *Auk*, **94**:1-17.

22. Crawley, M.C. (1972) Distribution and abundance of the New Zealand Fur Seal on the Snares Islands, New Zealand. *New Zealand Journal of Marine and Freshwater Research*, **6**:115-126.

23. Carey, P.W. (1998) New Zealand Fur Seals (*Arctocephalus forsteri*) at the Snares Islands: a stabilised population? *New Zealand Journal of Marine and Freshwater Research*, **32**:113-118.

24. McNab, R. (1907) William Smith, Invercargill.

25. Reischek, A. (1888) Notes on the islands to the south of New Zealand. *Transactions of the New Zealand Institute*, **21**:381.

26. Chilton, C. (1909) In: Chilton, C. (Ed) *The Subantarctic Islands of New Zealand Volume 1*. Philosophical Institute of Canterbury, Wellington. pp xiv-xxxv.

27. Warham, J. (1967) Snares Islands Birds. *Notornis*, **14**:122-139.

28. Miskelly, C.M. (1990) Effects of the 1982-1983 El Nino event on two endemic landbirds on the Snares Islands, New Zealand. *Emu*, **90**:24-27.

Macquarie Island

1. Selkirk, P.M., Seppelt, R.D. and Selkirk, D.R. (1990) Cambridge University Press, Cambridge.

2. Terauds, A. and Stewart, F. (2008) *Subantarctic Wilderness Macquarie Island*. Allen and Unwin, Sydney.

3. Brothers, N. and Ledingham, R. (2008) The avifauna of Bishop and Clerk Islands, its relationship to nearby Macquarie Island and implications of current management prescriptions. *Papers and Proceedings of the Royal Society of Tasmania*, **142**:117-122.

4. Hayes, D.E. and Talwani, M. (1972) Geophysical investigations of the Macquarie Ridge complex. In: Hayes, D.E. (Ed) *Antarctic Oceanography II, The Australian-New Zealand Sector. Antarctica*. American Geophysical Union, Washington. pp 211-234.

5. Williamson, P.E. (1988) Origin, structural and tectonic history of the Macquarie Island region. *Papers & Proceedings of the Royal Society of Tasmania*, **122**:27-43.

6. Daczko, N.R., Meckel, T.A., Mosher, S. and Coffin, M.F. (2005) Tectonic implications of fault-scarp-derived volcaniclastic deposits on Macquarie Island: sedimentation at a fossil ridge-transform intersection? *Bulletin of the Geological Society of America*, **117**:18-31.

7. Pollitz, F.F. (1986) Pliocene changes in Pacific plate motion. *Nature*, **320**:738-741.

8. Cumpston, J. (1968). Macquarie Island. *ANARE Scientific Reports, Series A(1) Narrative*. Antarctic Division, Department of External Affairs, Melbourne.

9. Adamson, D.A., Selkirk, P.M., Price, D.M., Ward, N., and Selkirk, J.M. (1996) Pleistocene uplift and palaeoenvironments of Macquarie Island: evidence from palaeobeaches and sedimentary deposits. *Papers and Proceedings of the Royal Society of Tasmania*, **130**:25-32.

10. Ledingham, R. and Petersen, J.A. (1998) Raised beach deposits and the distribution of structural lineaments on Macquarie Island. *Papers and Proceedings of the Royal Society of Tasmania*, **118**:223-235.

11. Christodoulou, C., Griffin, B.J. and Foden, J. (1984) The geology of Macquarie Island. *ANARE Research Notes*, **21**:1-15.

12. Quilty, P.G. (2007) *Papers and Proceedings of the Royal Society of Tasmania*, **14**:35-58.

13. Duncan, R.A. and Varne, R. (1988) The age and distribution of the igneous rocks of Macquarie Island. *Papers and Proceedings of the Royal Society of Tasmania*, **122**:45-50.

14. Goscombe, B.D. and Everard, J.L. (2001) Tectonic evolution of Macquarie Island: extensional structures and block rotations in oceanic crust. *Journal of Structural Geology*, **23**:639-673.

15. Wertz, K.L., Daczko, N.R., Mosher, S. and Coffin, M.F. (2003) Macquarie Island's Finch-Langdon fault: A ridge-transform inside corner structure. *Geology*, **31**:661-664.

16. Hamilton, A. (1895) Notes on a visit to Macquarie Island. *Transactions of the New Zealand Institute*, **17**:559.

17. Taylor, B.W. (1955) The flora, vegetation and soils of Macquarie Island. *ANARE Reports. B(2), Botany.* **19**.

18. Copson, G.R. (1984) An annotated atlas of the vascular flora of Macquarie Island. *ANARE Research Notes*, **18**.

19. Copson, G.R. and Whinam, J. (1998) Response of vegetation on subantarctic Macquarie Island to reduced rabbit grazing. *Australian Journal of Botany*, **46**:15-24.

20. Selkirk, P.M. and Seppelt, R.D. (1984) Fellfield on Macquarie Island. *Tasmanian Naturalist*, **78**:24-25.

21. Shaw, J.D., Hovenden, M.J. and Bergstrom, D.M. (2005) The impact of introduced ship rats (*Rattus rattus*) on seedling recruitment and distribution of a subantarctic megaherb (*Pleurophyllum hookeri*). *Austral Ecology*, **30**:118-125.

22. Seppelt, R.D. (2004) *The Moss Flora of Macquarie Island*. Australian Antarctic Division, Hobart.

23. Whinam, J. and Copson, G. (2006) Sphagnum moss: an indicator of climate change in the sub-Antarctic. *Polar Record*, **42**:43-49.

24. Ricker, R.W. (1987). *Taxonomy and biogeography of Macquarie Island Seaweeds*. British Museum (Natural History), London.

25. Vestjens, W.J.M. (1963) Remains of the extinct banded rail at Macquarie Island. *Emu*, **62**:249-250.

26. Rounsevell, D.E. and Copson, G.R. (1982) Growth rate and recovery of a King Penguin, *Aptenodytes patagonicus*, population after exploitation. *Australian Wildlife Research*, **9**:519-525.

27. Robertson, G. (1986) Population size and breeding success of the Gentoo Penguin, *Pygoscelis papua*, at Macquarie Island. *Australian Wildlife Research*, **13**:583-587.

28. Terauds, A., Gales, R., Baker, G.B., and Alderman, R. (2006) Population and survival trends of Wandering Albatrosses (*Diomedea exulans*) breeding on Macquarie Island. *Emu*, **106**:211-218.

29. Terauds, A., Gales, R. and Alderman, R. (2005) Trends in numbers and survival of Black-browed (*Thalassarche melanophrys*) and Grey-headed (*T. chrysostoma*) Albatrosses breeding on Macquarie Island. *Emu*, **105**:159-167.

30. Brothers, N. and Bone, C. (2008) The response of burrow-nesting petrels and other vulnerable bird species to vertebrate pest management and climate changes on subantarctic Macquarie Island. *Papers & Proceedings of the Royal Society of Tasmania*, **142**:123-148.

31. Brothers, N.P. (1984) Breeding distribution and status of burrow-nesting petrels on Macquarie Island. *Australian Wildlife Research*, **11**:113-131.

32. Schulz, M. and Gales, R. (2004) Breeding of the Antarctic Tern (*Sterna vittata bethunei*) on Macquarie Island. *Notornis*, **51**:114-116.

33. Norman, F.I. (1987) The ducks of Macquarie Island. *ANARE Research Notes*, **42**.

34. Lancaster, M.L., Gemmell, N.J., Negro, S., Goldsworthy, S. and Sunnucks, P. (2006) Ménage à trios on Macquarie Island: hybridization among three species of fur seal (*Arctocephalus* spp.) following historical population extinction. *Molecular Ecology*, **15**:3681-3692.

35. McMahon, C.R., Burton, H.R., Bester, M.N., Hindell, M.A., and Bradshaw, C.J.A. (2005) Population status, trends and a re-examination of the hypotheses explaining the recent declines of the southern elephant seal *Mirounga leonina*. *Mammal Review*, **35**:82-100.

36. Greenslade, P. (2006). *The Invertebrates of Macquarie Island*. Australian Antarctic Division, Hobart.

37. Palma, R.L. and Horning, D.S. (2002) The lice (Insecta: Phthiraptera) from Macquarie Island. *ANARE Research Notes*, **105**.

38. McNab, R. (1907) William Smith, Invercargill.

39. Ling, J.K. (1999) Exploitation of fur seals and sea lions from Australia, New Zealand and adjacent subantarctic islands during the 18th, 19th and 20th centuries. *Australian Zoologist*, **31**:323-350.

40. Mawson, D. (1915) *The Home of the Blizzard The Story of the Australasian Antarctic Expedition 1911-1914*. Heineman, London.

INDEX

A

Acheron 150
Adams Island (Auckland Islands) 117, *120*, 121, 122, 125, **128**, 131, 133, 134, 146, 147, 203
Adventure 166
Albatross 41, 63, 81, 102, 133, 159, 182
  Antipodean Albatross (*Diomedea antipodensis*) 71, 72, 81, 83, 89, 102
  Black-browed Albatross (*Thalassarche melanophrys*) 81, 102, 133, 159, 187
  Buller's Albatross (northern race) (*Thalassarche bulleri*) 41
  Buller's Albatross (southern race) (*Thalassarche bulleri*) 133, *157*, 159, *161*, 169
  bycatch/interactions with fisheries 81, 169
  Campbell Albatross (*Thalassarche impavida*) 22, 102, *103*
  census and/or research 63, 69, 89, 89, 102, 114, 115, 147, 169, 203
  Chatham Albatross (*Thalassarche eremita*) 41, *43*, 63, 159
  diet of castaways/sealers 87, 190
  effect on vegetation 79, 129
  foraging 25
  Gibson's Wandering Albatross (*Diomedea gibsoni*) *120*, 133, 147
  Grey-headed Albatross (*Thalassarche chrysostoma*) 102, *182*, 187
  Light-mantled Sooty Albatross (*Phoebetria palpebrata*) 82, *83*, 102, 106, 133, *178*, 187
  Northern Royal Albatross (*Diomedea sanfordi*) 41, *45*
  number of species in region 17
  Salvin's Albatross (*Thalassarche salvini*) 56, 62, 63, 159, *169*
  Shy Albatross (*Thalassarche cauta*) 63
  skua predation 187
  Southern Royal Albatross (*Diomedea epomophora*) 102, *104*, 115, 133, 197
  taxonomy 41, 81
  Wandering Albatross (*Diomedea exulans*) 81, 183
  White-capped Albatross (*Thalassarche steadii*) 63, 81, 133, 147
algae, marine *see marine plants*
algae, terrestrial 61, 68, 77, 79
alien (introduced) plants 34, 51, **100**, 101, **156**
  see also human impacts and vascular plants for species
American Museum of Natural History 86, 168
Amey, Jacinda 61, 63, 89
Amherst 68, 111, 145, 167
Anchorage Bay (Antipodes Islands) 74, 75
Anjou 145
Antarctic 111, 140, 166
Antarctic Convergence (Polar Front) 12, 23, 102, 174
Antarctica 88, 110, 140, 193, 200
  geology 58
  ice cap 23
  Marie Byrd Land 58
  surrounding oceanography 10, 12, 23
Archway Island (Antipodes Islands) 74, 81
Armstrong, Henry 86, 145, 167
Atkinson, Ian 35
Auckland, Lord 140
Aurora 190
Australian Antarctic Division 19
Australian National Antarctic Research Expedition (ANARE) 193
Azimuth, Mount (Campbell Island) 92, 94

B

Bailey, Alfred 114
Balleny, Captain John 110
Banded Dotterel (*Charadrius bicinctus*) 46, 134, *137*
Beeman Cove (Campbell Island) 114
Beeman Hill (Campbell Island) 95, *197*
Bell, Brian 9, 88, *204*
Bellbird (*Anthornis melanura*) 135
Bellinghausen, Admiral 192
Bencleugh 191
Benham, W. 145
Betsey 191
biodiversity 11, **12**, 47, 117, 195, 202, 203
biogeography 12
Biscoe, Captain J. 68
Bishop and Clerk (Macquarie Island) 174, 186
Black Robin (*Petroica traversi*) **44**, 46
Black Swan (*Cygnus atratus*) 45
Black, Alex 69, 88
Blackbird, European (*Turdus merula*) 107, 164
Bligh, Lieutenant 17, 67
Boat Harbour (The Snares) 155, 156
Bollons Island (Antipodes Islands) 74, 81, 82, 85
Booth, Andrea 63
Borchgrevink, Carsten 111
Bounty 17, 67
Bounty Platform 58, 74
Bremen 198
Bristow, Abraham 131, 140
British Museum 68, 86
Brittania 166
Brothers 67
Broughton Island (The Snares) 152, **157**
Broughton, Lieutenant William 17, *48*, 49, 166

214 GALAPAGOS OF THE ANTARCTIC

bryophytes 77, 100 *see also moss, liverworts*
Buchanan, John 96
Buckles Bay (Macquarie Island) 192, 199

C

Campbell Island Company 112
Campbell Island Syndicate 112
Campbell Macquarie 191
Campbell Plateau 15, 23, 58, 74, 94, 95, 121, 152, 202
Cape Expeditions 96, *113*, **114**, 115, *144*, **146**
Carnley Harbour (Auckland Island) 121, 122, 140, 142, 145, 146, *203*
Carnley Volcano (Auckland Islands) *120*, 122
Caroline 191
Caroline Cove 191, *192*
castaway depots 58, **69**, 86, 87, 88, **111**, 131, 145, 146, *167*, 196
Castle Island (Bounty Islands) 58
Castle Rock (Chatham Islands) 31, 32
cats *see introduced animals*
cattle *see introduced animals*
Cawthorn, Martin 147
Centre Group (Bounty Islands) 58, 61
Chace, Captain 67
Chaffinch (*Fringilla coelebs*) 108
Chapman, Frederick 68, 96, 167
Chatham 49, 166
Chatham Rise 23, 25, 31, 32
Chatham Schist 32
Chilton, Professor C. 112
Chudleigh, Edward 51
Clark, Gerry 69, 88, 89
Clifton, Les 114
climate 20, **21**, 22, 35, 48, 154, 176
climate change **21**, 180, 195

Clyde **192**
coastwatchers *see Cape Expeditions*
Cockayne, Leonard 69, 86, 96, *144*, 145
Coffin, Captain 166
collembola *see invertebrates, terrestrial*
Commerce 67, 140
Compadre 145
Complex Point (Campbell Island) 95
Conservation Management Strategy (NZ) 18, 53, 69, 198, 199
Cook, H.F. 112
cormorants *see Shags*
Countess Cimento 191
Courrejolles Point (Auckland Islands) 102
Crake, Marsh (*Porzana pusilla*) 45
Crake, Spotless (*Porzana tabuensis*) 45
Crater Bay (Antipodes Islands) 74
Crawley, M. 164
Crockett, David 41, *53*
Crozet Islands 12
Cumberland 110
cushion plants 77, 98, 99, 131, 156, 174, 176, *179 see also vascular plants for species*

D

Davis, Captain J.K. 193
de Roy, Tui 69
Delano, Captain Amasa 67, 166
Dent Island (Le Dent) (Campbell Group) 94, 106, 114
Denver Natural History Museum 114
Department of Conservation, New Zealand *see New Zealand Government Departments*
Depot Island 58, 66, 68
Derry Castle 145
Derry Castle Reef (Enderby Island) 121, 139, *144*

Dick, Mount (Adams Island) 121
Dieffenbach, Dr. Ernst 50
Disappointment Island (Auckland Islands) 121, 122, **131**, 133, 134, 139, *143*, 145
Discovery (1790s) 166, *167*
Discovery (1900s) 145, 193
Discovery II 88
Dominion Museum 146
Dougall, William 96
Dumas, Mount (Campbell Island) 94
Dundas Island (Auckland Islands) 139
Dundonald *143*, 145
Dunnock (*Prunella modularis*) 85, 107
Duris 111, 115
D'urville, Admiral Dumont 140, *141*

E

Eagle 191
Eagle Cave (Macquarie Island) 191
East Australia Current 23
East Group (Bounty Islands) 58, 61
Eastern Bar-tailed Godwit (*Limosa lapponica*) 164
Elizabeth and Mary 140, 190
Ellen Elizabeth Preece Conservation Covenant 45
Elliott, Graeme 19, 81, 89, 134, 146, *203*
Eltanin 88
Endeavour 192
endemic species 17, 35, 36, 37, 41, 42, 45, 46, 47, 65, 71, 77, 79, 81, 82, 84, 85, 102, 107, 108, 128, 131, 133, 134, 139, 154, 156, 158, 161, 164, 176, 179, 183, 187, 189
Enderby Island (Auckland Islands) 14, *118*, 121, *122*, *123*, *124*, 125, *126*, *127*, **128**, 131, 133, 134, 135, 142, 146, 147, *194*

Enderby Settlement **142**, *143*
Enderby Whaling Firm 140
Enderby, Charles 142
Enterprise 166
Epigwait 145
eradication operations *see introduced animals*
Erebus 96, 110, 133, *141*
Erebus Cove (Auckland Island) 131
Erlangen 146
Ewing Island (Auckland Islands) 131, 142, *144*

F
Fairchild, Captain 74
Fairchild's Garden (Adams Island) 128
Falcon, New Zealand (*Falco novaeseelandiae*) 135
Falkland Islands 12
Falla, Sir Robert 69, 88, 114, 146, 168
Fantail, Chatham Island (*Rhipidura fuliginosa penita*) 46
farming *see human impacts*
Faye, Mount (Campbell Island) 94
featherbed 174, *175*, 180, 181, 187
feldmark (or fell field) 80, 128, 131, 176, 180
feral animals *see introduced animals*
Fernbird, Snares (*Bowdleria punctata caudata*) 163, 164
ferns 36, 37, *38*, 76, 77, 78, 79, 88, 99, 100, 125, 128, 155, 156, 176, **180** *see also vascular plants for species*
Filhol, Dr. H. 111
fishing 52, 53, 202
 Blue cod, crayfish, paua 52
 long-lining 41, 81, 89, 169
 offal discards (and albatross) 159
 mooring of boats at The Snares 169

Figure of Eight Island (Auckland Islands) 139
Fizeau, Mount (Campbell Island) 94
flax 36, 142
Fleming, George 146
Fleming, Sir Charles 53, 123
Folger, Captain 49
Folly Island (Campbell Island) 94
Forty Fours, The (Chatham Islands) 31, 32, 35, 41, 42
fossils 31, **32**, *31*, 40, 95
Frontier Spirit 198
fungi 35, 77, 125, 155, **180**, 181
Funnel Island (Bounty Islands) 58, 61
Furious Fifties 20, 21

G
Galapagos of the Antarctic (island group) 10, 11, 12, 15, 17, 170, 196, 198
galaxiid fish 102
Galloway, Mount (Antipodes Islands) 74
Garden Cove 95
General Grant *143*, 145
Given, David 35, 96, 115
glacial action 15, 30, 75, 94, 95, *120*, 122, 123, 152
Godley, Eric 77, 96, 146
Goldfinch (*Carduelis carduelis*) 107
Gomez Island 94
Gondwana 12, 15, 32, 33, 54, 58
Goose, Feral (*Anser anser*) 45
Gordon, J. 111, 112
Grafton 142
Gratitude 192
Greenshank (*Tringa nebularia*) 164
Grey Duck (*Anas superciliosa*) 45, 107, 133, 135, 164, 188

greywacke 32
Gulls 63, 66
 Red-billed Gull (*Larus scopulinus*) 42, 64, 107, 134, 162
 Southern Black-backed (Kelp) Gull (*Larus dominicanus*) 42, 64, 82, 107, 134, 187

H
Hamilton, A. 193
Hamilton, Mount (Macquarie Island) 174
Handspike Point (Macquarie Island) 191
Hannah 141
Hapag Lloyd 198
Hardwicke 142
Harrier, Australasian (*Circus approximans*) 46
Harwood, Captain 50
Hasselburgh, Captain Frederick 110, 190
Hatch, Joseph 190, 191
Heard Island 12
Hector, Sir James 86
Henry 140
Heritage Expeditions 70, 88, 196, 198, 200
Hinemoa, S.S. 68, 69, 87, *143*
Ho Ho Bay 155
Honey, Mount (Campbell Island) 94, *197*
Hook Keys (Campbell Island) 94
Hooker Hills (Auckland Island) 147
Hooker, Sir Joseph 15, 96, 100, 110, 125, 141
Horning, Don 168
House Sparrow (*Passer domesticus*) 108
Hudson, G. 164
human impacts 27, 90, **131**, 195
 farming 28, 48, **50**, *51*, 90, **111**, **112**, **113**, 142, **143**, 166, 167
 fur seal industry *see sealing*

introduction of animals *see introduced animals*
introduction of disease 49
  on native fauna 41, 45, 51
  on native flora 35, 37, 51, 53, 71, 76, 86, 96, 99, 100, 116, 125, 131, 145, 167
Hunt, Frederick *48*, 51
Hutton, Professor Frederick 69, 86

I

Independence 86
International Geophysical Year (IGY) 224
International Union for the Conservation of Nature (IUCN) 42, 45, 63, 64, 81
introduced animals 17, 41, 63, 71, 85, 87, **108**, 128, 131, **139**, 141, 148, 169, **188**
  Brush-tailed Possum (*Trichosurus vulpecula*) 47, 51
  Cat (*Felis cattus*) 19, 42, 47, 51, 107, 108, 127, 133, 135, 139, 187, 188, 189
  Cattle 19, 37, 47, 91, 96, 108, 131, 146, 147, 188
  Dogs 188
  effect on native animals 19, 42, 47, 85, 107, 108, 116, 133, 134, 135, 139, 183, 187
  effects on native vegetation 35, 37, 96, 101, 108, 116, 125, 131, 139, 176, 179, 180, *181*, 187, 193
  eradication of 19, 90, 96, 107, 114, *115*, 127, 132, 134, 135, 147, 188, 193, 200
  European Hedgehog (*Erinaceus europaeus*) 47
  Goats 19, 47, 108, 147, 167, 188
  House Mouse (*Mus musculus*) 19, 47, 85, 135, 139, 147, 180, 183

Pigs 37, 42, 47, 50, 51, 108, 111, 117, 128, 131, 133, 135, *139*, 140, 142, 147, 202
  Rabbits, European (*Oryctolagus cuniculus*) 19, 47, 131, 134, 147, 176, 179, 180, *181*, 183, 187, 188, 193, 200
  Rats, Norway (*Rattus norvegicus*) 19, 47, 90, 96, 107, 108
  Rats, Polynesian (*Rattus exulans*) 47
  Rats, Ship (Black) (*Rattus rattus*) 47, 180, 183
  sheep 19, 37, 47, 51, 91, 96, 100, 108, 110, *111*, 112, 113, 114, 146, 188
  Stewart Island Weka (*Gallirallus australis scotti*) 20, 188, 193
  Stoats 47
Invercauld 145
invertebrates, terrestrial 47, **65**, **85**, 88, **108**, 134, 139, *162*, **164**, **189**
invertebrates, marine 33, 181
Isle de Jeannette Marie (Campbell Island) 94
Isthmus (Macquarie Island) *173*, 174, 175, 192, 193, 199

J

Jaquemart Island (Campbell Island) 94, 107
Jean Bart 50
Jessie Niccol 192
Jones, Mark 85
Judd, Norm 113
Judge and Clerk (Macquarie Island) 174

K

Kaingaroa, landing by Broughton 49
Kakanui 191
Keith, Captain 166

Kerguelen Islands 12
King George 67
Kirk, Thomas 68, 86, *87*, 96, 155, 167
Knights Island 166
Knox, Prof. George 168
krill 25

L

land birds **80**, 102, 107, 133 *see also specific species, Parakeets*
L'astrolabe 140, *141*
Leeward Island (Antipodes Islands) 74, 82
lichen 34, 61, 69, 77, 78, 96, 100, 125, *129*, 155, 175, 176, **180**
  Candelaria sp. 61
  crustose 61, 77, 98
  Pertusaria sp. 61
  Verrucaria manura 61
Linblad Travel 196
Lion Island (Bounty Islands) 58
Little Mangere (Tapuaenuku) 31, 32, 42, 45, 51, 53
Littlewood, Captain George 50
liverworts 77, 78, 79, 96, 125, 128
  see also Marchantia sp.
long-line fishing *see fishing*
Long-tailed Cuckoo (*Eudynamys taitensis*) 134
Lord Nelson 191
Lord Auckland 48
Lusitania Bay (Macquarie Island) *185*, 191
Lyall, Mount (Campbell Island) 94
lycopod 77, 78, 180

M

Macquarie Island Base *172*, 193
Macquarie Ridge Complex 23, 94, 121, 174

Main Group (Bounty Islands) 58
Mallard (*Anas platyrhynchos*) 45, 85, 107, 164, 188
Mangere Island (Chatham Islands) 31, 32, 42
Maori 27, **49**, 50, 52, 53, 67, **141**, 142, 152, 169 *see also Polynesian settlers*
Marchantia berteroana 79, 99, **130**, 155, **180**
marine plants 37, **61**, 79, **101**, **131**, **157**, **181**
    algae 37, 61, 69, 79, 101, 131, 181
    Antarctic bull kelp (*Durvillaea antarctica*) 37, 60, 61, 79, 101, 131, 157, 181
    Durvillaea chathamensis 37
    Durvillaea sp. (Antipodes Islands) 79
    Lessonia tholiformis 37
    Macrocystis pyrifera 37, 181
    Marginariella parsonii 61, 79
    red algae, coralline 37, 181
Mary and Sally 110
Matioro 141, 142
Matthewson 113
Mawson, Sir Douglas 193
McCormick, Dr. 110, 133, 141
McDonald Island 12
McGlone, M.S. 96
megaherbs 6, 15, 77, 79, 87, 96, 97, 99, 100, *101*, 125, 138, *130*, 131, *155*, 156, 176, *177*, *178*, *179*, **180** *see also vascular plants*
Menhir (Campbell Island) 94, 95
meteorological observations 21, 99, **114**, 115, 193
Meurk, Colin 61, 96
mica schist 95
Minerva 145
Miskelly, Colin 159
missionaries 50
Moffett, W.J. 146

Molly Cap (Bounty Islands) 58, 61
Monowai Island (Campbell Island) 94, 107
Monowai, H.M.N.Z.S. 69, 89, 114
Moody, Captain William 67
Moore, Peter 102
Moriori 27, 36, 48, **49**, 50, 52, 53, **141**, 142 *see also Polynesian settlers*
Moriori Kopinga Marae 53
Morrell, Captain B. 140, 166
moss 33, 35, 36, 77, 78, 96, 99, 125, 128, 154, 176, **180** *see also Sphagnum*
Murphy, Robert C. 168
Murray 113
Musgrave Peninsula (Auckland Island) 122

N

Neale, Henry 110
Nella Dan 192
New Zealand Company 50
New Zealand Forest and Bird Society 53
New Zealand Government Departments
    Department of Conservation 18, *19*, 35, 53, 63, 69, 81, 102, 108, 142, 169, 195, 198
    Department of Industrial and Scientific Research 146
    Lands and Survey 88, 115, 145, 146, 147, 169
    Ministry of Fisheries 89, 147, 169
    National Institute of Water and Atmospheric Research 81, 89, 169
    Oceanographic Institute 69, 88, 146
    Wildlife Service 53, 204
New Zealand Royal Society 115
Ngâti Mutunga 50, 141
Ngâti Tama 50
Nimrod 193

North Arm (Auckland Island) 142
North Rock (Bounty Islands) 58
North-east Harbour (Campbell Island) 94, 102, 112
North-east Island (The Snares) 152
North-west Bay (Campbell Island) 6, 94, 95, 112
Northwind, U.S.C.G. 88
Nuggets, the (Macquarie Island) 191, 192

O

Ocean 140
oceanography *see Southern Ocean*
oil, penguins 171, **190**
oil, elephant seals 171, **190**
oil, potential for mining 15, 202
orchids 77, 176
Orde Lees Islet (Antipodes Islands) 74
Outlying Islands Committee 18

P

Pacific Black Duck *See Grey Duck*
Parea (*Hemiphaga chathamensis*) 40, 45
Paris, Mount (Campbell Island) 94
Parakeets 45, 71, 80
    Antipodes Island (Antipodean) Parakeet (*Cyanoramphus unicolour*) 19, 71, 81, 82, 84
    Chatham Island Red-crowned Parakeet (*Cyanoramphus novaezelandiae chathamensis*) 44, **45**
    Forbes Parakeet (*Cyanoramphus forbesi*) 45
    in diet of sealers 190
    Macquarie Island parakeet (*Cyanoramphus novaezelandiae erythrotis*) extinct 183
    Red-crowned Parakeet (*Cyanoramphus novaezelandiae*) 134, *136*

Reischek's Parakeet (*Cyanoramphus novaezelandiae hochstetteri*) 81, 82, 83
research 19
speciation 17
Yellow-crowned Parakeet (*Cyanoramphus auriceps*) 134
Parker, Professor T.J. 86
Patagonian Toothfish (*Dissostichus eleginoides*) 202
peat 31, 32, 35, **36**, 37, 74, 75, 79, 81, 95, 100, 121, 142, 152, 156, 180
Pegasus 87
Penantipodes 71, 86
Penguins 63, 81, 102, 133, 159, 167, 171, 183
   census and/or research 69, 88, 102, 166
   diet of castaways/sealers 87, 190
   effect on vegetation 156, 176, 180
   Erect Crested Penguin (*Eudyptes sclateri*) 57, 63, 66, 69, 80, 81, 133, 159, 164
   evolution of 24
   Fiordland Penguin (*Eudyptes pachyrhynchus*) 159
   foraging 25
   Gentoo Penguin (*Pygoscelis papua*) 183, 186
   killed for their skins 86
   King Penguin (*Aptenodytes patagonicus*) 100, 160, 164, 190
   Little Blue Penguin (*Eudyptula minor chathamensis*) 42
   number of species 17
   oiling industry 18, 171, 183, **190**
   population declines 81, 102
   predation of 64, 187, 188
   Rockhopper Penguin (*Eudyptes chrysocome*) 81, 102, *106*, 133, 183, *186*
   Royal Penguin (*Eudyptes schlegeli*) 13, 183, *186*, 190, 191
   Snares Crested Penguin (*Eudyptes robustus*) 24, 158, 159, *201*
   Yellow-eyed Penguin (*Megadyptes antipodes*) 11, 102, *132*, 133
Penguin Island (Bounty Islands) 58
Petrels 37, **42**, 64, 81, 82, 102, **107**, 132, **134, 161**, 183 *see also* Albatrosses, Prions, Shearwaters
   Black-bellied Storm Petrels (*Fregetta tropica*) 64, 107, 134
   Black-winged Petrel (*Pterodroma nigripennis*) 42, 64, 82
   Blue Petrel (*Halobaena caerulea*) 187
   Cape Petrel (*Daption capense*) 161, 187
   Cape Petrel, Snares (*Daption capense australe*) 64, 82, 107, 134, 161
   census and research 89
   Chatham Petrel (*Pterodroma axillaris*) **41**, 64
   Common Diving Petrel (*Pelecanoides urinatrix*) 187
   Common Diving Petrel, southern (*Pelecanoides urinatrix chathamensis*) 42, 64, 82, 107, 134, 161
   Cook's Petrel (*Pterodroma cookii*) 64
   effect on vegetation 37, 79, 155
   evolution of 24
   Great-winged Petrel (*Pterodroma macroptera*) 64
   Grey Petrel (*Procellaria cinerea*) 82, 89, 107, 187
   Grey-backed Storm Petrel (*Garrodia nereis*) 42, 64, 82, 107, 134
   human impacts on 41
   in the diet of sealers 190
   Juan Fernandez Petrel (*Pterodroma externa*) 64
   Kerguelen Petrel (*Lugensa brevirostris*) 64
   Magenta Petrel (*Pterodroma magentae*) 27, **41**, *53*, 89
   Mottled Petrel (*Pterodroma inexpectata*) 161
   Northern Giant Petrel (*Macronectes halli*) 42, 64, 82, 83, 107, 134, 164, 187
   number of species 17
   predators 187, 188
   Soft-plumage Petrel (*Pterodroma mollis*) 64, 82, 187
   South Georgian Diving Petrel (*Pelecanoides georgicus*) 134
   Southern Giant Petrel (*Macronectes giganteus*) *186*, 187
   White-chinned Petrel (*Procellaria aequinoctialis*) 64, 82, 89, 107, 134
   White-faced Storm Petrel (*Pelagodroma marina maoriana*) 42, 64, 134
   White-headed Petrel (*Pterodroma lessoni*) 64, 82, 107, 134, 187
Perseverance 67, 110, 166, 190
Perseverance Harbour (Campbell Island) 94, 99, 100, 111, 114
Petrel Peak (Macquarie Island) 182
Philosophical Institute of Canterbury *see research expeditions*
phosphatic mudstone 59
phytoplankton 25
Pied Stilt (*Himantopus himantopus*) 45
pigs *see introduced animals*
Pilgrim 67, 166
pillow basalt 175

Pipits
    Chatham Island (*Anthus novaeseelandiae chathamensis*) 46
    NZ (*Anthus novaeseelandiae*) 106, 107
    NZ (Antipodes - *Anthus novaeseelandiae steindachneri*) 85
    NZ (Auckland Is. - *Anthus novaeseelandiae aucklandicus*) 134, 137

Pitt Island (Rangiauria) 32, 33, 37, 42, 45, 46, 47, *48*, 51, 52, 204
Pitt Strait 32
plants *see vascular plants or marine plants*
Polynesian visitors/settlers 17, 27, 47, 49, 110, 117, **140**
Port Ross (Auckland Island) 17, 121, 123, 138, *141*, 142, *143*, 145, 146
Port Ross Volcano 122, 123
Possession Island (Indian Ocean) 12
President Felix Faure 87
Prince Edward Islands 12
Prion Island (Bounties) 58

Prions
    Antarctic Prion (*Pachyptila desolata*) 134, 187
    Broad-billed Prion (*Pachyptila vittata*) 42, 64, 161
    Fairy Prion (*Pachyptila turtur*) 42, 82, 107, 161, 187
    Fulmar Prion, Chatham Island (*Pachyptila crassirostris pyramidalis*) 42
    Fulmar Prion (*Pachyptila crassirostris*) 23, 64, 161, 187
    research and/or census 69

Proclamation Island (Bounty Islands) 58, 69
Pukeko (*Porphyrio melanotus*) 45
Pyramid, The (Chatham Islands) 32, *33*, 35, 41

Q
quartz 95, 121, 152
Queen Charlotte 140

R
Rail
    Rail, Auckland Island (*Rallus pectoralis muelleri*) 134, 147
    Rail, Macquarie Pacific Banded (*Rallus philippensis macquariensis*) extinct 183

Raine, Thomas 192
Ranfurly Island (Bounty Islands) 58
Ranfurly, Earl of *68*, 69, 86
Rangatira *30*, 31, 32, 35, 42, 46, 47, 51, 53
Rangiauria *see Pitt Island*
Raven, Captain William 166
Red Bluff Tuff 33
Redpoll (*Carduelis flammea*) 85, 108, 164, 188
Reischek, Andreas 96, 145, 167, *168*
Rekohu 27, 31
Reliance, HMS 86
Remarkable Cave (Antipodes Islands) 74

research expeditions
    BAAS Expedition, NZ Wildlife Service (1974) 69, 88
    Dominion Museum (1954) 146
    French Transit of Venus Expedition (1874) 96, **111**, 115
    German Transit of Venus Expedition (1874) *144*, 145
    National Film Unit, HMNZS *Monowai* (1984) 89, 114
    NZ Dep. of Lands and Survey (1972) 146, *147*
    NZ Dep. of Scientific and Industrial Research (1954) 146
    NZ Oceanographic Institute (1962, 1963, 1964, 1973) 69, 88
    New Zealand Royal Society (2010) 115
    Philosophical Institute of Canterbury (1909) 96, 111, *144*, 145, 155, 164, 168
    Ross, Sir James Clark (1939-1942) 15, 96, **112**, 125, 132, **141**
    United States Exploring Expedition (1840) 140, 192
    Whitney South Sea Expedition (1926) 86

restorative management 202
Richdale, Lance 114, 168
Ritchie, Thomas *48*, 51
Roaring Forties 21
Robert Campbell and Co. 110
Robertson, Chris 63
Rose Island (Auckland Islands) 121, **129**, 131, 133, 147
Ross, Sir James Clark 125, 131 *see also research expeditions*
Round Island (Chatham Islands) 32
Royal Society (NZ) 115
Ruatara (Maori chief) 67
Ruatara Island 58
Russ, Rodney 107, *115*, 196, *204*
Russ, Shirley 196
Russian vessels 199

S
Sagar, Paul 159, 169
Sail Rock (Chatham Islands) 31
Sally 140
Samuel 140
Sandy Bay (Enderby Island) *118*, 121, 123
Sandy Bay (Macquarie Island) 199
Santa Anna 67

Sarah 140

Sarah W. Hunt 111

Sarah's Bosom (Auckland Island) 141

Scott, J. 193

Scott, Robert Falcon 193

Scown, Les *204*

seabirds 12, 15, 19, 23, 25, *33*, **42**, 55, **64**, 82, 102, **107**, 139, 148, 158, **161**, 170, 189 see also Albatrosses, Petrels, Prions, Shearwaters

sealing 16, 17
    Antipodes Islands 17, 71, 81, 85, **86**
    Auckland Islands 135, **140**, *141*
    Bounty Islands 55, 65, **67**, 68
    Campbell Island 91, **110**
    Chatham Island 47, 49, 50
    introduction of native animals 27
    legislation 87
    Macquarie Island 170, 183, **190**, 191, 192
    The Snares 149, 156, 159, 164, **166**

Seals 59, **65**, 85, 102, **164**, 183, 203
    Antarctic Fur Seal (*Arctocephalus gazella*) 188
    census and research 88
    diet of castaways 142, 190
    feeding 22, 25, 58
    impact on vegetation 180
    Leopard Seal (*Hydrurga leptonyx*) 47, 85, 188
    New Zealand (Hooker's) Sea Lion (*Phocarctos hookeri*) 47, 108, *109*, **118**, 120, 138, 139, 147, 159, 165, 188
    New Zealand Fur Seal (*Arctocephalus forsteri*) 47, 62, 65, 85, 108, 135, 159, 164, 188

Southern Elephant Seal (*Miroung leonina*) 47, 85, 99, 108, 139, 171, 188, *189*, **190**, 191

Subantarctic Fur Seal (*Arctocephalus tropicalis*) 85, 188, 190

sedimentary rock 15, 31, 32, *33*, 58, 95, 122, 202

Shags 62, 67, 164
    Auckland Island Shag (*Phalacrocorax colensoi*) 134, *137*
    Black Shag (*Phalacrocorax carbo*) 45
    Bounty Island Shag (*Phalacrocorax ranfurlyi*) 64, 82
    Campbell Island Shag (*Phalacrocorax cambelli*) 82, *106*, 107
    Chatham Island Shag (*Phalacrocorax onslowi*) 42
    Little Shag (*Phalacrocorax melanoleucos brevirostris*) 107
    Macquarie Island Shag (*Leucocarbo atriceps purpurascens*) 187
    Pitt Island Shag (*Phalacrocorax feathersoni*) 42
    speciation 16

Shand, Archibald 52

Sharp-tailed Sandpiper (*Calidris acuminata*) 164

Shearwaters 157, 177
    discovery of 68
    effect on vegetation 155
    harvesting 103
    Little Shearwater (*Puffinus assimilis*) 64
    Little Shearwater, Subantarctic (*Puffinus assimilis elegans*) 42, 64, 82, 174
    research and/or census 69, 169
    Sooty Shearwater (*Puffinus griseus*) 42, 82, 107, 134, 155, 159, *160*, 161, 169, 187

sheep see introduced animals

shipwrecks 86, **87**, 88, 110, **142**, 145, **191**, 192

Shoal Point Formation 95

Shorebirds 42
    Chatham Island Oystercatcher (*Haematopus chathamensis*) 42, *43*, 196
    New Zealand Shore Plover (*Thinornis novaeseelandiae*) *43*, 45
    White-faced Heron (*Ardea novaehollandiae*) 45

Silvereye (*Zosterops lateralis*) 108, 135, 164

Sirone, Captain 140

Sisters, The (Chatham Islands) 32, 35, 41, *45*

Skua Rock (Bounty Islands) 58

Skua, Subantarctic (Brown) (*Catharacta lonnbergi*) 42, 64, 82, 107, 134, *137*, 156, 161, 183, 187

Snipe
    Antipodes Island (*Coenocoypha meinertzhagenae*) 85
    Auckland Island (*Coenocorypha aucklandica*) 134, *136*
    Chatham Island (*Coenocorypha pusilla*) 45, 46
    Snares Island (*Coenocorypha aucklandica huegli*) *162*, 164
    Subantarctic (Campbell Is. *Coenocorypha* sp.) 107

Society Expeditions 198

Song Thrush (*Turdus philomelos*) 107, 164

Sorenson, Jack 96

South Bay (Antipodes Islands) 75, 88

South Georgia 12

South Temperate Zone 12, 23

South-east Island (Chatham Islands) see Rangatira

Southern Heritage Tours 196
Southern Ocean 23
    albatross foraging 63
    climate 20
    commercial fishing 88
    currents 23
    erosive force of 121, 174
    exploration 140
    flora 155, 157
    high productivity 12, 23, 25, 41, 51, 58, 64
    islands 10, 11, 12, 108, 116, 130, 154, 166, 167, 174
    marine life 25, 160, 182
    oceanography 23, 25
    research 168
    sealing 17, 111
    tourism 196, 198, 199, 200
Southern Volcanics (Chatham Islands) 32
Special Nature Reserve (Antipodes) 71
Sphagnum moss 36, 180
Spider Island (Bounty Islands) 58
Spirit of Dawn 87
Spirit of Enderby 118
Spur-winged Plover (*Vanellus miles novaehollandiae*) 46
squid 22, 25, 33, 202
Star 190
Star Keys (Chatham Islands) 31, 32, 35, 42, 45
Starling, European (*Sturnus vulgaris*) 60, 63, 85, 164, 188
Stella 167
Stella Bay (Antipodes Islands) 74
Subantarctic Tourist Guidelines (NZ) 198
Subtropical Convergence 21, 25
Sunday Islands 166
Survey Island (Campbell Island) 94
Sydney Cove 190

T
Taiko *see Petrels, Magenta Petrel*
Takatika Grit 33
Tapuaenuku *see Little Mangere*
Tasmanian Parks and Wildlife Service 18, 189, 198
Taylor, Rowley 65, 85, 88
Te Whanga Lagoon 31
Te Whanga Limestone 33
tectonic plates/movement 15, 174
Television NZ Natural History Unit 89
Teal
    Auckland Island (*Anas aucklandica*) 134, *135*
    Campbell Island Flightless (*Anas aucklandica nesiotis*) 19, *91*, 107, *115*
Terns
    Antarctic Tern (*Sterna vittata bethunei*) 64, 82, 107, 132, 161, 187
    White-fronted Tern (*Sterna striata*) 42, *43*, 134
Terror 96, 110, *141*
Terror Cove (Auckland Island) 145
Thomas, William 52
Tomtit
    Auckland Island (*Petroica macrocephala marrineri*) 135, *136*
    Black (Snares - *Petroica macrocephala dannefaerdi*) 150, 161, *162*
    Chatham Island (*Petroica macrocephala chathamensis*) *44*, 46
Topaz 49
Totorore 69, 88, 89
Townsend, I. 86
Transit of Venus Expeditions *see research expeditions*

Tourism 19, *194*, **196**, *197*, *199*, *201*
    A Turning Point 198
    advocacy 195
    Chatham Islands 53
    Heritage Expeditions 69
    history 19, **196**
    The Changing Face of Tourism 199
    Tourism Management 198
Tuanui family 41
Tucker Cove 101, 112
Tucker Cove Formation (Campbell Island) 95
Tucker, W.H. 113
Tui, Chatham Island (*Prosthemadera novaeseelandiae chathamensis*) 45, 47
Tui, New Zealand (*Prosthemadera novaeseelandiae*) 135
Tuku Valley 40, 41
Tula 68
Tupuangi Formation (Chatham Islands) 33

U
ultramafic rocks 175
Unity 190
University of Canterbury 168, 169
University of Otago 69, 79, 169
uplift 15, 32, 58, 175

V
Vancouver, Captain George 17, 166, *167*
vascular plants 61, *76*, 96, 125, 155, 176, 180, 181
    Acaena antarctica 78
    Acaena minor 79, 179
    Acaena magellanica 179
    Agrostis capillaris 99
    Agrostis magellanica 176

akeake (*Dodonaea viscose*) 36, 37
Anisotome acutifolia 156
Anisotome antipoda 78, 100
Anisotome latifolia 6, 98, 128, 131
Arrhenatherum elatius 101
Asplenium obtusatum 78, 155, 156
Azorella macquariensis 179
Baumea rubiginosa 36, 37
Blechnum capense 128
Blechnum durum 78, 79, 99, 100, 155, 156
Blechnum penna-marina 180
Blechnum sp. 36
Brachyglottis stewartiae 154, 155
Bulbinella rossii 6, 14, 92, 100, 124, 125, 128, 131
Callitriche antarctica 99, 156, 179
Cardamine corymbosa 179
Carex appressa 79, 100, 131
Carex sectiodes 79
Carex ternaria 78, 79
Carex trifida 36, 78, 131
Cassinia vauvilliersii 128
Cerastium fontanum 176
Chatham Island button-daisy (*Leptinella featherstonii*) 35, 36
Chatham Island forget-me-not (*Myosotidium hortensia*) 34, 35, 36
Chatham Island korokio (*Corokia macrocarpa*) 36
Chatham Island koromiko (*Hebe chathamica*) 35
Chatham Islands geranium (*Geranium traversii*) 35
Chatham Islands lacewood (hoho-*Pseudopanax chathamicus*) 37
Chatham Islands mingimingi (*Cyathodes robusta*) 36

Chionochloa antarctica 99, 128, 131
cocksfoot (*Dactylis glomerata*) 156
Colobanthus muscoides 77, 156, 179
Cook's scurvy grass (*Lepidium oleraceum*) 61, 156
Coprosma ciliata 128
Coprosma cuneata 128
Coprosma foetidissima 125
Coprosma perpusilla 79, 179
Coprosma rugosa (var *antipoda*) 77, 79
Coprosma spp. 99, 100, 129
Crassula moschata 77, 156
Damnamenia vernicosa 128
Deschampsia chapmanii 99
Deschampsia spp. 176
Dieffenbach's koromiko (*Hebe dieffenbachia*) 35
Disphyma papillatum 35
Dracophyllum longifolium 99, 125, 128
Dracophyllum scoparium 99
Dracophyllum spp. 36, 98, 129
Eleocharis acuta 36
Epilobium spp. 78, 79, 179
Festuca contracta 176
Festuca coxii 35
Fuschia excorticata 125
Gentiana antipoda 77, 79
Gentiana cerina 128, 130
Gentiana concinna 128
Grammitis hochbreutini 180
gully tree fern (*Cyathea cunninghamii*) 37
Hebe benthamii 100, 124, 128
Hebe elliptica 125, 156
Hebe odura 125
Histiopteris incisa 78, 128
Holcus lanatus 101

Huperzia australiana 180
Hymenophyllum falklandicum 180
Hymenophyllum multifidum 78
inaka (*Dracophyllum paludosum*) 36
Isolepis aucklandica 77
Isolepis cernua 156
Isolepis sp. 99
jointed rush (*Juncus articulatus*) 101
karamu (*Coprosma chathamica*) 36, 27
kawakawa (*Macropiper excelsum*) 36
keketerehe (*Olearia chathamica*) 36
kopi (*Corynocarpus laevigatus*) 36, 37
kowhai (*Sophora microphylla*) 37
Leptinella plumosa 77, 99, 179
Leptocarpus spp. 36
Luzula crinita 79, 176
mahoe (*Melicytus chathamica*) 36
marram grass (*Ammophila arenaria*) 36
marsh foxtail (*Alopecurus geniculatus*) 101
Marsippospermum gracile 100
matipo (*Myrsine chathamica*) 36, 37
monkey-flower (*Mimulus guttatus*) 101
Montia fontana 99, 179
Myosotis capita 130
Myrsine divaricata 125, 128, 129
Myrsine spp. 36, 37, 100, 125
New Zealand wild celery (*Apium prostratum*) 77
ngaio (*Myoporum* sp.) 37
Olearia lyalli 131, 154, 155, 157, 159, 164
Olearia spp. 125
orchids 77, 176
Oreobolus pecinatus 128
Oreobolus sp. 99
pingao (*Desmoschoenus spiralis*) 36

REFERENCES 223

Pleurophyllum criniferum 78, 79, 80, 100, 128, 131,
Pleurophyllum hookeri 100, *101*, 128, 176, *177*, 179
Pleurophyllum speciosum 97, 100, *101*, 125, 128, 131
Poa annua (annual meadow grass) 77, 156, 176
Poa astonii 156
Poa cookii 176
Poa foliosa 78, 99, 176
Poa litorosa 78, 131, 176
Poa tennantiana 156, 157
Poa chathamica 35
Poa ramosissima 99
Polystichum vestitum 78, 79, 125, 128, 155, 180
potatoes 50, 52, 142, 156, 166
Pseudopanax simplex 125
Puccinellia macquariensis 176
Ranunculus crassipes 179
ribbonwood (*Plagianthus regius* var *chathamicus*) 37
rye grass (*Lolium perenne*) 156
sand daphne (toroheke - *Pimelia arenaria*) 36
Senecio radiolatus antipodus 77, 79
Senecio radiolatus radiolatus 35
soft speargrass (*Aciphylla dieffenbachia*) 35, 36
Sonchus asper 77, 101
southern nettle (*Urtica australis*) 36
southern rata (*Metrosideros umbellata*) 125, *126*, *127*, 128, *129*, 131, 134, 146
sowthistle (*Embergeria grandiflora*) 36
Sporadanthus spp. 36
spruce 99

Stellaria decipiens var *angustata* 77, 79
Stellaria media 77, 79, 156, 176
Stilbocarpa polaris 79, 87, 99, 128, *130*, 155, 176, *178*
Stilbocarpa robusta 155, 156, 157
tarahinau (*Dracophyllum arboreum*) 36, 37
Tillaea moschata 157
Uncinia hookeri 79, 176
wheki (*Dicksonia squarrosa*) 37
wheki-pongi (*Dicksonia fibrosa*) 37
wild turnip (*Brassica rapa*) 77
Venus Cove (Auckland Islands) 111
Victoria 68, 111, 145
volcanic action/origins 15, 23, *30*, 31, 32, 33, 37, 58, 71, 74, 75, 94, 95, 118, 120, 121, 122, 123, 175

W

Waikato, H.M.N.Z.S. 69
Waitangi (Chatham Islands) *51*, 52
Waite, E.R. 145
Walker, Kath 19, 72, 76, 78, 81, 83, 84, 89, 120, 134, 147, 203
Warbler, Chatham Island (*Gerygone albofrontata*) 45
Warham, John 88, 159, 169
Warren, John 113
Wasp Island (Campbell group) 94
Waterhouse, Captain 86
Weka, Buff (*Gallirallus australis hectori*) 46, 47
Weka, Stewart Island (*Gallirallus australis scotti*) see introduced animals
Welcome Swallow (*Hirundo tahitica neoxena*) 47, 134
Wellington 140
Westerskov, Kaj 114

Western Chain (The Snares) 152, *153*, 159, 161
Western Reef (Chatham Islands) 32
Whales
   Killer Whales (*Orca orcinus*) 188
   Long-finned Pilot Whales (*Globicephala melas*) 47, 50
   Southern Right Whales (*Eubalaena australis*) 47, 50, 51, 108, 113, 139
   Sperm Whales (*Physeter macrocephalus*) 47, 50, 51, 52
Whaling 18
   Auckland Island 140, 142
   Bounty Islands 68
   Campbell Island 111, **112**, 113, 115
   Chatham Islands 50, **51**, 52
Wharekauri 27
Whitney South Sea Expedition
   see research expeditions
Wilkes, Charles 140, 192
Wilson, G. 164
Windward Islands (Antipodes Islands) 74
World Heritage Area 18, 170, 175, 193

Y

Yankee 140
Yellowhammer (*Emberiza citrinella*) 108

Z

Zelee 140, *141*
zooplankton 25